Ethics Without Intention

EZIO DI NUCCI

B L O O M S B U R Y

LONDON • NEW DELHI • NEW YORK • SYDNEY

Bloomsbury Academic

An imprint of Bloomsbury Publishing Plc

50 Bedford Square	1385 Broadway
London	New York
WC1B 3DP	NY 10018
UK	USA

www.bloomsbury.com

Bloomsbury is a registered trade mark of Bloomsbury Publishing Plc

First published 2014

© Ezio Di Nucci, 2014

British Library Cataloguing-in-Publication Data
A catalogue record for this book is available from the British Library.

ISBN: HB: 978-1-4725-2300-6
PB: 978-1-4725-3296-1
ePDF: 978-1-4725-2322-8
ePub: 978-1-4725-2579-6

Library of Congress Cataloging-in-Publication Data
A catalog record for this book is available from the Library of Congress.

Typeset by Deanta Global Publishing Services, Chennai, India
Printed and bound in India

Ethics Without Intention

BLOOMSBURY ETHICS SERIES

Bloomsbury Ethics is a series of books written to help students explore, engage with and master key topics in contemporary ethics and moral philosophy.

Intuitionism, David Kaspar
Moral Realism, Kevin DeLapp
Reasons, Eric Wiland
Virtue Ethics, Nafsika Athanassoulis

Forthcoming in the series:

Climate Ethics, Sarah Kenehan
Moral Principles, Maike Albertzart
Moral Skepticism, Basil Smith
Moral Psychology, Jay R. Elliott
Trust, Ethics and Human Reason, Olli Lagerspetz
Value Theory, Francesco Orsi

Series Editors:

Thom Brooks is Reader in Law at Durham Law School. He is the founding editor of the *Journal of Moral Philosophy* and runs a popular Political Philosophy blog called The Brooks Blog.

Simon Kirchin is Senior Lecturer in Philosophy at the University of Kent, UK. He is President of the British Society for Ethical Theory and co-editor of *Arguing About Metaethics* (Routledge, 2006).

ai miei figli, Eleonore e Francesco Paolo

CONTENTS

PREFACE

This book is a critical analysis of the *Doctrine of Double Effect*, a normative principle according to which sometimes an effect or consequence which is not morally permissible as an intended means or end is morally permissible as a merely foreseen side effect. Here I present the Doctrine and offer eight arguments against it. **First argument:** I show that the counterfactual test of intention fails to distinguish between intended means and merely foreseen side effects (Chapter 2). **Second argument:** I present the argument from marginally bad means, according to which the Doctrine implausibly rules against cases where the intended means are morally negligible (Chapter 3). **Third argument:** I dispute, both theoretically and empirically, the moral intuitions that are supposed to motivate the Doctrine, as, for example, killing one to save five in trolley cases (Chapters 4 and 5). **Fourth argument:** I show that the problem of closeness makes the Doctrine unworkable because we can always argue that the agent did not intend the bad means (Chapter 6). **Fifth argument:** I defend a counterexample to the Doctrine – the *Loop Variant* – from Frances Kamm's recent attempt to deal with it by arguing that means are not necessarily intended (Chapter 7). **Sixth argument:** I show that influential thought-experiments in the double effect literature, such as *Terror Bomber & Strategic Bomber*, face a dilemma: either there is no moral difference between the two consequentialistically identical cases – so that the Doctrine draws a moral distinction without a difference – or the moral difference is explained by more fundamental normative considerations rather than the distinction between intended means and merely foreseen side effects (Chapters 8 and 9). **Seventh argument:** I argue that the Doctrine provides no moral guidance because it cannot tell us what to do; it is therefore a useless normative principle (Chapter 11). **Eighth argument:** I argue that the Doctrine fails even if we water it down to a responsibility-attribution principle (Chapter 12). Summing up, this book argues that the Doctrine of Double Effect should be abandoned.

ACKNOWLEDGEMENTS

I would like to (try to) thank all those who have, more or less directly, supported this project. First of all, I thank my students at *Universität Duisburg-Essen*, especially those who were involved in winter semester 2011/2012 of my course on double effect and the students of the *Ethics Lecture* in summer semester 2012. I also wish to thank all the members of Neil Roughley's research group at *Universität Duisburg-Essen* (past and present), who have patiently heard me talk about double effect on many occasions; and I'm grateful to the participants to our *Mittelbaukolloquium*, where I presented an early summary of my work on double effect in 2012. My thanks also goes to various audiences in Germany, Holland, Hungary and the UK for helpful discussions on double effect on different occasions over the last couple of years. Also, some more targeted gratitude is called for: thanks to Chris Neuhäuser for reminding me of my interest in double effect; thanks to Michael Pakaluk for written comments on Chapter 3; thanks to Karo Sachs for helping during the early stages of the experimental work; thanks to Marcel Heusinger for talking about philosophy on so many occasions; thanks to Taha Laraki for helping me with the Index; and also my thanks goes to the series' editors, Simon Kirchin and Thom Brooks, and to everybody involved at Bloomsbury and its affiliates.

Finally, thanks to Ursula, without whom I couldn't do a thing.

Essen, 23.2.2014

An earlier draft of this book was submitted as my Habilitationsschrift *on the 23rd of September 2013 to* Universität Duisburg-Essen *under the title "Ethics without Intention: An Essay on Double Effect".*

CHAPTER ONE

Introductory remarks: We never do just one thing

We never really do just one thing. Political decisions, notoriously, will have financial consequences as well as electoral ones. Lovemaking is supposed to please both partners. Buying is such that we both acquire something and lose money. Oedipus marries the widowed Queen of Thebes Jocasta, but also his own mother. Little Boy killed more than 100,000 residents of Hiroshima, and also brought forward the end of World War II (probably). Of many of us it is true that we don't work just for the money but that we would also not work for free.[1] The infamous 'I was only following orders' is another example: famously following orders was not, tragically, the *only* thing that those who used such defence were doing.[2]

What all these examples have in common is not just that for each one there is more than one true description of what the agent(s) did – that much, as we said, would probably not identify them as a distinct group because it would apply to just about anything. What these examples have in common is also that there are, for each, at least two important descriptions. Whatever 'important' means here, there are also clear differences between the descriptions, both across cases and within the same case. Oedipus knew that he was marrying the widowed Queen of Thebes, for example, without knowing, though, that he was also marrying his own mother. So there is a clear epistemic difference between the two descriptions in question of what Oedipus did: Oedipus *intensionally* and *extensionally* married the Queen of Thebes but only extensionally married his own mother. This does not apply to other cases, where typically the agent is aware of both of the relevant consequences – politicians are a perfect example here; they never lose sight of the electoral consequences of their decisions, even though they like to claim that their decisions are not motivated solely by electoral considerations.

We have, then, identified the first difference, an epistemic one, between consequences that are foreseen and consequences that are not foreseen (like in the case of Oedipus). There are other differences: while the death of the 100,000+ residents of Hiroshima caused (probably) an anticipated end of World War II and the financial consequences of political decisions typically have causal influences on electoral outcomes, the same relationship does not hold for the relation between 'marrying the Queen of Thebes' and 'marrying his own mother': that is not a causal relation. The second difference, then, is that some but not all relations between different action descriptions are causal.

There are also differences in the direction of preferential attitudes, so that, typically, transactions are such that the buyer is motivated by the goods acquisition and not by the loss of money and the seller is motivated by the gain of money and not by the loss of goods (this may turn out to be short-sighted because in the long term there is interdependence, but that's beside the point here). Similarly, those using the 'I was only following orders' defence wanted to at least imply that their positive attitude was *only* towards following orders and not also towards the content of those orders – driving a train full of Jews to Auschwitz, say.

So far, we have then identified epistemic, causal and preferential differences between action descriptions. Those differences, mind you, are independent of each other, so that we can combine at will and get, say, a case of two action descriptions that are causally related but epistemically different (my turning on the radio early this morning woke up my neighbour but I did not expect that consequence because I thought she was on vacation) just as much as a case of two action descriptions that are neither epistemically different nor causally related ('typing' and 'working', say, as action descriptions of what I am doing just now).[3]

Once we add preferential attitudes to this mix, things get really interesting. The case of the radio waking up my neighbour, for example, could be one – as the above original – where I wanted to listen to loud music and thought that my neighbour was on vacation;

one consequence was foreseen – listening to music – while the other was not – waking up my neighbour. Alternatively, we can imagine a case where I really want to listen to loud music and I don't much care about the consequences for my neighbour, so I turned on the radio in order to listen to music while also knowing that the radio will likely wake up my neighbour – I simply don't care enough about my neighbour, at least relatively to how much I care about listening to loud music. This is a case where both consequences are foreseen but only one of them – listening to music – is motivating me.

Additionally, we can imagine a wicked case in which I turned on the radio in order to wake up my neighbour: again, a case in which both consequences are foreseen, my end is to wake up my neighbour and the consequence of listening to music motivates me only insofar as it is the way in which I am going to wake up my neighbour. Finally, we can imagine a case in which I would really like to listen to music but, out of respect for my neighbour, I wait until I am in the solitude of my own car to do so. This is the case in which the possible consequence of waking up my neighbour leads me to avoid listening to the radio in the flat. And within this framework, we can imagine other variants too, as, for example, the one in which I want to both listen to music and wake up my neighbour, so that I don't turn on the radio which is closest to where I am making coffee but rather the one which is closest to where I know my neighbour to be asleep.

How should we evaluate these different cases? It is plausible to think that whether the agent was aware of or had access to the relevant consequences or action descriptions will play a role by the evaluation: both responsibility and intentionality are, for example, often thought to depend on such criteria, so that the attribution of responsibility may vary depending on whether or not the agent was aware of some consequence of her action. It would make little sense, for example, to ask the agent *why* she woke up her neighbour in the case in which the agent thought that her neighbour was on vacation[4]; however, in the case in which the agent knows that her neighbour is there but does not consider this reason enough not to listen to music, we may ask why and the agent may reply that she wanted to listen to music.

Between these two cases we may have one where the question 'Why did you wake up your neighbour?' won't make much sense, but at the same time the agent may still be considered responsible for what she did because she had access to the relevant information: imagine a case in which the agent had been told that her neighbour wasn't on vacation yet and forgot; or a case where the agent had seen lights in the neighbour's flat the evening before but failed to draw the relevant inference. Those are cases where we may think that, even though the agent genuinely failed to realize that her listening to loud music would wake up her neighbour, still she may be held not only accountable but also liable for waking up her neighbour because she had easy access to the fact that her neighbour was still there – at the same time, in this kind of case we may still talk of the agent having unintentionally woken up her neighbour.[5]

What about the cases where there is no epistemic gap, where the agent knows that turning on the radio at 6 a.m. will wake up her neighbour just as well as she knows that turning on the radio at 6 a.m. will allow her to listen to music? Is there any difference between the three consequentialistically similar cases of (i) the agent turning on the radio in order to listen to music while at the same time knowing that this will wake up the neighbour and (ii) the agent turning on the radio in order to listen to music and in order to wake up her neighbour and (iii) the case of the agent turning on the radio in order to wake up her neighbour? This is where the *Doctrine of Double Effect*, the subject matter of this book, enters the scene.

One could draw the following distinction: one thing is if the agent actually set out to wake up her neighbour by means of listening to music; a different thing is if all that the agent was really interested in was listening to music even though she knew that this would also wake up her neighbour.[6] The suggestion being not only that there is an action-theoretical difference or a difference in terms of reasoning between the two cases, but that these differences may also be relevant when it comes to evaluating the different cases morally. And this is indeed what the Doctrine of Double Effect claims: that there is a moral difference – one that is traditionally made out in terms of moral permissibility and justification – between the case in which the foreseen negative consequence is an intended means or end and the case in which the foreseen negative consequence is a merely foreseen unintended side effect.[7]

The agent's intentions in bringing about a negative consequence are, according to the Doctrine of Double Effect, relevant to the moral permissibility of bringing about that negative consequence – this is both the topic of this book and the claim that I dispute throughout, arguing that the Doctrine of Double Effect fails to show that the difference between intended means and merely foreseen side effects is relevant to moral permissibility and justification.[8] As this whole book will analyse the Doctrine and its claims and discuss the relevant arguments, here I do not want to prematurely start that discussion but rather only illustrate the importance of double effect.

1 Thou Shalt Not Kill

Take the *Thou Shalt Not Kill* of the Judeo-Christian tradition: the Vatican explicitly appeals to double effect in its *Catechism of the Catholic Church* (part 3, section 2, chapter 2, article 5, I: 2263[9]) in order to explain the Commandment against killing. As it is easy to generate counterexamples to a Commandment against killing that, according to the *Catechism of the Catholic Church*, supposedly 'obliges each and everyone, always and everywhere' (part 3, section 2, chapter 2, article 5, I: 2261[10]), the appeal to double effect serves the purpose of showing that 'The legitimate defense of persons and societies is not an exception' (part 3, section 2, chapter 2, article 5, I: 2263[11]). That's where the *Catechism of the Catholic Church* directly quotes Aquinas on double effect: 'The act of self-defense can have a **double effect**: the preservation of one's own life; and the killing of the aggressor . . . the one is intended, the other is not' (part 3, section 2, chapter 2, article 5, I: 2263[12] – emphasis mine).

Those familiar with the Doctrine of Double Effect can also recognize more implicit references to double effect throughout the Catechism's discussion of the Commandment against killing: 'The fifth commandment forbids *direct and intentional* killing as gravely sinful' (part 3, section 2, chapter 2, article 5, I: 2268[13] – my own emphasis). The talk of 'direct' and 'intentional' killing is, as we shall see in the next chapter, an obvious reference to double effect, as is the talk of 'proportionate reasons': 'Unintentional killing is not morally imputable. But one is not exonerated from grave offense if, *without proportionate reasons*, he has acted in a way that brings about someone's death, even without the intention to do so' (part 3, section 2, chapter 2, article 5, I: 2269[14] – my own emphasis).[15]

The example of the Catechism of the Catholic Church is important not just because the Christian tradition has had and still has a large influence on society, but also because it helps illustrate the dialectical place of the Doctrine of Double Effect within moral philosophy in general: indeed, we have just seen how the Doctrine can be deployed to try to defend the generality of some moral principle from counterexamples. An obvious case would be the justification of war: it could even be argued that – without something like double effect – non-consequentialist moralities will not be able to justify any war. The argument could go something like this: the killing of innocents as collateral damage of armed conflict is – in war as we know it (forget about the infallibly precise *warbots* of the future) – unavoidable (this is a plausible empirical claim but I will not defend it here). In order to justify war, then, we need to find a way to justify this empirically necessary element of it: collateral damage. Without a justification of collateral damage, the only available justifications for war will be consequentialist ones.

Typically, the Doctrine of Double Effect will be deployed in order to justify collateral damages by saying that in such cases we do not intend to kill the innocent civilians who die as a foreseen result of our airstrike, say. And that – under certain circumstances, we have looked for alternatives, the war is just, etc. – we may bring about the death of these civilians as long as we do not intend to kill them. Now, a lot can be said here, and indeed a lot is said in this book about these and related issues; but this is not the place to do so. Here I just wanted to illustrate the important dialectical place that the Doctrine of Double Effect occupies along the classic frontlines in moral philosophy.

Let me say that the distinction between intending harm and merely foreseeing harm at the centre of the Doctrine of Double Effect should be kept separate from the distinction between doing and allowing (also often put in terms of the difference between actions and omissions); in the case of killing, for example, we must keep apart the distinction between intended killing and unintended killing from the distinction between killing and letting die. Even the Catechism of the Catholic Church recognizes as much when it says that 'The fifth commandment forbids doing anything with the intention of indirectly bringing about a person's death. the [*sic*] moral law prohibits exposing someone to mortal danger without grave reason, as well as refusing assistance to a person in danger' (part 3, section 2, chapter 2, article 5, I: 2269[16]). The point here is that one can have intended killing even in cases of omissions or letting die.

We should then not think that letting die is necessarily unintended or that killing is necessarily intended. We rather have the following possibilities:

- Intended killing;

- Unintended foreseen killing;

- Intended letting die; and

- Unintended foreseen letting die.

Deliberately shooting someone in the head from close range would be an example of intended killing, say; killing a protester while shooting into a crowd in order to disperse it may be taken to be an example of unintended but foreseen killing; not telling your climbing partner that they are about to step onto thin ice with the explicit intention of getting rid of them may be an example of intended letting die; finally, ignoring someone in need to avoid being late to work may count as a case of unintended but foreseen letting die. So let me clearly say at the outset that this book is only about the distinction between intended consequences and merely foreseen consequences and does not deal with the distinction between doing and allowing.

2 The book's contents

Having said what this book is about and what this book is not about, all that remains to be done in this chapter is to briefly illustrate the structure of this volume. The book is divided into three parts: in the first part I present the Doctrine of Double Effect and its central distinction between intended consequences and merely foreseen consequences; specifically, in Chapter 2 I analyse both classic and contemporary formulations of the Doctrine and its conditions, showing that classic formulations of the Doctrine in terms of four individually necessary and jointly sufficient conditions are in line with contemporary formulations of the Doctrine in terms of one crucial distinction between intended and merely foreseen negative consequences as something which *sometimes* justifies bringing about an unintended negative effect. I also offer my **first** argument against the Doctrine of Double Effect, showing that the so-called counterfactual test cannot distinguish between intended means and merely foreseen side effects.

In Chapter 3 I look at the origins of double effect, especially Aquinas and Aristotle, and discuss the relationship between the Doctrine and Aristotle's mixed actions, arguing that mixed actions cannot be dealt with by appeal to the Doctrine of Double Effect and that therefore Aristotle cannot be taken to be the father of double effect. This chapter also presents my **second** argument against double effect, derived from Aristotle's mixed actions: *the argument from marginally bad means.*

In Part II of the book I discuss the theoretical issues behind the Doctrine of Double Effect, especially the following elements: in Chapter 4 I argue that the Trolley Problem cannot be taken to be an argument in favour of the Doctrine of Double Effect because it is not obvious that it is morally permissible to kill the one to save the five. In Chapter 5 I then present my own data on moral intuitions on trolley cases that supplement the argument from Chapter 4. Chapters 4 and 5 together represent my **third** argument against double effect: the moral intuitions that are supposed to motivate the ethical relevance of the distinction between intended negative consequences and merely foreseen negative consequences are, at best, widely overrated.

My **fourth** argument against the Doctrine of Double Effect comes in Chapter 6 in the form of the so-called problem of closeness: there is no coherent way of formulating the distinction between intended consequences and merely foreseen consequences so as to avoid abuse of the Doctrine so that it can justify pretty much anything. In Chapter 7 I argue against Frances Kamm's suggestion that means are not necessarily intended: an issue that is important over and above the Doctrine of Double Effect as Kamm's is also meant to be a challenge to Kantian instrumental rationality. My critique of Kamm's proposed solution to the Loop Variant of the Trolley Problem constitutes my **fifth** argument against the Doctrine of Double Effect, as the Loop Variant is a counterexample to the Doctrine.

In Part III of the book I discuss some of the most influential practical applications of the Doctrine of Double Effect: I start in Chapter 8 with collateral damages; there I argue, by reference to the classic case of Terror Bomber and Strategic Bomber, that these kinds of thought-experiments that are supposed to both illustrate and motivate the Doctrine are typically underdetermined so as to allow for the following dilemma: either there is no moral difference between the two consequentialistically identical cases – so that the Doctrine draws a moral distinction without a difference – or the moral difference is explained by something more fundamental than the distinction between intended and merely foreseen consequences. This is also my **sixth** argument against the Doctrine of Double Effect. Chapter 9 supplements my argument from Chapter 8 with my own data on the moral intuitions behind the case of Terror Bomber and Strategic Bomber.

In Chapter 10 I discuss bioethical applications of the Doctrine of Double Effect. After reviewing different traditional bioethical applications, I choose the example of stem cell research and embryo loss for a more in-depth analysis, showing that the Doctrine fails to distinguish between the embryo loss involved in *in vivo* procreation and the embryo loss involved in stem cell research. In Chapter 11, then, I offer my **seventh** argument against the Doctrine of Double Effect, arguing that it is a useless moral principle because it cannot tell us what to do.

I conclude the book with Chapter 12, where I first offer my **eighth** argument against the Doctrine of Double Effect by showing that even reformulating it in terms of a principle about responsibility attribution rather than moral permissibility won't save the Doctrine; I then offer an alternative understanding of the normativity involved in double effect cases, what I call the *moral correlate of sentencing*. Finally, I distinguish between Ends, *Mends* and Means to put forward an alternative account of the reasoning involved when we do more than one thing.

3 Double effect cases

I would like to append at the end of this introductory chapter a list of the most influential cases and thought-experiments of the double effect literature that this book deals with. The cases will be presented again in detail in the coming chapters, so here I will not comment on them; indeed, I will sometimes throughout the book illustrate the same case more than once, because the details of these cases are often crucial to my discussion, so that I prefer the reader to have them always handy.

1   Terror Bomber and Strategic Bomber:

Both Terror Bomber and Strategic Bomber have the goal of promoting the war effort against Enemy. Each intends to pursue this goal by weakening Enemy, and each intends to do that by dropping bombs. Terror Bomber's plan is to bomb the school in Enemy's territory, thereby killing children of Enemy and terrorizing Enemy's population. Strategic Bomber's plan is different. He plans to bomb Enemy's munitions plant, thereby undermining Enemy's war effort. Strategic Bomber also knows, however, that next to the munitions plant is a school, and that when he bombs the plant he will also destroy the school, killing the children inside. Strategic Bomber has not ignored this fact. Indeed, he has worried a lot about it. Still, he has concluded that this cost, though significant, is outweighed by the contribution that would be made to the war effort by the destruction of the munitions plant. Now, Terror Bomber intends all of the features of his action just noted: he intends to drop the bombs, kill the children, terrorize the population, and thereby weaken Enemy. In contrast, it seems that Strategic Bomber only intends to drop the bombs, destroy the munitions plant, and weaken Enemy. Although he knows that by bombing the plant he will be killing the children, he does not, it seems, intend to kill them. Whereas killing the children is, for Terror Bomber, an intended means to his end of victory, it is, for Strategic Bomber, only something he knows he will do by bombing the munitions plant. Though Strategic Bomber has taken the deaths of the children quite seriously into account in his deliberation, these deaths are for him only an expected side effect; they are not – in contrast with Terror Bomber's position – intended as a means. . . . In saying this I do not deny that Strategic Bomber kills the children intentionally. (Bratman 1987: 139–40)

2   Trolley Problem:

Bystander at the Switch
In that case you have been strolling by the trolley track, and
you can see the situation at a glance: The driver saw the five on
the track ahead, he stamped on the brakes, the brakes failed, so
he fainted. What to do? Well, here is the switch, which you can
throw, thereby turning the trolley yourself. Of course you will
kill one if you do. But I should think you may turn it all the same.
(1985: 1397)

Fat Man
Consider a case – which I shall call *Fat Man* – in which you are
standing on a footbridge over the trolley track. You can see a
trolley hurtling down the track, out of control. You turn around
to see where the trolley is headed, and there are five workmen on
the track where it exits from under the footbridge. What to do?
Being an expert on trolleys, you know of one certain way to stop
an out-of-control trolley: Drop a really heavy weight in its path.
But where to find one? It just so happens that standing next to
you on the footbridge is a fat man, a really fat man. He is leaning
over the railing, watching the trolley; all you have to do is to give
him a little shove, and over the railing he will go, onto the track
in the path of the trolley. (1985: 1409)

3   Craniotomy:

It is said for instance that the operation of hysterectomy involves
the death of the foetus as the foreseen but not strictly or directly
intended consequence of the surgeon's act, while other operations
kill the child and count as the direct intention of taking an
innocent life, a distinction that has evoked particularly bitter
reactions on the part of non-Catholics. If you are permitted to
bring about the death of the child, what does it matter how it
is done? The doctrine of the double effect is also used to show
why in another case, where a woman in labour will die unless
a craniotomy operation is performed; the intervention is not to
be condoned. There, it is said, we may not operate but must let
the mother die. We foresee her death but do not directly intend

it, whereas to crush the skull of the child would count as direct intention of its death. (Foot 1967: 7)

4 Death-inducing pain alleviation:

A doctor who intends to hasten the death of a terminally ill patient by injecting a large dose of morphine would act impermissibly because he intends to bring about the patient's death. However, a doctor who intended to relieve the patient's pain with that same dose and merely foresaw the hastening of the patient's death would act permissibly (McIntyre, *Stanford Encyclopedia of Philosophy*).[17]

5 Self-Defence:

Nothing hinders one act from having two effects, only one of which is intended, while the other is beside the intention. . . . Accordingly, the act of self-defence may have two effects: one, the saving of one's life; the other, the slaying of the aggressor. (Aquinas, Summa II-II, Qu. 64, Art. 7)

PART ONE

The Doctrine of Double Effect

CHAPTER TWO

Definitions first: Classic formulations of the Doctrine

Abstract *In this chapter I analyse various representative formulations – both classic and contemporary – of the Doctrine of Double Effect which look superficially very different from each other. I show that, actually, those formulations are compatible as they all turn around a core distinction between intended and unintended harm (bad effect). The role of this chapter is to identify and clarify the subject matter of this book and to show that the arguments in the coming chapters do not depend on picking a particular formulation of the Doctrine. At the end of this chapter I also present my first argument against the Doctrine of Double Effect, showing that the counterfactual test of intention cannot distinguish between intended means and merely foreseen side effects.*

1 Introduction

This chapter defines the subject matter of this book by analysing different formulations and interpretations of the *Doctrine of Double Effect*. Here is a representative list of ways in which the Doctrine has been formulated in the literature:

1. McIntyre in the double effect entry for the *Stanford Encyclopedia of Philosophy* says that according to the Doctrine of Double Effect, 'sometimes it is permissible to bring about as a merely foreseen side effect a harmful event that it would be impermissible to bring about intentionally' (http://plato.stanford.edu/entries/double-effect/).

2. This is in line with classic formulations of the Doctrine such as Mangan's:

   > A person may licitly perform an action that he foresees will produce a good and a bad effect provided that four conditions are verified at one and the same time: 1) that the action in itself from its very object be good or at least indifferent; 2) that the good effect and not the evil effect be intended; 3) that the good effect be not produced by means of the evil effect; 4) that there be a proportionately grave reason for permitting the evil effect. (1949: 43)

3. Mangan follows Gury, which is the standard modern Latin source:

   > It is lawful to actuate a morally good or indifferent cause from which will follow two effects, one good and the other evil, if there is a proportionately serious reason, and the ultimate end of the agent is good, and the evil effect is not the means to the good effect. (Mangan's translation; 1949: 60)[1]

4. Aquinas is often credited with the first explicit version of the Doctrine in his discussion of self-defence: 'Nothing hinders one act from having two effects, only one of which is intended, while the other is beside the intention' (Summa II-II, 64, 7).[2]

5. Woodward in the *Introduction* to his standard anthology on double effect talks of the difference between: 'intentional

production of evil . . . and foreseen but unintentional production of evil' (2001: 2).

6   Finally, here is the definition of the *PhilPapers* Section on the Doctrine of Double Effect:

> The Doctrine of Double Effect is a normative principle according to which in pursuing the good it is sometimes morally permissible to bring about some evil as a side effect or merely foreseen consequence: the same evil would not be morally justified as an intended means or end (http://philpapers.org/browse/the-doctrine-of-double-effect).[3]

Let us analyse some of the differences between these various formulations. First of all, some formulations (such as, for example, McIntyre's, Woodward's and Aquinas's) focus on one crucial distinction which is supposed to be the core of the Doctrine, while others (such as, for example, Mangan's and Gury's) formulate a set of four conditions which are supposedly individually necessary and jointly sufficient for the permissibility of a certain action.

This difference between the more detailed and explicit formulations of the whole Doctrine and the more essential statements of one important distinction raises the question of whether the other three conditions mentioned by Mangan and Gury are truly all necessary, or whether they are just expressing one core distinction that does not need to be formulated in terms of three independent conditions: this latter option is the claim that I will be arguing for in this chapter.

One of these three conditions can be dealt with very quickly at the outset: this is because the proportionality condition is quickly accounted for by formulations such as McIntyre's by adding 'sometimes': '*sometimes* it is permissible to bring about as a merely foreseen side effect a harmful event that it would be impermissible to bring about intentionally' (my emphasis). Namely that the effect is merely foreseen and not intended isn't meant to be enough to make something morally permissible: there needs to be a proportional background, such as the difference between killing one and saving five in the Trolley Problem, only to mention an obvious example. What is going to count as a proportionately grave or serious reason in the relevant cases is a further normative issue that we do not need to settle here. But let me just say that it would be a mistake to assume that the proportionality condition needs to be cashed out in utilitarian or consequentialist terms, even though obviously some of the most clear examples (as kill one to save five in trolley cases) go in exactly that direction.

In Section 3 we will ask whether the other two conditions are necessary and claim that they are both redundant, but before we do that there are some other important interpretative issues to deal with.

2 Preliminaries

First of all, we should say that the talk of double *effect* is misleading if one takes it – metaphysically – seriously.[4] This is because what we are talking about are not necessarily effects: to see this, take Davidson's paradigmatic example from *Actions, Reasons, and Causes* (1963) of 'flipping a switch' – 'turning on the light' – 'illuminating the room' – 'alerting a prowler outside'.

Those are, according to Davidson and those who agree with Davidson about the individuation of action (e.g. Anscombe 1957 and Hornsby 1980), four different descriptions of the same action; whatever one thinks about individuation, though (for example, Goldman (1970) would say, contra Davidson, that those are different actions), it is clear that the relation between those four action descriptions is not always of cause and effect: so that 'flipping the switch' certainly causes 'alerting the prowler', but 'turning on the light' does not cause 'illuminating the room' in the sense that 'illuminating the room' is not an independent effect of the cause 'turning on the light' but rather just *is* 'turning on the light' or counts as 'turning on the light'. And one could imagine that Davidson's example is indeed a case where one could apply the Doctrine of Double Effect simply by stipulating something on the following lines: the agent turned on the light in order to illuminate the room; the agent foresaw that illuminating the room would also alert the prowler but that was not the agent's aim in illuminating the room. Now we have the two effects that double effect needs: 'illuminating the room' and 'alerting the prowler'; but, as we have just explained, those two count both as effects only of 'flipping the switch' but not, for example, of 'turning on the light', because the two descriptions 'turning on the light' and 'illuminating the room' are not in a cause and effect relation to each other.

The point is, then, that the application of the Doctrine does not depend on whether something really is an independent effect or just a consequence or result or alternative action description: independently of what one thinks of the Doctrine, for example, it would certainly be implausible to think that the Doctrine may be applied – in Davidson's case – to the action description 'flipping the switch' because that action description has two genuine effects but that the Doctrine may not be applied to the action description 'turning on the light' because this latter description does not have two independent effects because 'illuminating the room' is not an effect of the cause 'turning on the light' but rather a different description of the same event.

To put it briefly, then – and without having to enter the discussion on action individuation at all – we can say that talk of double *effect* is not meant to be taken literally, metaphysically speaking.[5]

2.1 Intentional and intended

A further preliminary issue: the reader will have noticed that some formulations of the Doctrine talk of 'intended' (Mangan and Gury[6]) while other formulations talk of 'intentional' (McIntyre and Woodward); on top of this, Aquinas himself talks of *praeter intentionem* (which in the translation I am adopting has been rendered with 'beside the intention').

Here I will leave the historical issue of whether 'intended' or 'intentional' is the best rendering of Aquinas's *praeter intentionem* and focus on the theoretical issue of whether it makes a difference to talk of 'intentional' instead of 'intended' – which, I am going to argue, it does. In contemporary philosophy of action, there is a continuing debate on the so-called *Simple View* of intentional action, according to which an action is intentional only if it is intended: 'For me intentionally to A I must intend to A . . . I will call this the Simple View' (Bratman 1987: 112).[7]

Even if one accepts the Simple View, then 'intended' and 'intentional' are still not interchangeable because the Simple View only offers necessary conditions rather than sufficient ones. But, more importantly, many if not most reject the Simple View of intentional action; and, interestingly, this rejection is not necessarily a sign of scepticism about double effect. Take Michael Bratman himself, who in discussing his friendly application of his planning theory of intention to double effect draws the distinction between the claim that the side effect is not intended and the claim that the side effect is not intentional:

> Though Strategic Bomber has taken the deaths of the children quite seriously into account in his deliberation, these deaths are for him only an expected side effect; they are not – in contrast with Terror Bomber's position – intended as a means . . . *In saying this I do not deny that Strategic Bomber kills the children intentionally.* (1987: 139–40 – my emphasis)[8]

What difference does it make to the Doctrine of Double Effect whether one formulates it in terms of an unintended effect or in terms of an unintentional effect? On the one hand, it could be suggested that it is rather friendly towards the Doctrine to formulate it in terms of unintentional effects, because the *agential* difference between intentional and unintentional effects is often taken to make a difference to important moral matters such as, say, responsibility; and so, it may be argued, if double effect is formulated as a principle about the moral value of unintentional effects rather than unintended effects, then it may be easier to claim that there is a moral difference.

I am not sure, though, that the talk of unintentional effects is really so sympathetic towards the Doctrine, because I think that one could easily turn the talk of unintentional effects against the Doctrine in the following way: if the Doctrine is, as it is traditionally thought to be (see, for example, the already mentioned Boyle 1980), a principle of justification and therefore a principle about the moral permissibility of actions (and it is clear that at least some famous applications of the Doctrine – such as, say, the Trolley Problem – are formulated in terms of moral permissibility), then talking about unintentional effects may turn out to be a problem for the Doctrine. This is because permissibility principles are meant for intentional actions: if one asks whether some action is morally allowed or not, one is asking whether one may perform some action and therefore is asking whether one may be allowed to intentionally perform that action. One is not asking about accidents or mistakes – which are two of the paradigmatic examples of unintentional actions.

Here we have already come to the decisive issue when it comes to whether we should interpret the Doctrine in terms of 'intended' or 'intentional': what we are asking, as already said, is whether the effect that the Doctrine wants to allow for should be interpreted to be an unintentional effect or merely an unintended effect; and this question must be addressed with the background that the relevant effect is not unforeseen. The relevant effect that the Doctrine wants to allow for is one that is both foreseen and avoidable: it is in this sense not a case of ignorance, false belief or coercion. The agent knows very well that the relevant effect will be a result of her actions and the agent is not coerced into bringing about that effect (at least not in the normal Aristotelian sense of being carried by the wind, even though some Kantians may want to say that the agent is coerced by her own principles or some such thing).

So whether or not one embraces the Simple View of intentional action, the real issue here is that it is problematic to think of the side effect that the Doctrine wants to allow for as an unintentional effect given that the agent foresees the effect and brings about it non-coercively. In this respect, then, we are deprived of some standard ways of arguing that this effect is unintentional. We have just seen, then, that the difference between 'intentional' and 'intended' is not merely terminological but rather theoretical and that it depends on what one makes of the Simple View of intentional action; but that we don't need to engage in a debate about the Simple View of intentional action in order to settle the issue of whether the side effect that the Doctrine wants to allow for is merely unintended or actually unintentional: since the side effect is both foreseen and non-coerced, then cannot argue that it is unintentional; and we are therefore left with just 'unintended'.

Here it could be objected that, notwithstanding our argument that the side effect cannot be unintentional, we need to deal with what a defender of the Simple View would say about the side effect. Here there seem to be different dialectical possibilities: the easiest and maybe also the preferred one if you think that intentional actions are necessarily intended may just be to claim that the side effect is also intended and be done with it. In that case, there would simply be no room left for something like the distinction which is at the core of the Doctrine of Double Effect. And this may indeed be the way to go if you are a Simple View sympathizer, since it is also a shortcut to rejecting double effect. But having argued elsewhere at length against the Simple View, this option is not available to those like myself (or Bratman, for that matter) who do not endorse the Simple View of intentional action (for my own discussion of the Simple View, see the following: Di Nucci 2008, 2009a, 2010a, 2013).

A different possibility for defenders of the Simple View may be to deny the points I have made above about unintentional actions being the result of an epistemic gap (ignorance or false belief) or of coercion. One could, for example, say the following: considerations such as an epistemic gap or coercion are decisive for responsibility but not for intentionality; what is decisive for intentionality is just the intention. This is quite obviously a possibility, but then one would no longer have any room left for the distinction between 'intended' and 'intentional', so that 'intentional' would then just mean 'intended' and the Simple View would be a conceptual truth. I am not going to say why I find this approach problematic (just see my other writings on this), because we do not need to deal with this approach given that, on this approach, all the different formulations of the Doctrine that we have listed, whether they use 'intended' or 'intentional', really refer to the same concept and the distinction between 'intended' and 'intentional' would then merely be a terminological one. This last option, by the way, is at least historically quite plausible: namely it is quite plausible that those who formulate the Doctrine in terms of 'intentional' are just not very familiar with or interested in contemporary debates in the philosophy of action about intentional action and the Simple View and just take 'unintentional' to mean 'unintended'.

Let us take stock: so far we have clarified two important aspects of the different formulations of the Doctrine of Double Effect: the first issue being whether we should take the talk of 'effects' metaphysically seriously and the second being how we should interpret the diverging talk of 'intended' and 'intentional' in the different formulations of the Doctrine.

2.2 Intending the good effect

There is another action-theoretical issue that needs dealing with which is related to what we have just said about the difference between *intentional* action and *intended* action. In at least one formulation of the Doctrine – Mangan's – the intention requirement is not merely formulated in negative terms, so that the bad effect should not be intended; the intention requirement is also formulated in positive terms, so that the good effect should be intended: '2) that the good effect and not the evil effect be intended' (1949: 43). This is a potential limitation to the application of the Doctrine which, depending on your views on agency, may actually turn out to be either a very large limitation or a pretty insignificant one.

The issue is whether the Doctrine should really only be applicable to those cases where the agent positively intends the good effect but does not intend the bad effect or whether it should also be applicable to cases where the agent neither intends the good effect nor she intends the bad effect. You may think that intention in particular and mental states in general have a more limited role in action explanation than most philosophers of action grant them, because there are plenty of agential phenomena which are not intended; here are some: automatic actions, habits, emotional and spontaneous reactions, omissions, social conventions, primed behaviours.

If you think that at least some of those agential phenomena cannot be explained in terms of mental states such as intentions (and I do: I have written two books on this and related issues – Di Nucci 2008 and Di Nucci 2013), then you may also think that on Mangan's formulation of double effect the Doctrine has limited application because it cannot be applied to cases such as automatic actions. This is not the place to discuss this issue in any detail (just check my books mentioned above if you are interested); but these considerations are a reason why we should focus only on the negative formulation of the Doctrine which requires that the bad effect be unintended and ignore Mangan's additional condition that the good effect be intended. Admittedly, there is a further issue here which I will not discuss at length: if one believes – like I do – that sometimes when we act automatically or habitually we act intentionally but without the relevant intention, then that would allow one – at least according to the Doctrine of Double Effect – to get away with a lot of bad things as long as these things were done both habitually and within the proportionality condition; and this can be in itself taken to be an argument against the Doctrine of Double Effect, because it can't be that the moral permissibility of an action depends on whether the agent was acting automatically at the time; I will not explore this in any detail here; as I mentioned, I have defended the premise of this argument elsewhere (especially Di Nucci 2008 and Di Nucci 2013).

2.3 Permissibility

A further issue that has emerged during our preliminary discussion is what we should take the Doctrine to want to do. This is a very important point but one that we can deal with pretty quickly because there is no disagreement on this issue between the different formulations of the Doctrine that we are here comparing and also no disagreement in the literature on double effect more in general: the Doctrine of Double Effect is a principle about justification and permissibility, as we gather from McIntyre's talk of 'permissible', Mangan's talk of 'licitly' and Gury's talk of 'lawful'.

Here it is maybe easier to illustrate this point by mentioning what the Doctrine is NOT meant to do: first of all, in saying that it is a principle of moral permissibility we are saying that it is a purely *moral* principle. It is not, for example, a legal principle nor is it an agential principle about the attributability of certain effects. It is just a standard moral principle about whether some action is morally justified/permissible. Secondly, in saying that it is a principle of moral permissibility we are also saying that it is only about permissibility and not, say, about what we ought to do or about our moral duties and obligations.

The quickest way to see this is to look at one standard application of double effect, namely the Trolley Problem, where the original question is whether it is morally permissible to divert a trolley onto a side track where it will kill one person if we are doing so in order to save the five people on the main track. The question here is NOT whether we ought to divert the trolley but only whether we are allowed to divert it: one could think, for example, that the Doctrine of Double Effect provides us with an argument why we are morally allowed to divert the trolley (so that we could appeal to the Doctrine to justify our actions) but that at the same time the Doctrine does not bind us so that we are also allowed not to intervene. For example, one may think that since the Doctrine does explicitly recognize the permissible effect as a bad or evil one, then that would be the reason why we are not obliged to bring about the evil effect but only allowed to. Again, here we don't need to enter into any big debate about the nature of moral permissibility as opposed to moral obligation: the point is only that all standard formulations of the Doctrine make it out in terms of moral permissibility and not in terms of moral obligation.

Finally, in saying that double effect is a principle of moral permissibility, we are also saying that it is not a principle about responsibility, excuse or mitigating reasons: it is really about justi-fication. As I dedicate an entire chapter to this issue (Chapter 12), I will not discuss it here any further than just stating that double effect is about justification and not about responsibility – for the further question of whether double effect *may* be made out to become a principle about responsibility, just wait for Chapter 12 please.

In the next section I deal with the other interpretative issue mentioned at the outset, namely how many conditions the Doctrine really needs.

3 Too many conditions?

The Doctrine of Double Effect as it has been historically formulated involves both a distinction between 'means' and 'side effects' (or at least 'means' anyway, as the term 'side effects' does not normally feature in formulations of the Doctrine's conditions) and a distinction between 'intending' and 'merely foreseeing' (or at least 'not intending'; as, again, the term 'foreseeing' does not normally feature in formulations of the Doctrine's conditions; see Davis 1984: 121[9] for an exception). In the classic formulations of the Doctrine, there is a stipulation both that the bad effect may not be a means to the good effect and that the bad effect may not be intended; and, importantly, these two points are made in different conditions. Mangan's second and third conditions are the standard example: '2) that the good effect and not the evil effect be intended; 3) that the good effect be not produced by means of the evil effect' (1949: 43). That the stipulation about 'intention' and the stipulation about 'means' come in different conditions must suggest that intention and means are, at least traditionally, understood to be independent from one another to the extent that they warrant different necessary conditions.

This suggests at least the following two ways in which the two are independent: that the bad effect may be intended but not a means to the good effect, and that the bad effect may be a means to the good effect but not be intended. Not many people would endorse the by-conditional between 'means' and 'intended', simply because we may also intend other things, such as, for example, ends. So that we intend an effect does not imply that this effect counts as a means. That this conditional is false explains why the by-conditional is false, but this leaves open the possibility that the other conditional be true, namely that if an effect counts as a means, then it must be intended. This position can be found in the literature on the Doctrine of Double Effect: Boyle (1980) argues that the means condition (3) is simply implied by the intention condition (2) because by stipulating that the bad effect may not be intended, then – if the above conditional is true – we also imply that the bad effect may not be a means to the good end or effect.

> If the evil effect is brought about as a means to the good effect, then the evil effect must be intended, and the bringing about of the instrumental state of affairs is morally impermissible. The bad effect is intended if it is chosen as a means because it becomes something which the agent is committed to realizing. The bringing about of this instrumental state of affairs is a morally impermissible act because this state of affairs – the bad effect – determines the moral character of the undertaking. Thus, the third condition is implied by the first condition and the definition of a "means". (Boyle 1980: 11[10])

Boyle's point is that if the bad effect were a means, then it must have been intended; but then it would already violate the 'intention' condition; so the 'means' condition is implied by the 'intention' condition plus our above conditional that an effect can count as a means only if it is intended (that is what Boyle refers to with the definition of 'means': it is part of the definition of 'means' that they are intended).

The question is not just whether means are necessarily intended. It is also whether side effects are necessarily not intended – merely foreseen, as it is normally put in the literature. But if we answer the first question affirmatively, then the means condition is implied by the intention condition. But then we needn't worry about the means/side effect dichotomy anymore, because the means condition would then be superfluous and we could focus the discussion only on the intending/foreseeing dichotomy. Here there is a more important point at stake: applying the principle of charity, those in the tradition systematized by Gury and Mangan could not have just overlooked the redundancy of the 'means' condition on the 'intention' condition given that means are necessarily intended. Therefore, they must have thought that means were not necessarily intended. And even if we granted that means are necessarily intended, therefore ridding the Doctrine of the means/side effects dichotomy, we would still need a coherent distinction between intending and merely foreseeing: one may argue that the talk of means/side effects helps us with the intending/foreseeing dichotomy whether or not 'means' feature in the conditions of the Doctrine.

In asking the question if means, as opposed to side effects, are necessarily intended, we must distinguish between a *intensional* understanding of 'means' and an *extensional* understanding of 'means': Davis (1984: 129–30) talks of 'agent-interpretation' and 'event-interpretation'. On the event-interpretation, some causal condition counts as a means irrespective of the agent's awareness. Suppose I am on the bridge with the fat man. I haven't realized that there are rail tracks under the bridge. I haven't seen the runaway trolley or the five workmen on the tracks. I am just on the bridge with this fat man, and I hate his guts. So I push him, thereby saving the five. Now on the extensional interpretation of 'means', my pushing him is a means to save the five just because it was a causal condition to save the five. But I didn't even know that these people existed. So the event-interpretation will not do.[11]

On the agent-interpretation, some event counts as a means only if it features in the agent's psychology. Two points here: it is one thing to say that an event features in the agent's psychology, and another thing to say that an event is intended by the agent. Merely foreseen side effects also feature in the agent's psychology: the agent has, at the very least, a belief that some action of hers will have a certain side effect. So talking about awareness does not go very far in distinguishing between means and side effects; and it does not answer the question of whether means are necessarily intended. It only shows – and this is important – that the Doctrine should be understood intensionally and not extensionally.

Here is not the place to answer the question of whether means are necessarily intended, as I dedicate a chapter to this issue (Chapter 7). The point here was to illustrate the relationship between the different conditions and also to show that the Doctrine must be understood intensionally. Having done so, we see that Mangan's and Gury's formulations – which are made out in terms of four conditions – are not that different, really, from McIntyre's and Woodward's, which only mention one distinction. To illustrate this even more explicitly, take Boyle's translation of Gury's version of the Doctrine:

> It is licit to posit a cause which is either good or indifferent from which there follows a twofold effect, one good, there other evil, if a proportionately grave reason is present, and if the end of the agent is honourable – that is, if he does not intend the evil effect. (1980: 8)

Here, in line with Boyle's argument about the redundancy of the means condition on the intention condition, we no longer have four conditions but only three (in the order in which they are mentioned in the text):

1 the cause must be either good or indifferent;
2 proportionality;
3 the end of the agent is honourable: that is, he does not intend the evil effect.

Here Mangan's translation of Gury again:

> It is lawful to actuate a morally good or indifferent cause from which will follow two effects, one good and the other evil, if there is a proportionately serious reason, and the ultimate end of the agent is good, and the evil effect is not the means to the good effect. (Mangan's translation; 1949: 60)

What has happened to Gury's Doctrine moving from Mangan's translation to Boyle's? Boyle simply takes the last statement ('the evil effect is not the means to the good effect', which Boyle formulates as 'he does not intend the evil effect' to eliminate all talk of 'means') to be an illustration of the previous one rather than an addition onto the previous one: Boyle translates with 'that is' rather than 'and' as it was in Mangan; three conditions rather than four. And given what we have said about intended means and also about the intensional nature of the Doctrine, we now see why Boyle's move is a legitimate one.

We have now eliminated one further difference between Gury's original and modern formulations such as McIntyre's. Having already dealt with the proportionality condition, all that is left to distinguish modern from classic formulations is, then, the first condition which is made out in terms of 'posit a cause which is either good or indifferent' (Boyle's Gury) or 'actuate a morally good or indifferent cause' (Mangan's Gury) or 'that the action in itself from its very object be good or at least indifferent' (Mangan). Here I will show that the first condition is also redundant so that classic formulations in terms of four conditions and contemporary formulations in terms of one single distinction are indeed equivalent (Boyle also argues against the first condition (1980: 11–12)).

One thing about the first condition has already been said: even though it is traditionally often put in terms of 'cause', it need be no cause because, as we have argued in this chapter, the relation does not need to be one of cause and effect, as in 'turning the light on' and 'illuminating the room'. And indeed the translation of Aquinas mentions an 'act' rather than a 'cause'. What we can agree on is that the first condition is a condition about the action of which the Doctrine wants to say that, despite its bad effect, it is under certain conditions morally permissible. So it is not a condition about the side effect but a condition about the action of which that effect is predicated. And the first condition constraints the kind of actions to which the Doctrine may be applied by saying that it can only be successfully applied to actions that are 'good or indifferent'; which means, in short, that it cannot be applied to actions which are bad/evil.

The first objection to the first condition is pretty simple: how can we mention the moral status of the action (good or indifferent) in the first condition if the moral status of the action is exactly what the whole Doctrine is meant to establish? Namely, the first objection to the first condition is that it is question-begging, because it already establishes in one part of the Doctrine what the whole Doctrine is meant to establish, namely that the action is not bad/impermissible.

In order to deal with the above objection, someone who wanted to defend the independence of the first condition would then have to argue that the 'good or indifferent' mentioned in the first condition is something other than the 'morally permissible' that the whole Doctrine is meant to establish. One way of doing that would be to argue that 'good or indifferent' is being predicated of the action itself (as Mangan explicitly puts it), while 'morally permissible' – if the Doctrine is successful – is predicated of the whole action including the effects. The idea would be to distinguish the action in itself from the complex action which includes certain effects that it produces.

Here one could say, with Boyle, that since the talk is of positing or actuating a cause, it is hard to see how the cause should be evaluated independently of the effects that it produces, as the first condition appears to suggest: 'cause and effect are correlative, and "positing a cause" can be immoral only because it brings about some effect which it is impermissible to bring about' (1980: 11). I agree with Boyle here, but since we have shown that the success or failure of the Doctrine does not depend on a strict metaphysical understanding of 'effect', we should be able to make Boyle's point independently of appealing to causes and effects. And indeed Boyle himself suggests a way which I think is independent of talking of causes and effects being correlative: if the act itself is supposed to be impermissible independently of the effects that it will generate, then intending that act would mean that the agent would intend something bad/ evil, which is already ruled out by the other condition so that this condition is now superfluous (again, see here Boyle 1980: 11).

I think that there are also other ways of showing why condition 1 is superfluous which are independent of Boyle's critique. Let us ask ourselves what kind of cases condition 1 is supposed to rule out: the idea seems to be that there are actions which have an intrinsic negative value (independent of their positive or negative effects) which cannot be compensated by grave reason even if their negative effect is not intended and that there are actions which do not have such negative intrinsic value so that they are permissible if there is a grave reason and the negative effect is not intended.

Take the trolley problem as an example of this supposed intrinsic value of actions. One could think, for example, that diverting trolleys from one track to another is intrinsically morally good or indifferent (the latter, I guess) but that pushing people off bridges is intrinsically morally bad and that therefore whatever grave reason one has for doing it and even if the bad effect of it is unintended, pushing people off bridges will not be the kind of act to which the

Doctrine can be applied to. But this talk of intrinsic value is both too weak and too strong at the same time: too weak because one does not want to rule out all 'pushing people off bridges': think of bungee jumping; think of diving if you are disabled and need some support; think of collapsing bridges and various other terrible things that can happen on a bridge and that can be avoided by being pushed off it. But even if one wanted to hang on to some sort of intrinsic badness of 'pushing people off bridges' and tried to rule out the above counterexamples one by one, the problem is that the Doctrine is also supposed to apply to things that are much worse – intrinsically – than pushing people off bridges, such as, for example, dropping bombs. So it is not clear how actions such as dropping bombs (independently of their consequences, naturally) are going to be included if the first condition is interpreted as strictly as it is being suggested here.

Also – and this will be my last word on the issue of the first condition – it seems that the work that this first 'intrinsic value' condition is supposed to do in ruling out some cases can easily be done by the proportionality condition: if the action is just too bad, then that will just mean that the reason in favour of it will simply be not grave enough. So that what the first condition was supposed to rule out is ruled out by the proportionality condition and the first condition is – again but for different reasons – redundant.

4 One final clarification: The counterfactual test

In conclusion to this chapter, I want to clarify one more aspect of the Doctrine. I do so by arguing that the *counterfactual test* for intention does not work in distinguishing intended means from merely foreseen side effects and that therefore the doctrine cannot appeal to it. Even though this is already a rebuttal of a possible argument in favour of the Doctrine, the point that is being made here is so uncontroversial that this section should rather be understood as further clarifying what the Doctrine of Double Effect consists in by avoiding one common misunderstanding. Still, my rejection of the counterfactual test of intention in this section counts as my first argument against the Doctrine of Double Effect.

The counterfactual test is one (superficial) way in which one could try to distinguish between intended means and merely foreseen side effects, and therefore one possible argument for the fundamental distinction behind the Doctrine of Double Effect. The idea is that to test whether some effect is intended, one should ask what the agent would do in a parallel scenario where everything is the same apart from the fact that somehow the agent's action no longer brings about that effect: if the agent would no longer perform the relevant action, then that effect was intended.[12] Take *Bystander at the Switch*: one could use the counterfactual test to argue that the bystander does not intend to kill the one.

The argument would go as follows: in the actual case, the bystander did bring about the effect of killing the one; but that was only because of ugly necessity, since there was no way to avoid killing the one in saving the five by redirecting the trolley. What shows that the bystander did not intend to kill the one and therefore that the killing of the one was only a merely foreseen side effect – so would the argument based on the counterfactual test continue – is that the agent would still act in a counterfactual case where, everything else being equal, diverting the trolley would somehow not kill the one.

The counterfactual test, though, won't do to distinguish cases that are supposed to involve merely foreseen side effects such as *Bystander at the Switch* from cases such as *Fat Man* that are supposed to involve intended means rather than merely foreseen side effects. Here is why: let us ask the same question we asked for *Bystander at the Switch* also for *Fat Man*, namely whether the bystander intends to kill the (fat) one. We find that we can say for *Fat Man* exactly what we said for *Bystander at the Switch* too: namely, that in the actual case the bystander did bring about the effect of killing the one; but that was only because of ugly necessity, since there was no way to avoid killing the one in saving the five by *stopping* the trolley. What shows that the bystander did not intend to kill the one and therefore that the killing of the one was only a merely foreseen side effect is that the agent would still act in a counterfactual case where, everything else being equal, *stopping* the trolley would somehow not kill the one (note that the two 'stopping' in italics are the only differences between what we said here and what we said above for *Bystander at the Switch*, where we had 'diverting').

Here it makes no sense to appeal to other possible differences: that's not at issue here and it is discussed at length elsewhere within the whole book; the point here is only to assess the value of the counterfactual test. Before we explain why the test fails, let me run it for the other classic example in the double effect literature to show that the failing of the counterfactual test does not depend on particular features of trolley cases.

Enter Strategic Bomber and Terror Bomber: one could try to apply the counterfactual test in order to show that Strategic Bomber does not intend to kill the children while Terror Bomber does by saying the following: if somehow Strategic Bomber's plan turns out to no longer depend on the effect of killing the children because the munitions factory turns out to be further from the school than previously thought, that will make no difference to Strategic Bomber because it is only the munitions factory that she cares about; but Terror Bomber's plan depends on killing the children so that if the planned bombing turned out to no longer have that effect, then Terror Bomber could no longer go ahead and would have to reconsider. But think of this: just as Strategic Bomber only needs the children's death as long as they are necessary to destroy the munitions factory, so Terror Bomber only needs the children's death as long as they are necessary to demoralize the enemy too; if somehow the enemy turned out to be demoralized/demoralizable independently of the children's death – as with Strategic Bomber the munitions factory turned out to be destroyed/destroyable independently of the children's death, then Terror Bomber would no longer have any reason to kill the children.

Here, again, it makes no sense to appeal to other possible differences or to enter the whole closeness debate, because we are only assessing whether the counterfactual test alone can do the trick, which it cannot (for the issue of closeness, see Chapter 6).[13] Let us now briefly explain why the counterfactual test fails: it should be no surprise that one can eliminate the relevant effect in both the cases that are supposed to be intended means and the cases that are supposed to be merely foreseen side effects, because both means and side effects are such that they only have dependent value: namely they are only valuable insofar as they enable some further means or ends; means, just like side effects, are not valuable in themselves. That is the simple reason why the counterfactual test does not work in distinguishing between means and side effects;

because it actually appeals to a feature which means and side effects have in common, namely that they are not valuable in themselves but only in virtue of their supposed relation to the achievement of some further means or ends.

Let me clarify that the point of this section is only to show that the counterfactual test alone will not distinguish between intended means and merely foreseen side effects; it is neither to claim that we cannot distinguish between intended means and side effects (otherwise, the book would be already over with this section), nor is it to claim that the counterfactual test is in itself useless. Indeed, at least the latter point is probably false: compare Terror Bomber with Sadistic Bomber.

The former is someone who intends to kill school children in order to demoralize the enemy; given that the involvement of school children in her plan only serves the purpose of demoralizing the enemy, Terror Bomber would not intend to kill the school children in a counterfactual scenario where she does not have the end of demoralizing the enemy nor would she intend to kill the children in a counterfactual scenario where she can demoralize the enemy without killing the children – whatever you make of these counterfactuals, they can certainly be stipulated.

Sadistic Bomber, on the other hand, may be imagined as someone who also intends to kill the children in order to demoralize the enemy; differently from Terror Bomber, though, Sadistic Bomber would also still intend to kill the children in counterfactual scenarios where the goal of demoralizing the enemy can be achieved differently; this is because the value of killing school children, for Sadistic Bomber, does not entirely depend on it serving the purpose of demoralizing the enemy; Sadistic Bomber values killing school children also independently of that further purpose.

Having distinguished Terror Bomber from Sadistic Bomber, we can say at least the following: it may be that the counterfactual test can distinguish between the attitudes of Terror Bomber and Sadistic Bomber to killing school children by running counterfactual scenarios in which killing school children does not serve the *actual* goal of the two bombers. I think that what I have said above does suggest this conclusion and I will not dispute this point here. Further, it may be that one may be able to convincingly use the counterfactual test in a moral argument which distinguishes Terror Bomber from Sadistic Bomber. Again, I will not dispute this point.

The only point I have disputed in this section is the claim that the counterfactual test can alone distinguish between intended means and merely foreseen side effects: it cannot do that.

This section has hopefully also served the purpose of further clarifying the scope of my arguments in this book: I do not want to deny that motivation in general may make a moral difference; I only want to deny the truth of the Doctrine of Double Effect, namely that the same effect can be permissible if a merely foreseen side effect but impermissible if an intended means; and in this section I have shown that this distinction cannot be drawn by appeal to the counterfactual test.

5 Conclusion

Summing up, in this chapter we have shown that even though traditional formulations of the Doctrine of Double Effect look very different from contemporary statements of it and are made out in terms of four individually necessary and jointly sufficient conditions against the single distinction of contemporary statements of the Doctrine, the two really are equivalent insofar as in both cases it comes down to a principle that sometimes allows for unintended harm (bad effect). Boyle comes to the same conclusion when he trims the four traditional conditions down to two: '(1) the state of affairs is not intrinsic to the action undertaken – that is, it is not intended – and (2) there is a serious reason for undertaking the action' (1980: 12). Finally, we have further clarified the role of the distinction between intended means and merely foreseen side effects in the Doctrine of Double Effect by rejecting the so-called counterfactual test of intention as a way of drawing that distinction.

CHAPTER THREE

Back to the beginning: Aristotle, Aquinas and the origins of double effect

Abstract *Where did the Doctrine of Double Effect come from? Despite standard attributions to Aquinas's discussion of self-defence in* Summa II, *there are some interesting similarities between the actions often thought to be justifiable by the Doctrine of Double Effect and Aristotle's 'mixed actions' in* Book III *of the* Nicomachean Ethics. *After casting doubts on the attribution of double effect to Aquinas, in this chapter I compare Aristotle's examples of mixed actions with standard cases from the literature on double effect such as, among others, strategic bombing, the trolley problem and craniotomy. I find that, despite some common features such as the dilemmatic structure and the inevitability of a bad effect, Aristotle's mixed actions do not count as cases justifiable through application of the Doctrine of Double Effect because they fail to meet the crucial necessary condition of the Doctrine according to which the bad effect can only be a merely foreseen side effect and not an intended*

means. The upshot of my discussion of Aristotle's mixed
actions in this chapter is my second argument against the
Doctrine: the argument from marginally bad means.

1 Introduction

The Doctrine of Double Effect is normally traced back to Aquinas:
'Nothing hinders one act from having two effects, only one of
which is intended, while the other is beside the intention' (*Summa
II-II*, 64, 7). The attribution of the Doctrine of Double Effect to
Aquinas's treatment of self-defence in *Summa II* has sometimes
been denied – notably by Anscombe – but double effect is not
normally thought to go further back than Aquinas. Now, I am
not an historian, but Anscombe's arguments against attributing
double effect to Aquinas seem pretty convincing to me. Indeed,
even louder than Anscombe's arguments speaks Aquinas's own
text which Anscombe quotes:

> If it (the consequent event) is pre-conceived, it manifestly adds
> to the goodness or badness of the action. For when someone
> considers that much that is bad can follow from what he does,
> and does not give it up on that account, this shows that his will is
> more inordinate. But if the consequent act is not pre-conceived,
> then it is necessary to distinguish. For if it follows from that kind
> of action *per se* and in most cases, then the consequent event
> does accordingly add to the goodness or badness of the action;
> for it is clear that action is better in kind, from which more
> goods can follow, and worse, from which more evils are liable to
> follow. But if it is *per accidens*, and in rather few cases, then the
> consequent event does not add to the goodness or to the badness
> of the action: for there isn't judgment on any matter according
> to what is *per accidens* but only what is *per se*. (Anscombe 2001:
> 66; Aquinas's original is in I-II, 20, 5)

Now, this isn't exactly inconsistent with double effect, but there
are two elements in what Aquinas is quoted as saying above which
point in a very different direction: first, Aquinas says explicitly that
if a bad effect is foreseen, that adds to the badness of the action.
Secondly, Aquinas talks of *per accidens* rather than unintended,

thereby identifying a class of cases (unintentional actions) that we have, in the previous chapter, distinguished from the unintended but foreseen and avoidable effects that the Doctrine wants to allow for.

Here I am not interested in adjudicating the issue: let us just say that the attribution to Aquinas has been historically very common and influential but that, at the same time, the evidence brought by Anscombe does at least cast some serious doubts on this classic attribution. But what I am interested in more in this chapter is to look at a much less discussed link, namely the one between double effect and Aristotle's discussion of mixed actions in Book III of the Nicomachean Ethics: only recently scholars have started to point out a possible connection (Pakaluk 2011[1]).

In discussing *hekousion* and *akousion* (normally translated with 'voluntary' and 'involuntary'), Aristotle offers some examples – of what he calls 'mixed actions' – which are strikingly similar to the sort of examples which are put forward in discussions of the Doctrine of Double Effect. Here I look at this connection between mixed actions and double effect and argue that – despite the similarities – nothing like the Doctrine of Double Effect can be possibly attributed to Aristotle. In reading this chapter, please keep in mind that the scope is not primarily historical but rather to further illustrate the Doctrine and some of its classic cases by looking at Aristotle's mixed actions.

Here are Aristotle's two examples in the classic translation of Ross (1925):

> . . . if a tyrant were to order one to do something base, having one's parents and children in his power, and if one did the action they were to be saved, but otherwise would be put to death . . .
>
> Something of the sort happens also with regard to the throwing of goods overboard in a storm; for in the abstract no one throws goods away voluntarily; but on condition of its securing the safety of himself and his crew any sensible man does so. (1110a5–20)

Let us look at the similarities between those two examples: both cases are such that the agent is under external pressure to do something that she would normally not do – 'do something base' and 'throw goods overboard'. Both are cases where capitulating to the external pressure appears to be prima facie morally preferable to not capitulating: 'do something base or your family will be killed' and 'throw goods overboard or you and your crew will die'. In this respect the latter example is even clearer than the former, contrasting goods with persons; the former is more problematic because we may imagine base things that are not prima facie outweighed by rescuing one's family.

We may indeed for both examples talk of two effects or consequences: doing something base against rescuing my family in the first case, and throwing goods overboard against rescuing myself and my crew in the second case.[2] These cases are similar to Double Effect cases in that in both cases there is a prima facie good effect – rescuing my family and rescuing my crew – and a prima facie bad (or evil) effect – doing something base and throwing goods overboard.

Here I first explain what Aristotle means by 'mixed actions' by looking at his discussion of *hekousion* in NE III and then compare mixed actions with the standard scenarios in the double effect literature.

2 Aristotle

Aristotle thinks that these sorts of actions are 'mixed' because they are both *hekousion* and *akousion* (voluntary and involuntary). Here is the passage on mixed actions in full:

> But with regard to the things that are done from fear of greater evils or for some noble object (e.g. if a tyrant were to order one to do something base, having one's parents and children in his power, and if one did the action they were to be saved, but otherwise would be put to death), it may be debated whether such actions are involuntary or voluntary. Something of the sort happens also with regard to the throwing of goods overboard in a storm; for in the abstract no one throws goods away voluntarily, but on condition of its securing the safety of himself and his crew any sensible man does so. Such actions, then, are mixed, but are more like voluntary actions; for they are worthy of choice at the time when they are done, and the end of an action is relative to the occasion. Both the terms, then, 'voluntary' and 'involuntary', must be used with reference to the moment of action. Now the man acts voluntarily; for the principle that moves the instrumental parts of the body in such actions is in him, and the things of which the moving principle is in a man himself are in his power

to do or not to do. Such actions, therefore, are voluntary, but in the abstract perhaps involuntary; for no one would choose any such act in itself. (1110a5–20)

Here we must briefly say something about Aristotle's general discussion of hekousion in NE III.1 and III.2. Aristotle distinguishes among at least five kinds of actions:

a Chosen actions
b Voluntary actions
c Not voluntary actions
d Involuntary actions and
e Mixed actions

Aristotle starts with (d), involuntary actions: 'Those things, then, are thought involuntary, which take place by force or owing to ignorance' (1110a1). This is pretty intuitive: the only thing to note is perhaps that, in the contemporary action theory literature, what happens as the result of physical coercion is normally distinguished by behaving in ignorance. Davidson (1963, 1971, 1978), the trailblazer of contemporary causalism, holds that some movement is an action only if it is intentional under at least one description. On this account, movements that happen under physical coercion (Aristotle's own example is 'if he were to be carried somewhere by a wind, or by men who had him in their power' (1110a2)) are intentional under no description; therefore these movements are not actions, following Davidson.

On the other hand, on Davidson's account, cases of ignorance will count as actions, precisely unintentional actions. Oedipus knowingly kills the man at the junction and unknowingly kills his father. Here killing his father is unintentional because Oedipus does not know (nor does he believe) that the man at the junction is his father; but it is an action because it is intentional under another legitimate description, namely killing the man at the junction. So this is an example, on Davidson's account, of unintentional action. And this is different from the examples of physical coercion because those are not even actions.

Aristotle also distinguishes between involuntary actions and actions that are simply not voluntary: 'Everything that is done by reason of ignorance is not voluntary; it is only what produces pain and repentance that is involuntary' (1110b18–25). After having offered various examples of involuntary actions, Aristotle puts forward a definition of voluntary action: 'Since that which is done under compulsion or by reason of ignorance is involuntary, the voluntary would seem to be that of which the moving principle is in the agent himself, he being aware of the particular circumstances of the action' (1111a21).[3]

David Charles (1984) in his book on Aristotle's philosophy of action formalizes Aristotle's voluntary action as follows:

z is a voluntary action of S's at t1 iff;
z is a bodily movement of S's at t1;
S knows the relevant particulars involved in doing z (what he is doing at t1; to whom; with what: 1110b33); and
z is caused efficiently by one of S's desires at t1. (1980: 58)[4]

This formulation is interestingly similar to the kind of Humean causal account of action Davidson puts forward in *Actions, Reasons, and Causes* (1963 – and indeed there Davidson takes himself to be defending an 'ancient' (1963: 4) view, referring presumably to Aristotle). In this respect it is then no surprise that Charles thinks that 'voluntary' action in Aristotle is *intentional action*. But there is an important technical difference: Davidson's account is left as a set of necessary conditions because of deviant counterexamples. Presumably, Charles's formulation of Aristotle's account, given as a set of necessary and sufficient conditions, would also be subject to deviant counterexamples (1963: 12 and also Davidson's essay *Freedom to Act* (1973)).[5]

Voluntary actions, according to Aristotle, can be attributed to children and other animals too, and Aristotle introduces a further kind that seems to be reserved only to adult human agents, (a) choice: 'Both the voluntary and the involuntary having been delimited, we must next discuss choice; for it is thought to be most closely bound up with virtue and to discriminate characters better than actions do. Choice, then, seems to be voluntary, but not the same thing as the voluntary; the latter extends more widely. For both children and the lower animals share in voluntary action, but not in choice, and acts done on the spur of the moment we describe as voluntary, but not as chosen' (1111b5–10).[6]

Having now looked at Aristotle's understanding of action, we have a better idea of why Aristotle claims that 'mixed actions' are voluntary: the agent is neither physically coerced to act in the case of 'mixed actions' nor does the agent act in ignorance. Less clear, it would seem, is why Aristotle says that 'mixed actions' are also in some sense involuntary. But take notice of the following two aspects: first, mixed actions are also, in an important way, forced upon the agent. Even though the agent is not physically coerced as when she may be carried by the wind, the agent is forced by the circumstances to act the way she does.[7] Take the tyrant's example: the point is that it is *only* because of the tyrant's threat that the agent may consider doing something base. And that it is *only* because of the threat of the storm that the agent will throw goods overboard. Secondly, Aristotle says in distinguishing involuntary actions from actions that are merely not voluntary, that involuntary action requires 'pain and repentance'; mixed actions are certainly also a cause of pain; and the sort of difficult choices involved may provoke sometimes repentance and almost always lingering doubts.

Aristotle's suggestion, then, is that mixed actions are voluntary actions that have important features in common with involuntary actions: external circumstances force the agent in a dilemmatic situation out of which the agent cannot come without some bad consequences. Indeed, even when the balance of reasons may be clear as in the case of throwing goods overboard, the agent's only way out of the difficult situation involves some necessary bad consequences. Those are the very features of the sort of cases that are often tackled by the Doctrine of Double Effect: dilemma situations where there are no good effects without bad effects.

There is another similarity between Aristotle's mixed actions and standard cases from the literature on double effect: we have seen that Aristotle says that mixed actions are *hekousion* but also, in some sense, *akousion*. And we have seen that Charles's seminal treatment of Aristotle's action theory takes *hekousion* to be intentional action. At the same time, we find, in discussions on double effect (take, for example, Bratman's statement already quoted in the previous chapter), that the actions that the Doctrine is supposed to justify (Strategic Bomber's killing of the children, say) are intentional but not intended.

Let us now look at some classic double effect cases and compare them to Aristotle's mixed actions.

3 Double effect

Aristotle's two cases are strikingly similar to the classic examples in the Double Effect debate. I will mention here five kinds of examples which I take to be the most common ones[8] – the details of the cases have already been introduced in Chapter 1:

1 *Terror Bombing*. A good illustration of this case is provided by Bratman (1987: 139–40, already illustrated in Chapter 1);

2 *Trolley Problem*. The Trolley Problem was first introduced by Foot (1967[9]) even though its most influential formulation is Thomson's (1976 and 1985) variation on Foot's original case – the next chapter will deal with the trolley problem in more detail;

3 *Craniotomy*, which goes back to Foot's influential discussion (1967);

4 *Death-inducing pain alleviation*. This is another classic of the literature on double effect, even though there is overwhelming evidence that the sort of dosages of opioid drugs which are effective against pain do not actually hasten death (Sykes and Thorns 2003);

5 *Self-defence*, the original double effect case from Aquinas.

Let us now compare these classic examples from the double effect literature to Aristotle's two examples. Notice the similarity between, say, Strategic Bomber and Aristotle's captain. Both do things that might be thought to be absolutely forbidden (at least relatively to their role). Both do them unwillingly. Both seem to think that their wider goal is worth the sacrifice: in Strategic Bomber's case the wider goal of weakening enemy is supposedly worth the sacrifice of killing the children; and in Aristotle's Captain's case the wider goal of guaranteeing the safety of the crew is supposedly worth the sacrifice of the cargo.

Also, in both cases we can imagine alternative characters who might do the thing in question willingly: Terror Bomber on the one hand, and a Captain who might want to compromise the profitability of that particular route by throwing goods overboard. Also, importantly, Aristotle endorses the captain's throwing goods overboard by saying that 'any sensible man does so' just as the Doctrine of Double Effect provides a justification for what Strategic Bomber does.[10]

I will not go through the comparison of Aristotle's examples with all of the aforementioned scenarios, but just summarize the structural similarities:

Scenario	Good effect	Bad effect
Doing something base	Family is saved	The base thing
Throwing goods	Crew is saved	Goods are lost
Strategic Bomber	Factory is destroyed	Children are killed
Trolley Bystander	Five are saved	One is killed
Hysterectomy	Mother is saved	Foetus is killed
Pain alleviation	Pain relief	Death is hastened
Self-defence	I am saved	Attacker is killed

While it is not in all cases clear that the good effect is prima facie to be preferred to the bad effect, it is in all cases clear that there is a prima facie good effect and a prima facie bad effect. Pakaluk suggests the following in relation to the case in which one's family is hostage to a tyrant:

> if in the second case one refused to do the disgraceful thing, then one might wish to defend this by an appeal to DE [Double Effect], claiming that the death of one's family, although foreseen, was not intended, and that the agent cannot be held responsible for the bad actions of others, when there are merely incidental to what he was aiming to do, that is, act always in an upright way: in avoiding the disgraceful action, one both gains an honourable good (the kalon) and incurs a loss (of philoi); it makes sense to prefer the one over the other; there is no third way out (ex hypothesi); and certainly one takes no pleasure in the death of one's spouse and children. (2011: 215–16)

This is different from my classification, but it is also a different course of events – so that the two are not necessarily incompatible with each other. I have been comparing the case in which the agent saves his family with cases of double effect, while Pakaluk compares the case in which the agent does not save his family with cases of double effect. Here then the bad effect is the death of the family while the good effect is that the agent does an honourable thing in refusing to do something base, supposedly.

There are two things to note about Pakaluk's alternative reading: first, notice that here the proposed application of the Doctrine of Double Effect is for an intentional omission rather than for an action: the agent refuses or omits to do the base thing; none of the standard scenarios in the debate on double effect are such that the Doctrine is used to justify an omission; the Doctrine is rather normally used to justify an intervention: think, for example, of the bystander who may omit to divert the trolley from the five to the one but who, according to the Doctrine, may justifiably divert the trolley from the five to the one. Think of the surgeon who may omit to practise a hysterectomy but who, according to the Doctrine, may justifiably intervene to save the mother even though that kills the foetus.

Secondly, notice that Pakaluk's reading depends on supposing that 'one both gains an honourable good (the kalon) and incurs a loss (of philoi); it makes sense to prefer the one over the other' (2011: 216). Here, as we have said, because the course of events is different, there is no problem with Pakaluk's claim that refusing to do something base is an honourable good and that losing one's family is a loss; indeed, the two are both very plausible. But Pakaluk's next claim is less plausible, where he says that it makes sense to prefer the honourable good to avoiding the loss. The problem is not just moral intuition, which suggests that most people would probably rather save their family than obtain the honourable good of not doing something base (but, again, that does depend on what this base action consists in). The problem is rather that this would not be a clear-cut case, even if we inserted instead of the variable base action something pretty bad, say killing someone or betraying an important secret or something like that. Normally, in cases of double effect, the prima facie moral balance is, however, very clear: five workers as opposed to one in the trolley problem, or thousands of lives saved by shortening the war as opposed to some children in strategic bomber.[11]

Another thing that all the Double Effect scenarios have in common is that there are parallel cases also involving a comparable good effect and a comparable bad effect which do not meet the conditions to be justified by the Doctrine of Double Effect.

Scenario	Justified case	Unjustified case
Bomber	Strategic Bomber	Terror Bomber
Trolley	Bystander	Fat Man
Abortion	Hysterectomy	Craniotomy
Euthanasia	Pain relief	Intended killing
Killing	Self-defence	Intended killing

Here the structure of the Double Effect cases starts to emerge: it isn't simply that there are two effects, one good and the other bad, and that the good effect overwhelms, at least prima facie, the bad effect. That is because those two things are also true of all the above cases that are not supposed to be justifiable with the Doctrine. The idea is that, in each case, both the justifiable and unjustifiable cases are consequentialistically identical but that there is an intensional difference between each pair of cases: the justifiable case, in each pair, is one in which only the good effect was intended while the bad effect was merely foreseen as a side effect. Namely, the good effect may be an end in itself or a means to another good effect, while the bad effect may be neither an end in itself nor a means to the good effect – it can only be an unintended side effect. It is this intensional difference that is supposed to explain why the Doctrine justifies one but not the other in each pair.

So, to cite just one case, Strategic Bomber intends to destroy the munitions factory and foresees that destroying the munitions factory (as a means to shortening the war) will also cause the death of the children as a side effect. Strategic Bomber does not intend to kill the children either as an end in itself or as a means to shortening the war (nor is the death of the children supposed to be, according to double effect, a means to destroying the munitions factory). Terror Bomber, however, intends to kill the children as a means to shortening the war. Killing the children is, for Terror Bomber, an intended means to his end of shortening the war, and not merely a foreseen side effect of his plan.

In the next section, I will analyse Aristotle's mixed actions to see whether the distinction between intended means and merely foreseen side effects applies to mixed actions.

4 Means and side effects

Can we apply the distinction between intended means and merely foreseen side effects to Aristotle's examples? We may try to say the following: the captain, in throwing goods overboard, only intends to save the crew and does not actually intend to throw goods overboard: throwing goods overboard is merely a side effect of saving the crew. Similarly, we may say, of the agent who is asked by a tyrant to do something base otherwise his family will be killed, that he does not intend to do the base thing; he rather only intends to do save his family, and doing the base thing is just a foreseen side effect of saving his family. We may, indeed, try to say the above: but it does not sound as plausible as it does with the previously illustrated double effect examples such as strategic bombing or *Bystander at the Switch*. Can we really deny that throwing goods overboard is a means to save the crew? Can we really deny that doing the base thing is a means to save the family? It could be suggested that we look for parallel examples: after all, it may be said, to say that Strategic Bomber does not intend to kill the children is not in itself plausible; its plausibility depends on contrasting Strategic Bomber with Terror Bomber, who *clearly* intends to kill the children.

What are, then, the equivalent parallel cases for Aristotle's examples of mixed actions? Let us take throwing goods overboard. Take an alternative captain who may throw goods overboard because he wants to compromise the profitability of the route, or because he may be opposed to the goods in question (suppose they are transporting alcohol or neuroenhancements). The consequences of the two cases are supposed to be the same: the ship's cargo is lost. And we can certainly say that the two captains have different attitudes to throwing goods overboard. But is this difference in attitude a matter of intention? It seems to be rather a matter of having different reasons or goals: Aristotle's captain's goal is to save the crew; the new captain's goal is to prevent the dissemination of intoxifying substances.

We may argue about who has the morally preferable goal, but, again, the difference does seem to be in their goal and not in their intending to throw goods overboard. It seems, indeed, that in both cases the captains intend to throw goods overboard as a means to their respective goals of saving the crew and preventing the dissemination of intoxifying substances. We may try to say that Aristotle's captain does not really intend to throw the goods overboard because he would no longer throw goods overboard if the tempest would quiet down. But, as we have already shown in the previous chapter, this strategy – the so-called *counterfactual test* – does not go very far, because the other captain would also no longer throw the goods overboard if he realizes that he is actually carrying medicines; or maybe he reads a convincing argument in favour of the use of neuroenhancements. The counterfactuals are similarly close in both cases.

What would Aristotle's case have to look like so that we may convincingly talk of side effects as opposed to means? Before attempting to modify Aristotle's example, we should look at his other scenario, involving someone who has been blackmailed by a tyrant to do something base: if he does not comply, the tyrant will execute his family. Suppose that the one in question is a security official and that the base thing in question is to reveal a sensitive secret to the tyrant. Can we say that, when the security official passes the relevant information to the enemy, he does not intend to do so and that passing information to the enemy is not a means to save his family but only a side effect of saving his family? Again, that does not seem convincing, and this impression does not change even when we contrast our security official with another one who simply betrays his country for money. Again, they have different attitudes in that they have different reasons or goals; but that does not seem enough to be able to say that the former official does not pass on information as an intended means to save his family.

Maybe, it could be objected, we are just comparing Aristotle's examples to the wrong double effect case. Maybe if we compare them to a different case, we will get the relevant similarity. In this respect, self-defence looks promising. Indeed, Aristotle's case of doing a base thing does not seem far from a case of self-defence, as the victim is defending his own family from a threat. The structure is similar: if I don't do something that is prima facie base, such as killing or passing sensitive information to the enemy, I will lose something that is paramount to me (either my own life or the life of my children). Indeed, why think that the emergency in the case of self-defence is greater: most people would probably prioritize the life of their children over their own life. How is double effect supposed to justify self-defence and can we apply the same justification to Aristotle's case?

In applying the Doctrine of Double Effect to self-defence, we would probably say something like the following: I did not really intend to kill the attacker; I only intended to save my own life. And we can indeed say of Aristotle's example that the agent did not really intend to pass on the sensitive information, he only intended to save the life of his children. But the problem was that we cannot plausibly say that the agent did not pass sensitive information to the enemy as a means to save the life of his children. Similarly, though, we cannot plausibly say that the victim who kills in self-defence does not kill the attacker as a means to save his own life.

Recall Mangan's Condition 3 in his classic definition of the Doctrine of Double Effect: 'that the good effect be not produced by means of the evil effect' (1949: 43). The evil effect is not allowed to be a means to the good effect: so the killing of the attacker (bad effect) cannot be a means to save my own life (good effect), and the base betrayal of my country (bad effect) cannot be a means to save the life of my children (good effect). What that shows, though, is not just that Aristotle's example does not meet Condition 3 of the Doctrine of Double Effect. It also shows that the standard account of self-defence fails to meet Condition 3 of the Doctrine of Double Effect. And, after all, if the Doctrine's most influential example is Aquinas's discussion of self-defence, it cannot be that self-defence does not fit the Doctrine. Should we then just drop Condition 3?

This seems to be, for example, Pakaluk's position in arguing in favour of a significant relationship between Aristotle's examples and the Doctrine of Double Effect:

The class of actions which Aristotle would describe as "necessitated" is evidently the very same class to which a DE [Double Effect] analysis would apply. Both involve acting so as to bring about (or not acting to prevent) something bad, in circumstances of constraint such that this could not be done except by being responsible for something taken to be worse. Suppose there are two goods such that each is reasonably wanted but one is correctly preferred to the other, and suppose that circumstances are such that the goods have become so bound together that the only action which suffices to preserve the one is something which destroys the other; then we may say either that in the circumstances the agent is necessitated, by fear of losing the greater good, to act so as to destroy what he usually would want to preserve, or that in the circumstances the only action by which the agent may, as usual, preserve the greater good happens also to destroy the lesser good. An upshot is that DE applies to a much broader range of actions than is typically thought. (2011: 224–5)

Suppose we ignore Condition 3 and we say that, just as the attacked did not intend to kill the attacker but only intended to save his life, so in Aristotle's first example, I did not intend to do the base thing but only intended to save my family, and similarly in Aristotle's second example, I did not intend to throw the goods overboard but only intended to save my crew. The problem is that this is just an endorsement of some form of utilitarianism, as the above can be said of all the classic counterexamples to utilitarianism. Take the judge who knowingly puts to death an innocent man to avoid a riot (Rawls 1955; Foot 1967): the judge did not intend to put to death an innocent man but only intended to avoid a riot. Take the surgeon who kills a healthy hospital visitor to save five patients in desperate need of organs. The surgeon did not intend to kill the one but only intended to save the patients. Even if one thinks that the Doctrine of Double Effect is a concession of the absolutist to utilitarian counterexamples, then if there is to be anything to the Doctrine of Double Effect then there must be cases that it does not allow despite their utility.[12]

Pakaluk's suggestion of extending double effect has exactly the same problem, which we can illustrate by looking at his example of the two goods who happen to be bound together: 'two goods such that each is reasonably wanted but one is correctly preferred to the other, and suppose that circumstances are such that the goods have become so bound together that the only action which suffices to preserve the one is something which destroys the other' (2011: 225).

This is too broad: take the surgeon and the judge. The surgeon is also faced with two goods that are bound together: saving the lives of five patients on the one hand and not killing the healthy hospital visitor on the other. To use Pakaluk's own language: the circumstances are such that the goods have become so bound together that the only action which suffices to preserve the lives of the five patients is something which destroys the life of the other. Similarly with the judge: circumstances are such that the goods have become so bound together that the only action which suffices to preserve the public peace is something which destroys the life of the innocent man.

So if we water down double effect as proposed by Pakaluk so as to preserve the coincidence between Aristotle's examples and the standard cases of double effect, then we have just gone all the way utilitarian. Indeed, Pakaluk's two goods bound together identify just about any genuine dilemma. Sure, the Doctrine of Double Effect can be considered, dialectically, to be a sort of concession on the grounds of plausibility that the absolutist Kantian makes to utilitarian counterexamples: at least sometimes numbers must count, insists the utilitarian. And the Kantian absolutist may reply with the Doctrine of Double Effect that indeed sometimes, under the right conditions, numbers *can* count. But if we follow the suggestion discussed above, then numbers always count. But then we could no longer distinguish the Doctrine of Double Effect from utilitarianism. And that cannot be what the Doctrine of Double Effect was ever meant to do even if, as I said, one does concede that the Doctrine could be a compromise position between absolutism and utilitarianism.

In the next section, I consider whether there is a plausible interpretation of Aristotle's examples of mixed actions on which they may be equivalent to the sort of cases that the Doctrine of Double Effect justifies.

5 Mixed actions and double effect

The question remains whether we can interpret Aristotle's examples so that they may more plausibly meet Condition 3 and be assimilated to the classic scenarios in the Double Effect debate that we have been discussing. In order for Aristotle's captain's scenario to meet Condition 3, it must be the case that the bad effect – throwing goods overboard – is not an intended means to the good effect – saving the crew. The bad effect of throwing goods overboard must be just a side effect of saving the crew or of the action which results in saving the crew. Indeed, we need not imagine Aristotle's captain as standing on the edge of his ship literally throwing boxes in the water so as to reduce the ship's weight in order to increase the chances of withstanding the storm.

We may imagine that, in order to withstand the storm, the captain operates a sudden turning manoeuvre so as to direct the ship towards less dangerous waters. The captain knows that this sudden turning manoeuvre is likely to result in loss of cargo. Still, the captain does not want to or intend to lose cargo; he rather wants to and intends to save ship and crew from the storm. This scenario appears to be structurally similar to prominent side effects scenarios from the double effect debate, such as *Bystander at the Switch* or *Strategic Bomber*. The captain foresees loss of cargo but does not intend to get rid of his cargo; were there to be a different available manoeuvre with similar probabilities to save ship and crew from the storm but which did not involve likely loss of cargo, the captain would rather have chosen this other manoeuvre. But this possibility is just not there, so that the captain, if he wants to do his best to try and save ship and crew, must choose the sudden turning manoeuvre that he knows will likely also cause loss of cargo. In this scenario, just like in *Bystander at the Switch* and the Trolley Problem, loss of cargo (the bad effect) appears to be a side effect of the rapid turning manoeuvre to save ship and crew (the good effect). Notice the similarity with *Bystander at the Switch* and the Trolley Problem:

Scenario	Action	Bad effect	Good effect
Aristotle's Captain	Sudden turning manoeuvre	Loss of cargo	Crew is saved
Bystander	Flipping switch	One dies	Five are saved
Strategic Bomber	Dropping bombs	Children are killed	War is shortened

Now compare this interpretation of Aristotle's example to the following alternative possibility: the captain has been paid by a rival company to compromise the profitability of the route, of his ship, and of his shipping company. Luck has it that the current storm gives the captain the perfect chance to realize his plan without being caught. The captain opts for a sudden turning manoeuvre which will according to his calculations cause the cargo to fall in the water and be lost at sea. He suddenly turns the ship in order to drop as much cargo as possible. As it happens, the captain knows that this manoeuvre will also direct the ship towards less dangerous waters and minimize the chances of losing members of the crew.

But this captain does not really care about that; indeed, he is being paid by the rival company in order to compromise his own shipping company. For all he knows, the loss of crew members may have also been an effective strategy; but his deal involved only loss of cargo and he is personally indifferent to what happens to crew members. Now, this captain does not appear to have just lost cargo as a foreseen side effect to his attempt to save the crew. On the contrary, he is indifferent to what happens to crew members and cares only about getting rid of as much cargo as possible so as to increase economic damage to his current employer.

This story emphasizes the side effect character of the loss of goods in my previous interpretation of Aristotle's example. In this respect, then, given the equivalence between my interpretation of Aristotle's example and Strategic Bomber and *Bystander at the Switch*, then this new story should in turn be equivalent to scenarios such as Terror Bomber and *Fat Man*. But it is not. Here we certainly have an agent who intends the bad effect, loss of cargo. But here the bad effect is not an intended means to the good effect, saving the crew; while in *Fat Man* the bad effect – pushing the fat guy down the bridge – is a means to the good effect, saving the five. Similarly in Terror Bomber, the bad effect, killing the children, is a means to the good effect of shortening the war.

In both the trolley problem twin scenarios and in the terror bombing and strategic bombing twin scenarios, the overall good goal remains stable: shortening the war is both Terror Bomber's goal and Strategic Bomber's goal, and saving the five workers is the goal of the bystander in both *Bystander at the Switch* and *Fat Man*. But in my reading of Aristotle's captain, saving the crew is not the overall goal in both cases, once pursued through bad means and the other time pursued through good or indifferent means but a bad side effect.

Ironically, though, it is not difficult to find the candidate reading of Aristotle's example which is supposed to be equivalent to Terror Bomber and *Fat Man* so as to be contrasted with the side effect case in which the captain operates a sudden turning manoeuvre in order to bring the ship in less dangerous waters while knowing that the sudden manoeuvre is likely to cause loss of cargo. The equivalent to Terror Bomber and *Fat Man* is just Aristotle's original case, in which the captain throws goods overboard in order to save his crew. Recall Aristotle's own words and contrast them to my side effect reading of the scenario:

> Something of the sort happens also with regard to the throwing of goods overboard in a storm; for in the abstract no one throws goods away voluntarily; but on condition of its securing the safety of himself and his crew any sensible man does so. (1110a5–20)

Here we have a case in which the agent brings about the bad effect (throwing goods overboard) as a means to achieve the good effect – saving the crew. Contrast this with my reading in which the captain suddenly turns the ship in order to direct it towards safer waters while knowing that the sudden manoeuvre will likely result in loss of cargo.

We have now identified two parallel scenarios – Aristotle's original example and my sudden manoeuvre reading – which are equivalent to the classic twin cases in the double effect debate such as the Trolley Problem and Terror and Strategic Bomber in respect to a common good goal (saving the crew, saving the five, shortening the war). But, it may be objected, there is a difference between the two parallel scenarios from Aristotle and the others in the double effect literature: namely, the agents in the two parallel scenarios from Aristotle no longer perform the same action. One throws goods overboard, the other one suddenly turns the ship. But that's not a problem because, even if indeed in Terror Bomber and Strategic Bomber the two perform the same action of dropping bombs, in the Trolley Problem the two do not perform the same action, as the bystander in *Bystander at the Switch* must only flip a switch while the bystander in *Fat Man* must push the fat guy down the bridge.

Here it won't do to insist that the Trolley Problem is still different because one can reformulate *Fat Man* so as to have the bystander just flip a switch, which will cause the fat guy to fall off the bridge (see Kamm 2007; Otsuka 2008); because the same reformulation can be offered for Aristotle's parallel examples, by stipulating, say, that the captain in both cases must just operate a lever, which will in the one case direct the ship towards safer waters and in the other case throw goods overboard.[13]

Summing up, then, we could read Aristotle's throwing goods overboard example as the sort of case that is normally used in the debate on the Doctrine of Double Effect, but there are at least two important notes of caution against doing so: first, we have seen that in reading Aristotle's example as a double-effect-type scenario, it comes out that Aristotle's own case, in its most basic and natural reading, is rather like the sort of cases that the Doctrine of Double Effect does not justify because they involve bad means to good ends, such as Terror Bomber and *Fat Man*. Still, we have put forward a plausible reading of Aristotle's example where the bad effect (loss of goods) is not a means to the good effect (saving the crew).

The second note of caution is related: the above implies that, on the most natural reading of Aristotle's example, Aristotle gives the opposite verdict than the justifying verdict that the Doctrine of Double Effect normally gives to these examples. While the Doctrine's verdict on the scenarios in which the bad effect is a means to the good end is that they cannot be justified, Aristotle's verdict is that any sensible man would do it, which, in Aristotle's language, ought to count as a moral justification. And, indeed, Aristotle's verdict that any sensible man would do it also fits common moral intuition, as it would be preposterous to prioritize goods over people. Is that a point against the Doctrine of Double Effect's verdict against cases in which bad means are chosen for good ends? Not really, because Aristotle's example is different to the standard double effect examples in another important respect, its moral implications.

In Aristotle's example, the agent must choose between goods and people, while in standard double effect scenarios the agent must rather choose between people and people: in the Trolley Problem, it is a choice between the life of the one and the lives of the five. In Terror Bomber and Strategic Bomber, it is a choice between the lives of the children and the lives that will be spared by shortening the war. So it is life against life in classic double effect scenarios[14] while it is life against goods in Aristotle's scenario. So the bad effect, in Aristotle's scenario, is just too far, morally speaking, from the good effect – and that would explain why we find Aristotle's verdict of moral permissibility plausible.

6 Intended means, bad effects and the argument from marginally bad means

Three questions emerge that need dealing with:

1 Can we say that Aristotle's example is a counterexample to the Doctrine of Double Effect because it posits a case in which it is just intuitively morally obvious that it is permissible to choose a bad means to a good end?

2 Can we reformulate Aristotle's example so as to find the kind of moral balance between bad effects and good effects that we have in other double effect scenarios?

3 Aristotle's other example, of having to do something base in order to save one's family, may be more promising with respect to establishing the normal moral balance between bad effects and good effects that we find in standard double effect cases.

Aristotle says that any sensible man would throw goods overboard to save his crew. This must imply that Aristotle had in mind goods whose moral value cannot be compared with the lives of crew members. As we already said, we must suppose that, were the captain not to throw goods overboard, the lives of crew members would be lost but the goods themselves would not be necessarily lost (if one were to suppose that the goods would be lost no matter what, then the situation is obviously relevantly morally different). Now suppose the goods in question are the only boxes still in circulation of some life-saving medicine. People will die if these goods were to be lost. Now, on this supposition, Aristotle's example would have the sort of moral connotations of the standard double effect cases, where there is an alternative between life and life (see point (2) above). And then it is just a matter of getting the proportion right, according to Condition 4: 'that there be a proportionately grave reason for permitting the evil effect' (Mangan 1949: 43). In the Trolley Problem, the proportionately grave reason for permitting the evil effect of killing the one is the five lives that would be saved. In Terror Bomber and Strategic Bomber, the proportionately grave reason for permitting the killing of the children is the many lives that would be saved by shortening the war. Similarly, in Aristotle's example, the proportionately grave reason for throwing goods overboard that would save the lives of some sick patients at home is saving the lives of the sailors.

But what if the goods in questions were just, to use modern examples, mobile phones? Then, just as Aristotle says, any sensible man would throw them overboard to save the crew. The moral imbalance between mobile phones and human lives is such that any sensible man would throw mobiles phones overboard to save the crew. The idea, here, is that if the proportionately grave reason is indeed grave enough (proportionately speaking, again), such as in the case of, say, the lives of 10 sailors against boxes containing hundreds of mobile phones, then it is irrelevant whether the throwing of the goods overboard is an intended means or a merely foreseen side effect. Any sensible virtuous person would allow that throwing hundreds of mobile phones overboard to save the lives of 10 human beings is not just morally permissible but morally obligatory, and that such is the case even if throwing the goods overboard is indeed an intended means.

The problem for the Doctrine of Double Effect seems to be that there must be some sort of minimal threshold for the sort of bad effects that are not allowed to be intended means; if just any bad effect is not allowed to be an intended means, then the Doctrine runs into some serious problems of plausibility (see point (1) above). Let us illustrate this by looking at the four conditions of Mangan's classic definition:

A person may licitly perform an action that he foresees will produce a good and a bad effect provided that four conditions are verified at one and the same time: 1) that the action in itself from its very object be good or at least indifferent; 2) that the good effect and not the evil effect be intended; 3) that the good effect be not produced by means of the evil effect; 4) that there be a proportionately grave reason for permitting the evil effect. (1949: 43)

The point is that if the case of throwing mobile phones overboard as an intended means to save the lives of ten crew members cannot be morally justified by the Doctrine, then the Doctrine is implausible. Here a defender of the Doctrine will have to say that throwing mobile phones overboard is not an evil effect. And, indeed, one may want to argue that the loss of goods is not evil even if it has negative economic consequences that will affect the lives of human beings. But the problem with this reply is that, if throwing goods overboard is not evil, then Aristotle's case is no double effect scenario. And if throwing goods overboard *is* evil, then Aristotle's case is a counterexample to the Doctrine because the Doctrine would not allow one to throw goods overboard in order to save the crew. As we saw, there are two possible ways to resist this conclusion, both of which are problematic: one could try to argue that throwing goods overboard is not an intended means to save the crew – we saw a possible reading along these lines, even though the most basic and natural interpretation of Aristotle's example is as an intended means.

The other strategy consists in denying that the goods are morally irrelevant and suppose, for example, that they are indispensable medicines which will save lives. But that does not sit very well with Aristotle's remark that any sensible man would throw the goods overboard. Here one would have to suppose that the medicines would save some lives but that the number of lives that the medicines would save is clearly inferior to the number of crew members that would die. On this interpretation, then, Aristotle's case would be somewhat like *Fat Man*: there is a relatively clear utility on the side of the good effect (saving the five, saving the crew) but the Doctrine still says that the agent is not morally permitted to intervene because the agent would bring about an evil intended means (killing the fat guy, throwing the medicines overboard).

Still, in Aristotle's example, if the balance of utility is clear in favour of the lives of the crew, intuition still tells us that the agent is permitted to intervene (and, indeed, may be morally obligated to intervene) despite the fact that throwing goods overboard would be an intended means. So that the only way to get moral intuition on the side of the Doctrine of Double Effect, in this case (viz. to deny that it is permitted to throw goods overboard), appears to be to stipulate that the number of sick people that would be saved by the medicines is clearly greater than the number of crew members that would be saved: namely, overturning the balance of utility. But that, and here we are back at the beginning, would mean that the case is not one of double effect because then Condition 4 would not be met as then there is no proportionately grave reason to permit the evil effect.

What with Aristotle's other example, having to do something base to avoid your family being killed (as of point (3) above)? '. . . if a tyrant were to order one to do something base, having one's parents and children in his power, and if one did the action they were to be saved, but otherwise would be put to death . . .' (1110a5–20). This seems to be indeed an example in which there is the kind of balance between good and bad effect which is typical of double effect cases. But this seems to be, again, a case in which the agent who would submit and do the base thing would do it as an intended means to the end of saving one's family from the tyrant's menace.

Here the issue, as it should be clear by now, goes well beyond the interpretation of Aristotle's mixed actions; so that we are now able to formulate the second argument against the Doctrine of Double Effect, the *argument from marginally bad means*: if the Doctrine rules against all bad consequences as long as they are intended no matter what, then the Doctrine is forced to rule against countless cases where intuition tells us that acting is not only morally permissible but also morally obligatory, as in the obvious choice – for any sensible person – between a cargo of mobile phones and the lives of crew members.

Let us take stock of our argument so far: we have looked in some detail at two examples of mixed actions from Aristotle and we have compared them with the classic examples that are brought to bear in the double effect debate. We have found that Aristotle's examples could be revised so as to be interpreted as the sorts of examples that the Doctrine of Double Effect could justify, but that the most basic and natural reading of Aristotle's examples is one in which the agent brings about the bad effect (throwing goods overboard, doing something base) as an intended means to the good effect (saving the crew, saving one's family). Our discussion of Aristotle has also produced an important upshot: namely, one can fill in the details of Aristotle's mixed actions so as to produce countless counterexamples to the Doctrine of Double Effect by generating cases where the bad means (such as dropping a cargo of mobile phones) is not even remotely morally comparable to the good effect (such as saving the crew). And the problem for the Doctrine is that it would not allow for such cases of marginally bad means.

Now it may be objected to the claim that the most basic and natural reading of Aristotle's example is as intended means to a good end that the debate on the Doctrine of Double Effect shows that the distinction between means and side effects is itself problematic and that it can therefore not be argued, on grounds of the distinction between means and side effects, that Aristotle's cases are not structurally equivalent to standard double effect cases. Sure enough, a lot of the debate around the Doctrine of Double Effect centres on whether it is at all possible to offer a coherent working distinction between intended means and merely foreseen side effects: much of the rest of this book, indeed, is dedicated to precisely this issue. But that whole debate is beside the point here because, if we do give up on the distinction between intended means and merely foreseen side effects (or on the moral relevance of such a distinction for moral permissibility and moral justification), then we are just giving up on the Doctrine of Double Effect as a whole because, as the four conditions of the Doctrine make clear, the Doctrine depends on the distinction between intended means and merely foreseen side effects. So the option of denying the claim that Aristotle's examples are cases of intended means on the grounds that there is no coherent working distinction between intended means and merely foreseen side effects cannot rescue the thesis that Aristotle's examples of mixed actions are cases of double effect, because then there would be no double effect left at all.

7 Conclusion

In conclusion, we have here investigated the possibility that Aristotle's examples of mixed actions in NE III.1 could be early cases of double effect. We have found that Aristotle's examples of mixed actions have some important features in common with standard cases of double effect such as, among others, Strategic Bomber and the Trolley Problem: examples of mixed actions, just like double effect cases, involve dilemma scenarios with both bad effects and good effects so that the agent cannot solve the dilemma without incurring in bad effects. We have also found, however, that there are some crucial difficulties in interpreting Aristotle's two examples of mixed actions as genuine double effect cases: namely, as cases that the Doctrine of Double Effect could offer a moral justification for. Briefly, the most significant problem is that both of Aristotle's examples of mixed actions appear to be cases where the agent brings about the bad effect as an intended means to the good effect. An upshot of our discussion of Aristotle's mixed actions is that we were able to put forward another clear argument against double effect: namely that it cannot justify marginally bad means. Summing up, then, Aristotle's mixed actions cannot be justified by appeal to the Doctrine of Double Effect. And that, mind, may say more about the Doctrine of Double Effect than it does about Aristotle's mixed actions – as the rest of this book is going to show.

PART TWO

Double Effect in Theory

CHAPTER FOUR

The Trolley Problem

Abstract *In this chapter I analyse the relationship between the Doctrine of Double Effect and the Trolley Problem: the Trolley Problem provides three distinct dialectical arguments in favour of the Doctrine of Double Effect: summarizing, (1) the Doctrine of Double Effect offers a solution to the Trolley Problem; (2) the two scenarios which constitute the Trolley Problem illustrate the distinction between 'means' and 'side effects' which, according to the Doctrine of Double Effect, is morally relevant; (3) widespread moral intuitions about the Trolley Problem suggest that, just as the Doctrine of Double Effect says, the distinction between 'means' and 'side effects' is indeed morally relevant. But here I argue that the Trolley Problem does not actually support the Doctrine of Double Effect because – apart from the theoretical problems that the Doctrine faces and that I discuss in the other chapters of this book – intervening in* Bystander at the Switch *is, differently from what the Doctrine suggests, not permissible.*

1 Introduction

In one of the infamous thought-experiments of analytic philosophy, a runaway trolley is about to kill five workmen who cannot move off the tracks quickly enough; their only chance is for a bystander to flip a switch to divert the trolley onto a side track, where one workman would be killed. In a parallel scenario, the bystander's only chance to save the five is to push a fat man off a bridge onto the tracks: that will stop the trolley but the fat man will die. Why is it permissible for the bystander to divert the trolley onto the one workman by pressing the switch while it is not permissible for the bystander to stop the trolley by pushing the fat man off the bridge? This is the so-called Trolley Problem, resulting from Judith Jarvis Thomson's (1976 and 1985) adaptation of an example from Philippa Foot (1967). *If* it is permissible to intervene in the so-called *Bystander at the Switch* scenario while it is not permissible to intervene in the so-called *Fat Man* scenario, then the Trolley Problem arises and we must explain the moral difference between these two cases.

As we have seen in Chapter 2, according to the *Doctrine of Double Effect*, 'sometimes it is permissible to bring about as a merely foreseen side effect a harmful event that it would be impermissible to bring about intentionally', as McIntyre puts it in her introductory essay on the Doctrine for the *Stanford Encyclopedia of Philosophy*.[1] The Doctrine, it could be argued, offers a possible answer to the Trolley Problem, because it can be deployed to argue that the difference in moral permissibility results from the one being killed as a means to save the five in *Fat Man*, while in *Bystander at the Switch* the killing of the one is a mere side effect of saving the five. In this respect, as long as the Trolley Problem remains 'unsolved' it offers dialectical support to the Doctrine.

So the connection between double effect and the Trolley Problem is dialectically very simple: the Trolley Problem counts as an argument in favour of the Doctrine of Double Effect insofar as it remains an unresolved problem and in so far as the Doctrine offers a possible solution to this unresolved problem. But double effect is just one small corner of moral philosophy, and the wider dialectic of the Trolley Problem is a touch more complicated.

Originally, Thomson's (1976 and 1985) *Bystander at the Switch* scenario, put forward as an argument against Foot's (1967) deontological solution to her Tram version of the problem (negative duties to avoid harm are stronger than positive duties to bring aid), could have been thought of as a consequentialist argument. But once we contrast *Bystander at the Switch* with *Fat Man*, formulating the problem as we have done above (why is it permissible for the bystander to divert the trolley onto the one workman by pressing the switch while it is not permissible for the bystander to stop the trolley by pushing the fat man off the bridge?), it is no longer clear that the Trolley Problem supports consequentialism over deontology.

This much we can say: there is a deontological dissolution of the problem – arguing that it is impermissible to intervene in both *Bystander at the Switch* and *Fat Man*; in a slogan: *killing is killing* – and there is a consequentialist dissolution of the problem: arguing that it is permissible to intervene in both *Bystander at the Switch* and *Fat Man*; in a slogan: *it's the numbers, stupid*. Note that these two are dissolutions rather than solutions because they don't actually answer the question formulated above as the Problem: they rather claim that there is no problem, either because intervening is in both cases permissible or because intervening is in neither case permissible.

What this shows, importantly, is that it isn't at all clear that the problem, as a problem, constitutes an argument for either deontology or consequentialism. What it is, as countless philosophy lecturers have learnt, is a very simple way of distinguishing two general approaches to normative ethics. But, understood as a genuine unresolved problem, the Trolley Problem is not an argument for either deontology or consequentialism. Looking at the Trolley Problem from the wider dialectical perspective of normative ethics, then, it does not look as though the problem, as a problem, constitutes an argument for either approach. Indeed, it might be argued that the persistence of the Trolley Problem suggests that we should abandon both approaches (it can be no coincidence if Philippa Foot turned to virtue ethics, one may think).

If the Trolley Problem is a genuine problem, then we should abandon deontology because it does not allow us to intervene in *Bystander* and we should abandon consequentialism because it tells us to intervene in *Fat Man*. Let us be more precise here: it isn't even the problem as a problem which, it may be argued, speaks against both deontology and consequentialism. It is rather only its components: that it is permissible to intervene in *Bystander* may be taken to be a general counterexample to deontology; and that it is not permissible to intervene in *Fat Man* may be taken to be a general counterexample to consequentialism. However, we saw that looking at the Trolley Problem from the narrower dialectical perspective of double effect, the problem, as a problem, speaks in favour of the Doctrine. And if the Doctrine of Double Effect belongs to the deontological camp, then the Trolley Problem does in the end favour one general approach to normative ethics over the other.

Where to place the Doctrine of Double Effect in normative ethics is an interesting issue. The Doctrine has in general an ambivalent relation with the Kantian tradition: on the one hand, the Doctrine is in contrast with the Kantian tradition in that it represents an exception to the kind of absolutism that is often identified with Kantian morality.[2] On the other hand, the Doctrine is, from the point of view of moral psychology, Kantian in that it emphasizes the role of motivation in moral agency, as opposed to consequentialism (more on Kant and double effect in Chapter 7).

2 Trolleys

There is a simple objection to the claim that the Trolley Problem constitutes an argument in favour of the Doctrine of Double Effect. Surely the Trolley Problem has to do with asymmetries such as doing and allowing, actions and omissions, and killing and letting die; and these must be kept separate from double effect. It is historically true that the Trolley Problem was originally dealt with in terms of a sort of doing/allowing asymmetry, Philippa Foot's distinction between the negative duty to avoid injury and the positive duty to bring aid.

Still, if we are talking about the history of this debate, it must also be said that Foot's article, where the first trolley thought-experiment appears, is entitled *The Problem of Abortion and the Doctrine of the Double Effect* (1967); and that Foot explicitly introduces the thought-experiment to motivate double effect. The paragraph in which the first trolley thought-experiment appears begins with 'It is now time to say why this doctrine should be taken seriously' (1967: 146[3]). Foot originally uses the thought-experiment to motivate the Doctrine against Hart, whose article (1967) in the previous issue of the *Oxford Review* she is replying to (more on Hart in Chapter 12).

Still, in that article Foot ends up rejecting the Doctrine if favour of a different principle, according to which the negative duty to avoid injury is stronger than the positive duty to bring aid.

Here is Foot's original example:

> . . . he is the driver of a runaway tram which he can only steer from one narrow track to another; five men are working on one track and one man on the other; anyone on the track he enters is bound to be killed. . . . The question is why we should say, without hesitation, that the driver should steer for the less occupied track. (1967: 147)[4]

Foot asks readers to imagine the driver of a runaway tram who can't stop the tram but only steer it away from a track where five workmen would be killed to a track where only one workman would be killed. Foot contrasts the scenario with another, in which a judge must frame an innocent man and have him executed in order to prevent rioters from taking their revenge on five hostages. The idea is that it would be permissible for the driver to steer while it would not be permissible for the judge to frame the innocent man. Foot uses the contrast between these two scenarios to motivate the Doctrine, supposedly because the driver does not intend killing the one as a means to not killing the five, while the judge would intend to kill the one as a means to save the five (Foot talks of obliquely intending something as opposed to aiming at something, borrowing Bentham's classic terminology).

In the end, though, Foot rejects the Doctrine of Double Effect as a solution to this first trolley problem, proposing instead that we distinguish between the negative duty to avoid injury and the positive duty to bring aid (1967: 151). The tram driver faces a dilemma between two negative duties, the negative duty to avoid injuring the five against the negative duty to avoid injuring the one. On the other hand, the judge faces a dilemma between his negative duty to avoid injuring the one and his positive duty to bring aid to the five. If negative duties to avoid injury are stronger than positive duties to bring aid, then that explains why the judge may not act on his positive duty to bring aid over his negative duty to avoid injury.

On the other hand, for the tram driver there is only a contrast of negative duties (both with regard to the one and with regard to the five); supposedly in the case of the tram driver, in the absence of a qualitative difference between the duties, a quantitative difference may be a reasonable solution to the dilemma, and that is why it may be permissible for the tram driver to choose to kill one rather than five. This is the difference between the two cases which would explain, according to Foot, why we would say that the driver may steer to kill the one but not say that the judge may have the innocent man executed.

So the thought-experiment that would then be developed in the Trolley Problem emerged from the debate on double effect. Let us make explicit how the Doctrine may have been taken to be able to distinguish between the judge and the tram driver. In Foot's cases, the good effect would be, in both scenarios, that the five survive while the evil effect would be, in both scenarios, that the one is killed. The doctrine says that a person (the tram driver) may 'licitly' perform an action (steering) that he foresees will produce a good (the five survive) and a bad effect (the one is killed) provided that the four conditions of the Doctrine of Double Effect are met. Let us take Condition 3, that the good effect not be produced by means of the evil effect.

Foot's scenario of the tram driver as contrasted with the judge is exactly supposed to illustrate a case in which the good effect of saving the five is not produced by means of the evil effect of killing the one; because while the judge needs the death of the one to save the five, all the tram driver needs is diverting his tram. As Foot says,

> Perhaps he might find a foothold on the side of the tunnel and cling on as the vehicle hurtled by. The driver of the tram does not then leap off and brain him with a crowbar. The judge, however, needs the death of the innocent man for his (good) purposes. If the victim proves hard to hang he must see to it that he dies another way. (1967: 147)

This is supposed to illustrate the difference between the death of the one being a means to the judge's good end in the one case, while it is supposed to be only a side effect of the driver's good end in the other case.

In the end, Foot goes a different way: 'At one time I thought that these arguments in favour of the Doctrine were conclusive, but

I now believe that the conflict should be solved in another way' (1967: 149); and she goes on to put forward the solution that we have seen above. This is an important passage in the debate: the Doctrine, as we have seen, may be deployed to answer the question posed by Foot's original thought-experiment. But, according to Foot, there is a better answer to that question. If there is a better answer to the questions posed by trolley thought-experiments, then these do not speak in favour of double effect simply because, as we have explained at the beginning, the sense in which the Trolley Problem is an argument for the Doctrine of Double Effect is simply that double effect has an answer to the problem; so that in the absence of better answers, that is a consideration in favour of the Doctrine. Therefore, whether Foot's solution works is crucial to whether the Trolley Problem speaks in favour of the Doctrine of Double Effect. And, as Thomson has famously shown, Foot's solution does not work.

The first thought-experiment actually involving a 'trolley' was put forward by Judith Jarvis Thomson (1976 and 1985) as a counterexample to Foot's solution of negative duties to avoid injury overriding positive duties to aid.

> In that case you have been strolling by the trolley track, and you can see the situation at a glance: The driver saw the five on the track ahead, he stamped on the brakes, the brakes failed, so he fainted. What to do? Well, here is the switch, which you can throw, thereby turning the trolley yourself. Of course you will kill one if you do. But I should think you may turn it all the same. (1985: 1397)

Thomson's scenario is very similar to Foot's, with the crucial novelty that the agent who faces the moral dilemma is no longer the trolley's driver, but rather a bystander who has taken in the whole situation and finds himself able to operate a switch that would divert the runaway trolley from the track with five workmen to the track with just the one workman. Should the bystander operate the switch, thereby killing the one workman? This scenario is problematic for Foot's solution because most have the intuition that the bystander, just like the trolley driver in Foot's original scenario, may divert the trolley. Some data on these intuitions: 76.85 per cent of respondents to a BBC News online poll answered YES to the question 'Should you flip the switch?', and 23.15 per cent answered NO.[5] About 90 per cent of respondents to Marc Hauser's Moral Sense Test[6] thought that diverting the trolley by pressing the switch was permissible (2006: 128). Hauser reports that at the time of writing *Moral Minds*, already sixty thousand people had taken the online Moral Sense Test.

The bystander, by diverting the trolley, would kill the one, just like the trolley driver. But the bystander, if she does not divert the trolley, would not kill the five, just letting them die – it may be said; while the trolley driver would kill the five. So for the bystander, Foot's solution of negative duties to avoid injury overriding positive duties to aid will not do; because if negative duties to avoid injury did indeed override positive duties to aid, then the bystander ought not to intervene. The case of the bystander is supposed to be more like Foot's judge case: a dilemma between a negative duty to avoid injury to the one and a positive duty to aid the five. So Thomson's *Bystander at the switch* is a counterexample to Foot's solution of negative duties to avoid injury overriding positive duties to aid.

Foot's proposal to distinguish between the moral significance of the negative duty to avoid injury and the moral significance of the positive duty to bring aid, quantifiable in 'Killing one is worse than letting five die' as Thomson puts it (1985: 1399), can be characterized as an anti-consequentialist constraint which, at the same time, does not go as far as double effect, at least according to Foot. The proposal is firmly in Kantian territory in recognizing the moral difference that agency makes. According to this dialectic, then, Thomson's *Bystander at the Switch* counterexample counts as a consequentialist argument, in that it shows that the (loosely) Kantian principle that 'killing one is worse than letting five die' is false, and that, in general, the consequentialist body count (five to one) has moral priority over agency.

Thomson's case is not just a counterexample to Foot's solution; it also puts to bed the objection that the Trolley Problem does not speak in favour of double effect because the former, but not the latter, has to do with the asymmetry between doing and allowing. So the asymmetry between doing and allowing put forward by Foot cannot explain why it is permissible for the bystander to intervene. Can the Doctrine of Double Effect do that? It may be argued that the Doctrine can explain why it is permissible to kill the one in *Bystander at the Switch* because killing the one is not a means to the end of saving the five. The Doctrine says that it may be sometimes legitimate to bring about an evil effect as long as this is not the means to the good effect (and other conditions are met). In *Bystander at the Switch*, it may be argued, the killing of the one is not a means to the saving of the five because, were the one not on the side track, diverting to the side track would still save the five.

Remember Foot's remarks: 'Perhaps he might find a foothold on the side of the tunnel and cling on as the vehicle hurtled by. The driver of the tram does not then leap off and brain him with a crowbar. The judge, however, needs the death of the innocent man for his (good) purposes. If the victim proves hard to hang he must see to it that he dies another way' (1967: 147). The idea that these remarks try to bring out is that killing the one is not a means *to* save the five, but merely a side effect *of* saving the five. Were it a means, then the Doctrine would not allow for it. But it is morally permissible exactly because the one is not treated as a mere means to the good deed of saving the five.

From the general point of view of moral philosophy, it is interesting to note that the permissibility of *Bystander at the Switch* is deployed by Thomson to show that Foot's anti-consequentialist solution will not do. So the permissibility of *Bystander at the Switch* should count as a point for consequentialists. But then the permissibility of *Bystander at the Switch* poses its own problem, namely why it is morally permissible to intervene, and a proposed solution comes from no less anti-consequentialist quarters than double effect.

The asymmetry between doing and allowing does not explain why it is permissible to intervene in *Bystander at the Switch*, while the Doctrine, if the one workman is not treated as a means to the end of saving the five, does explain the permissibility of the intervention. And the *Fat Man* scenario is supposed to illustrate the idea that the killing of the one workman in *Bystander at the Switch* is not a means to the end of rescuing the five.

> Consider a case – which I shall call Fat Man – in which you are standing on a footbridge over the trolley track. You can see a trolley hurtling down the track, out of control. You turn around to see where the trolley is headed, and there are five workmen on the track where it exits from under the footbridge. What to do? Being an expert on trolleys, you know of one certain way to stop

an out-of-control trolley: Drop a really heavy weight in its path. But where to find one? It just so happens that standing next to you on the footbridge is a fat man, a really fat man. He is leaning over the railing, watching the trolley; all you have to do is to give him a little shove, and over the railing he will go, onto the track in the path of the trolley. (Thomson 1985: 1409)

The *Fat Man* scenario brings out the problem of the permissibility of intervention in *Bystander at the Switch*. The idea is that it would be impermissible to push the fat man to save the five. This intuition is corroborated by the results of Hauser's Moral Sense Test, as around 90 per cent of respondents thought that it would not be permissible to kill the *fat* man to save the five (2006: 128). Pretty similar data comes from the BBC News poll, where 73.12 per cent of respondents answered NO to the question 'Should you push the fat man?' (26.88 per cent answered YES).

Combining *Bystander at the Switch* and *Fat Man*, we obtain the Trolley Problem as we know it: why is it that killing the workman on the side track is permissible in *Bystander at the Switch* while killing the fat man is not permissible? The asymmetry between doing and allowing, specified as a moral difference between killing and letting die, does not solve this problem because in both scenarios we kill one instead of letting five die, so that the distinction between killing and letting die has no application to these scenarios; furthermore, if we accepted the principle that killing one were morally worse than letting five die, because our negative duties to avoid harm are morally stronger than our positive duties to bring aid, then we ought not to kill the one in both scenarios. Therefore, this principle does not explain the difference between the two scenarios.

The Doctrine of Double Effect, on the other hand, does explain this difference: we may not intervene in *Fat Man* because if we intervened we would kill the one as a means to save the five, and the Doctrine does not allow to bring about a bad effect (kill the one) as a means to bringing about the good effect (saving the five). On the other hand, we may intervene in *Bystander at the Switch* because we would not be killing the one as a means to save the five.

What is this difference between killing the one as a means to save the five in *Fat Man* on the one hand and killing the one as a side effect of saving the five in *Bystander at the Switch* on the other hand? This could be cashed out by the thought that I can perfectly well explain how I saved the five in the bystander case without mentioning the death of the bystander – all I need to tell is that I diverted the trolley onto a side track; while I cannot explain how I saved the five without mentioning the fat man in the other case. People often talk of how I actually need the death of the fat man but I do not need the death of the workman on the side track, and we have already seen that Foot makes this point in her original formulation too.

Thomson herself did not think that this distinction between means and side effects could explain why it is permissible to intervene in one case but not in the other. Her argument relies on a further variant on the trolley thought-experiment:

> Consider now what I shall call "the loop variant" on this case, in which the tracks do not continue to diverge – they circle back, as in the following picture:

> Let us now imagine that the five on the straight track are thin, but thick enough so that although all five will be killed if the trolley goes straight, the bodies of the five will stop it, and it will therefore not reach the one. On the other hand, the one on the right-hand track is fat, so fat that his body will by itself stop the trolley, and the trolley will therefore not reach the five. (Thomson 1985: 1402–3)

This variation on *Bystander at the Switch* challenges the idea that the Doctrine may answer the question regarding the permissibility of intervening in *Bystander at the Switch*. The scenario is the same, but the two tracks are connected so that if the bystander operates the switch diverting the trolley from the main track with five workmen to the side track with just the one workman, and for some reason the one workman would manage to get out of the way or maybe his body would not stop the trolley, then the trolley would continue his journey and still hit and kill the five from behind. This case is supposed to bring out the idea that, this time, the killing of the one is indeed a means to the end of saving the five, differently from the classic *Bystander at the Switch*. And if this case is similarly permissible as *Bystander at the Switch*, then that is a problem for the Doctrine, which would then not be able to explain the permissibility of *Bystander at the Switch* by appealing to the difference between means and side effects, because this case, which supposedly does involve means, is similarly permissible; the Doctrine of Double Effect could then in this case not appeal to the notion of side effects to explain why the Loop Variant is also permissible.

The issue of the permissibility of diverting the trolley in the Loop Variant is then crucial: that it is permissible to divert the trolley in the Loop Variant is the reason why, supposedly, the Doctrine cannot explain the permissibility of *Bystander at the Switch*; more generally, it could be argued that the permissibility of the Loop Variant is a general argument against double effect's proposal that the difference between 'means' and 'side effects' is morally relevant. Thomson appears to take it for granted that the Loop Variant is just as permissible as *Bystander at the Switch*:

> we cannot really suppose that the presence or absence of that extra bit of track makes a major moral difference as to what an agent may do in these cases, and it really does seem right to think (despite the discomfort) that the agent may proceed. (1985: 1403)

But the data from Hauser's Moral Sense Test suggests that respondents are split around 50–50 about the permissibility of diverting the trolley in the Loop Variant (Otsuka 2008: 95; Hauser 2006: 128–9). Liao et al. (forthcoming) also surveyed intuitions on the Loop Variant, finding that answers were dependent on whether the Loop Variant was presented after a version of *Bystander* (66 per cent say that intervening in the Loop Variant is permissible when they answer the Loop Variant after having answered *Bystander*) or after a modified version of *Fat Man* (56 per cent say that intervening in the Loop Variant is not permissible when they answer the Loop Variant after having answered a modified version of *Fat Man*).

One may argue about the significance of the effect identified by Liao et al. (forthcoming), as their numbers are not exactly staggering; but it seems clear, putting together both Hauser's data and Liao et al.'s data, that intuitions on the Loop Variant are far from obvious or univocal, especially when compared with the data on *Bystander* and *Fat Man*.

Here we don't seem to be able to rely on a pretty uncontroversial intuition according to which diverting the trolley in the Loop Variant is permissible. And as the permissibility of diverting the trolley is a necessary element of an argument that would use the Loop Variant to argue against the Doctrine, then such an argument needs more than just inconclusive data on moral intuitions for the Loop Variant. If it were indeed obvious that the Loop Variant were similarly permissible as *Bystander at the Switch*, then we may argue that double effect (and in particular its distinction between 'means' and 'side effects') could not explain the permissibility of *Bystander at the Switch*, because the Doctrine gives the wrong answer to the Loop Variant, namely that it is impermissible to intervene. But it is not clear that the Doctrine of Double Effect does give the wrong answer, given the experimental philosophy data. So we may not conclude that the Loop Variant shows that the Doctrine cannot answer the Trolley Problem.

Before someone complains that all I have said about the Loop Variant is mention some data on intuition, then let me remind them that I dedicate a whole chapter to the Loop Variant and Kamm's discussion of it – so for a proper theoretical discussion of the Loop Variant, readers should just wait for or jump to Chapter 7.

We have shown that the distinction between doing and allowing cannot be used to answer the Trolley Problem while the Doctrine of Double Effect does explain why it is permissible to intervene in one case but not in the other, at least if there is a difference in terms of 'means' on the one hand and 'side effects' on the other between *Fat Man* and *Bystander at the Switch*. But, it may be objected, one of the crucial issues in the debate on double effect is exactly the distinction between 'means' and 'side effects': we can't very well assume this distinction to argue that the Trolley Problem speaks in favour of the Doctrine. To put it another way, the claim that the Trolley Problem speaks in favour of the Doctrine cannot be conditional on the distinction between 'means' and 'side effects' because, if the claim is conditional on that distinction, then we have made no progress at all, since we always knew that the Doctrine itself was conditional on the distinction between 'means' and 'side effects', which is one of the necessary conditions of the Doctrine at least because Gury's already cited nineteenth-century formulation.

But this can be easily turned around: the point is rather that the trolley thought-experiments offer a vivid example of the distinction between 'means' and 'side effects' that, according to double effect, is morally relevant. And the striking differences in intuitive permissibility (confirmed by the experimental philosophy data) between *Fat Man* and *Bystander at the Switch* tell us today exactly what the Doctrine has always told us: that there is a difference between 'means' and 'side effects', and that this difference is morally relevant. And that just is the sense in which the Trolley Problem speaks in favour of the Doctrine of Double Effect.

Here it could be said that there are then three different arguments that the Trolley Problem offers in favour of the Doctrine: first, as an unsolved problem, the Trolley Problem speaks in favour of the Doctrine because the Doctrine offers a solution to the problem; secondly, the Trolley Problem illustrates the distinction between 'means' and 'side effects' which is a crucial part of double effect; thirdly, the moral intuitions on the Trolley Problem suggest that, just as the Doctrine claims, the distinction between 'means' and 'side effects' is morally significant.

3 A dialectical asymmetry

Let us take stock: we have analysed the relation between double effect and the Trolley Problem, showing that the Trolley Problem represents an argument for the Doctrine insofar as, (1) the two scenarios which constitute, together, the Trolley Problem illustrate the distinction between 'means' and 'side effects' which, according to the Doctrine, makes a difference in terms of moral permissibility; (2) the permissibility of *Bystander* as opposed to the non-permissibility of *Fat Man*, which seem to be widely shared moral intuitions, suggest that the distinction between 'means' and 'side effects' is indeed morally relevant, just as double effect says; (3) the Doctrine of Double Effect provides an answer to the Trolley Problem – and we have shown how distinctions such as doing/allowing (and the related killing/letting die) cannot, on the other hand, answer the Trolley Problem. Still, this all depends on being able to coherently distinguish between intended means and merely foreseen side effects: the Doctrine, for example, must be coherently formulated so that it is immune to the problem of 'closeness' (see Chapter 6). But here there is an important dialectical asymmetry between defenders of the Doctrine and critics, such as those who raise the problem of closeness and related objections against the Doctrine, as I do in this book. Namely, defenders of the Doctrine maintain the dialectical advantage of offering answers to the Trolley Problem and related intractable cases. That is why merely criticizing attempts at coherently formulating the Doctrine, without at the same time offering solutions to the Trolley Problem and related cases, leaves critics of the Doctrine such as myself to a disadvantage.

To avoid a continuing philosophical stall, critics of the Doctrine must offer a solution to the Trolley Problem and related dilemmas; otherwise, we will have to balance coherence against explanatory power, in such a way that, certainly in society at large and often even in philosophy, the latter may prevail. A good example of this is Thomas Nagel's coming out in favour of double effect in *The View from Nowhere*:

> I believe that the traditional principle of double effect, despite problems of application, provides a rough guide to the extension and character of deontological constraints, and that even after the volumes that have been written on the subject in recent years, this remains the right point of convergence for efforts to capture our intuitions. (1986: 179)

Nagel is a perfect example of my above diagnosis: he is not too subtly saying that, whatever the philosophical details (such as the problem of closeness, for example), the Doctrine captures our intuitions; and the latter consideration trumps the former. Now we may question the philosophical legitimacy of Nagel's judgement here, but it just reinforces the need for critics of the Doctrine to answer the Trolley Problem and related moral intuitions.

It is clear that Foot herself, for example, had understood that the stakes were too high for critics to simply dismiss the Doctrine as a view that could not be coherently applied: she introduces the original trolley case to motivate the Doctrine and raises the problem of closeness against the Doctrine.[7] In the end, crucially, she offers an alternative – which has been shown by Thomson to fail to address the Trolley Problem. The point here is simply that critical discussions of double effect cannot afford any lesser dialectical structure than Foot's *The Problem of Abortion and the Doctrine of Double Effect*: they must feature the intuitive motivation sustaining the Doctrine; they must feature a critical analysis of the Doctrine itself; and, crucially, they must feature, if the Doctrine has to be rejected, an alternative view that successfully captures our moral intuitions.

It is because too many discussions of double effect have failed to provide all three of these aspects that it remains possible, with Nagel, to endorse the Doctrine despite its problems. That is why the next and last task of this chapter is to offer a solution to the Trolley Problem, which I do by defending Thomson's recent turn (2008) from both theoretical and empirical challenges that have been raised against it.

4 Self-sacrifice

There are two obvious ways to go about the Trolley Problem: one can either explain the moral difference between the two scenarios, or one can deny that there is such a difference, by either denying that it is permissible to kill the one workman in *Bystander at the Switch* or by denying that it is not permissible to kill the fat man in the other scenario. Interestingly, Thomson (2008) herself has recently argued that there is no Trolley Problem by denying that it is permissible to intervene in *Bystander at the Switch*. Thomson's argument moves from a variant in which you also have the chance to divert the trolley onto yourself (you are on a third track and you can't move off it quickly enough). If you would not be willing to divert the trolley onto yourself – sacrificing your own life to save the five – then it would be preposterous to sacrifice someone else: it is just not fair.

Someone who would not sacrifice herself in this new scenario ought not to sacrifice someone else in the original *Bystander at the Switch*; or so Thomson argues 'Since he wouldn't himself pay the cost of his good deed if he could pay it, there is no way in which he can decently regard himself as entitled to make someone else pay it' (2008: 366). Here folk intuitions aren't clear-cut: 43 per cent would still kill the one; 38 per cent would commit self-sacrifice; and

19 per cent would not act, letting the trolley kill the five (Huebner and Hauser 2011).

If these numbers are to be believed, they can be used against Thomson's argument, because more than 40 per cent would still kill the one; but also in favour of it, since almost 40 per cent would commit self-sacrifice; and, perhaps more importantly, the majority (almost 60 per cent) would now not kill the one, while in the traditional *Bystander at the Switch* it was only around 10 per cent.[8]

But there is another respect in which the numbers are not decisive: Thomson's argument is about the effect of this new three-way scenario on the traditional two-way *Bystander at the Switch*. And these numbers are silent on that – what should then be tested is how folk intuitions would respond to the traditional scenario after having been subjected to the new three-way scenario: if the 9 to 1 proportion would even out somewhat, that would speak in favour of Thomson's argument.

Experiments that I conducted suggested just that participants who were not previously familiar with any of the trolley scenarios were presented first with Thomson's new three-way scenario and then with the traditional *Bystander at the Switch*. Answers to *Bystander at the Switch* were radically different from the 9 to 1 proportion identified by Hauser, so much so that the majority (**61.34 per cent**) opted to let the five workmen die – for details on my experiments and their results, please see the next chapter. So it seems that the apparently overwhelming intuition that intervening in *Bystander* is permissible disappears when subjects are presented with *Bystander* only after they have been asked about Thomson's new scenario. Indeed, after having considered a scenario in which they could also sacrifice themselves, a majority of subjects appear to think that intervening in *Bystander* is not permissible. As anticipated above, these results support Thomson's claim that her new scenario has a bearing on the permissibility of intervening in *Bystander*: we can suppose that subjects who have just been asked about the self-sacrifice scenario may overwhelmingly opt to let the five die in *Bystander at the Switch* because they now recognize that they may not do to the one what they would not do to themselves.

It may be objected that these results do not support Thomson's new argument; they rather just show that the relevant moral intuitions are very unstable. This is after all the conclusion Swain et al. (2008) drew following their own experimental philosophy studies where the order in which the cases were presented affected results (see also, for other examples of this sort of effect, Petrinovich and O'Neill 1996; Sinnott-Armstrong 2008; Wiegmann et al. 2010). I think that the dialectic of Thomson's argument is such that our results do support it, because her argument is about the effect of the new case on the old one – again, see the next chapter for details on this; but even if you disagree, then our results would show, in line with Swain et al. (2008), that the *Bystander* intuition is unstable and that it depends on the order of presentation so heavily that it disappears (less than 40 per cent have it) when *Bystander* is first introduced after the Thomson's new self-sacrifice case.

Even if Hauser's data are reliable, then, these numbers are not decisive one way or another for Thomson's argument, because they can be interpreted both in favour of Thomson's argument and against it, and because the more relevant questions have not been asked – when the right questions are asked, then, as our numbers above show, intuitions seem to support Thomson's argument. My argument about the data has been admittedly very quick here; the reader should wait for or jump to the next chapter for details and the compete version of my argument about moral intuitions on the trolley problem.

The empirical challenges against Thomson fail; but there has also been a theoretical critique of Thomson's new argument. According to Thomson, her new case brings out the principle that 'A must not kill B to save five if he can instead kill himself to save the five' (2008: 365). William J. FitzPatrick has recently argued (2009) against this principle by suggesting that the values of equality and fairness that Thomson's argument appeals to can be captured by a weaker principle that does not support Thomson's conclusion. According to FitzPatrick, we need not accept, with Thomson, that 'A's respecting B as a moral equal requires that A not sacrifice B (without B's consent) for end E unless A would be willing to sacrifice himself for E if he could do so instead' (2009: 639). Moral equality may be satisfied by appeal to the weaker principle according to which 'A's respecting B as a moral equal requires that A not sacrifice B for end E unless A recognizes B's equal right to sacrifice A for E if their positions were reversed' (639). On the former principle, I may not sacrifice the bystander if I would not be willing to sacrifice myself; but on the latter principle I may, as long as I recognize the bystander's right to sacrifice me if our positions were reversed.

On this latter understanding, then, fairness would not support Thomson's argument that it is not permissible to intervene in *Bystander at the Switch*.

It may be argued that employing FitzPatrick's latter principle in the debate on the Trolley Problem is methodologically suspect because it introduces 'rights': what's at stake are exactly the sort of fundamental principles that may be deployed to justify rights, rather than the other way around. But there is a bigger worry with FitzPatrick's alternative principle: the problem is that this is no principle to capture fairness or, as FitzPatrick puts it, 'respecting others as moral equals' (2009: 639). His principle amounts to the Law of the Jungle: it just says that whoever happens to find herself at the switch may take advantage of this (lucky or otherwise) circumstance and kill the other. It doesn't have anything to do with fairness or equality; it is sheer power and privilege. The point is not whether this perspective is defensible; it is just that, even if it is, this is not the point of view of fairness or 'respecting others as moral equals'. Here the dialectic of the argument is important: FitzPatrick doesn't argue for his alternative principle on the grounds that Thomson's own principle is flawed, but only on the grounds that his own less-demanding principle also accounts for fairness and 'respecting others as moral equals'. That is why what is crucial is whether his principle does indeed account for fairness and 'respecting others as moral equals' rather than whether it is, in absolute terms, defensible.

This alternative principle does not support FitzPatrick's argument. What about the principle's intrinsic value, so to speak? In some particular set of circumstances, I may kill you only if I recognize your equal right to kill me if our positions were reversed. What may my recognition of your equal right to kill me amount to? Maybe if you were at the switch and diverted the trolley towards me, my recognition of your equal right to kill me means that I may not, as I die, swear at you; or that, as the trolley approaches, I should quickly try to write a note saying that I don't blame you. But wouldn't that problematically amount to consent? This would be problematic because the question is whether I may divert the trolley onto your track irrespective of your consent. But I think it is both complicated and uncharitable to test the principle's intrinsic value on the Trolley Problem. What about its more general application? The idea that I recognize your right to kill me if our positions were reserved must mean, for example, that if our positions were reserved, and you were threatening to kill me, I should not defend myself or try to stop you, because I recognize your right to kill me, after all. And this isn't just weird, it is also against the spirit of the principle itself: if whoever gets to the switch first may kill the other, then you would expect that we are allowed to take advantage of our privileged positions; but then why should I let you kill me? In short, the principle bears contradicting responses: it asks us, on the one hand, to recognize the other's right to kill us, and on the other hand, it justifies this right with the other's privileged position.

The principle is too Machiavellian to count as a principle of fairness or 'respecting others as moral equals', but it isn't Machiavellian enough to function as a workable and coherent moral or political principle. Therefore, it works neither against Thomson's argument nor generally.[9] All in all, its absurdity as a principle of fairness explains why the principle yields the 'surprising' and 'paradoxical' (FitzPatrick's (2009: 640) own words) conclusion that it is permissible to divert the trolley onto another even if we are able but unwilling to divert it onto ourselves instead.

FitzPatrick's objection to Thomson does not work, then. But that, clearly, does not mean that Thomson's argument goes through. Specifically, FitzPatrick challenges also another aspect of Thomson's argument, where she argues that even those who would divert the trolley onto themselves in the three-way scenario, sacrificing their own lives, are not allowed to divert the trolley onto the one workman in the traditional *Bystander at the Switch*. Thomson claims that this sort of altruism is not 'morally attractive' (2008: 366), and that anyway the bystander may not suppose that the workman is similarly altruistic.

As we have seen, almost 40 per cent of respondents to the Moral Sense Test declare that they would commit self-sacrifice in the three-way scenario; that's why this part of Thomson's argument is important. If Thomson's argument would apply only to those who would not be willing to commit self-sacrifice, and if the numbers are to be taken seriously, then that would be a problem for her general conclusion that intervening in *Bystander at the Switch* is not permissible: indeed, that conclusion could not be generalized to a large part of the population.[10] That is why, this second part of Thomson's argument in which she argues that even those supposed altruists may not intervene in *Bystander at the Switch* also matters.

FitzPatrick challenges this part of Thomson's argument by arguing that her appeal to the notion of consent 'beg[s] the interesting questions. . . . Those who believe that it is generally permissible to turn the trolley obviously think that this is a special case where consent isn't necessary. So Thomson's quick appeal to consent won't gain any traction with those who don't already share her view' (2009: 642).

Thomson writes that 'the altruistic bystander is not entitled to assume that the one workman is equally altruistic, and would therefore consent to the bystander's choosing option (ii). Altruism is by hypothesis not morally required of us. Suppose, then, that the bystander knows that the one workman would not consent, and indeed is not morally required to consent, to his choosing option (ii)'[11] (2008: 367).

Here FitzPatrick is right to point out that appealing to consent is problematic – because the whole point of the Trolley Problem is the intuition that killing the one workman may be permissible even against his consent – but wrong to think that consent is what the argument actually relies on. In criticizing the sort of altruism that may motivate the bystander to turn the trolley towards herself in the three-way scenario, Thomson argues that dying for the sake of five strangers is not morally valuable. Thomson says that 'I would certainly not feel proud of my children if I learned that they value their own lives as little as that man values his' (2008: 367). It is this claim, which she cashes out in terms of altruism by devising her new three-way scenario, which is doing the philosophical work for Thomson: it is because dying for the sake of five strangers is not morally valuable that even the bystander that would sacrifice herself may not sacrifice someone else. Consent doesn't actually matter, as shown by the counterfactual that if dying for the sake of five strangers were morally valuable, then the bystander may turn the trolley against the one workman irrespective of the workman's consent.

In defusing FitzPatrick's challenge, then, we have uncovered the deep structure of Thomson's argument[12]: it is not about consent, but rather about the moral value of dying for strangers. Let me just say that here it will not do to object that in the traditional *Bystander at the Switch* both the one and the five are strangers for the bystander: that is addressed by Thomson's new scenario, which supposedly shows that the bystander may not sacrifice the one if she is not willing to sacrifice herself. This is just a point about fairness and treating others as moral equals, which we have here defended from FitzPatrick's weaker principle. But it is when Thomson addresses those who would be willing to sacrifice themselves that her stronger normative claim emerges: dying for the sake of strangers is not morally valuable. Because it is not morally valuable, those who wish to do it will have to appeal to individual liberty to justify it; but liberty will only justify self-sacrifice, and not sacrificing others. That is then why even those who would, in the three-way scenario, sacrifice themselves, may not sacrifice the one workman in the traditional *Bystander at the Switch*.

I have not only rebutted FitzPatrick's critique; I have also made explicit the crucial normative premise upon which Thomson's new argument is built: that it is not morally valuable to die for the sake of strangers. We see now that the real novelty in Thomson's new discussion of the Trolley Problem is not just the new three-way scenario involving self-sacrifice and its implications for the traditional scenario; Thomson has shown that we must defend the value of dying for the sake of strangers in order for the Trolley Problem to even arise. And because there is no moral value in dying for strangers, then there is no Trolley Problem. Here it is neither possible nor necessary to deal in depth with this sort of radical altruism: it is enough to have shown that the very existence of the Trolley Problem depends on taking a particular position on this radical altruism (and anyway, how many people do you know, for example, who have committed suicide so that their organs may be deployed to save the life of five strangers?[13]).

It may be objected that Thomson's dissolution of the Trolley Problem crucially depends on the characters involved being strangers. But, the objection goes, we can reformulate the Trolley Problem without this requirement, so that Thomson's argument would fail to dissolve this new version of the Trolley Problem because it could no longer rely on the point about dying for the sake of strangers. Let us then look at a variant on the Trolley Problem which includes the kind of features that, according to Thomson, may make self-sacrifice morally valuable: 'They're my children', 'They're my friends', 'They stand for things that matter to me', 'They're young, whereas I haven't much longer to live', 'I've committed myself to doing what I can for them': these and their ilk would make sacrificing one's life to save five morally intelligible.

> Consider, by contrast, the man who learns that five strangers will live if and only if they get the organs they need, and that his are the only ones that are available in time, and who therefore straightway volunteers. No reputable surgeon would perform the operation, and no hospital would allow it to be performed under its auspices. I would certainly not feel proud of my children if I learned that they value their own lives as little as that man values his. (2008: 366–7)

Let us then take it that the five stuck on the main track are volunteers who have been trying to reach an isolated village in desperate need of water after an earthquake. And let us further suppose that the bystander knows the good work that the five have been doing through the years; the bystander thinks that the five are virtuous examples who must continue to provide an inspiration to society. The bystander concludes that, were she stuck on a third track towards which she could divert the runway trolley, she would sacrifice herself for the sake of the five. In order to maintain the symmetry of the original Trolley Problem, let us suppose that the one was also on her way to help the same isolated village, and that the bystander considers the one a virtuous example who must continue to provide an inspiration to society too. Is it now permissible for the bystander to sacrifice the one in order to save the five?

I see two problems here: first, once we have described the victims as exceptionally virtuous so as to provide an argument for self-sacrifice which the traditional Trolley Problem lacks, then the bystander may reasonably assume that the one would consent to being sacrificed; and on the other hand if the bystander were to think that the one would not consent, then she may no longer regard it as exceptionally virtuous – so that the symmetry with the traditional Trolley Problem would be lost one way or the other. The second problem is with *Fat Man*: apart from the plausibility of a very fat man taking part to a rescue operation, in this version of the Trolley Problem it is no longer clear that it would be clearly impermissible to shove the fat man off the bridge – indeed, for the considerations above, it may have to be supposed that the fat man would himself jump; and that if he didn't (jump or just give his consent to being pushed, as he might be too fat to climb the railing himself), the symmetry would no longer hold.

Here it may be objected that it is only by modelling the new variant on 'They stand for things that matter to me' (2008: 366) that we run into problems; other variants will work better. Let us try: 'They're my children' (ibid.) will not do because, if all six have to be my children, then I can't compare myself to the one, which has a different relation to the five than I do. And in general we would be contaminating the Trolley Problem with parental and fraternal commitments and responsibility which would make the problem non-basic in a way so as to radically change its role in normative ethics. These two kinds of considerations also apply, respectively, to 'They're young, whereas I haven't much longer to live' (ibid.) and 'I've committed myself to doing what I can for them' (ibid.): the former because the symmetry between my relation to the five and the one's relation to the five would be altered; the latter because of the special responsibilities with which we would alter the Trolley Problem. Finally, 'They're my friends' (ibid.) will also not do because of reasonable assumptions about consent in both *Bystander* and *Fat Man*. What this suggests is that it is constitutive of the Trolley Problem that it features strangers; but, as Thomson argues, because it features strangers, the Trolley Problem is not a problem because it is not permissible to kill the one in *Bystander at the Switch*.

I have argued that criticizing the Doctrine of Double Effect will, alone, not do. We must also offer an alternative explanation for the cases, such as the Trolley Problem, that the Doctrine can deal with. On these grounds, I have defended a proposed dissolution of the Trolley Problem. It may be objected that the Doctrine may still be preferred to Thomson's dissolution on the grounds that the former, but not the latter, explains the Trolley Problem by accounting for lay intuitions that *Bystander* is permissible but *Fat Man* is not permissible; the latter challenges lay intuitions by arguing that *Bystander* is not actually permissible. So only the Doctrine really does justice to lay intuitions; my proposed alternative does not. And on this ground one may still hang on to double effect.

It is true that the conclusion of Thomson's new argument, which I have here defended, is that *Bystander* is not permissible, while empirical evidence suggests that *the people* (as Steinbeck would have said) think that *Bystander* is permissible. But the relationship between Thomson's new argument and intuitions which I have suggested here is different: my own experimental philosophy data suggest that the *Bystander* intuition is not basic in the way in which it has until now been suggested. When subjects answer the self-sacrifice scenario before they answer the *Bystander* scenario, then they no longer report the intuition that *Bystander* is permissible. So my proposal is not at a disadvantage against double effect on the grounds that the Doctrine does justice to wide-spread moral intuitions while my proposal does not: I have done justice to intuitions too by deploying Thomson's new argument to demonstrate that people don't really have the intuition that *Bystander* is permissible – as the next chapter shows in some detail.

5 Conclusion

Before turning to that, let us sum up what we have achieved in this chapter. We have argued that the Trolley Problem dialectically supports the Doctrine of Double Effect, and that therefore endless debates about shortcomings of double effect (many of which are discussed in this book) will not do, *alone*, as an argument against the Doctrine: we must, in the spirit of Philippa Foot, offer an alternative. To this end, we have defended Thomson's dissolution of the Trolley Problem, according to which it is not permissible to kill the one workman in *Bystander at the Switch*.

CHAPTER FIVE

An experimental approach to the permissibility of killing one to save five

Abstract *This chapter presents my own data on trolley cases. Bryce Huebner and Marc Hauser have recently put Thomson's argument for the impermissibility of killing the one to the empirical test by asking people what they should do in the new trilemma case in which they may also sacrifice themselves. They found that the majority judge that they should either kill the one or sacrifice themselves; Huebner and Hauser argue that those numbers speak against Thomson's argument. But Thomson's argument was about the dialectical effect of the new trilemma on the traditional dilemma, rather than about the trilemma itself. Here I present the results of a study in which I asked subjects first what they should do in the trilemma and then what they should do in the traditional Trolley Problem. I found that, if asked first about the trilemma, subjects have the intuition that killing the one in the traditional* Bystander at the Switch *is not permissible – exactly what Thomson's argument had predicted.*

1 Introduction

In the last chapter, we looked at the relation between the Trolley Problem and the Doctrine of Double Effect. There I mentioned some experiments of mine on trolley scenarios. This chapter is dedicated to presenting those experiments in detail. Let us start by reminding ourselves where moral intuition is supposed to stand when it comes to trolley cases. Intuitions on the Trolley Problem are very clear: if the results of Marc Hauser's *Moral Sense Test* are to be believed, then according to public opinion it is permissible to intervene in *Bystander at the Switch*: around 90 per cent of respondents to the Moral Sense Test thought as much (Hauser 2006: 139). On the other hand, respondents say that it is not permissible to intervene in *Fat Man*: only around 10 per cent of respondents thought it is permissible to intervene.[1]

The folk, then, are due an answer: why is it permissible to intervene in *Bystander at the Switch* while it is not permissible to intervene in *Fat Man*? The literature on double effect and the Trolley Problem – as we have seen in the last chapter – is very large, because the question drives straight at the heart of the disagreement between deontological and consequentialist approaches to normative ethics. There are three possible approaches here: one can (1) try to answer the question; or (2) deny the question on the grounds that it is permissible to kill the *Fat Man*; or (3) deny the question on the grounds that it is not permissible to kill the one in *Bystander at the Switch*.

Here I will ignore both 1 and 2: on 2, biting the consequentialist bullet and denying that it is not permissible to kill the fat man is, whatever the merits of such a strategy, not a very original way to go: these kinds of counterexamples have always been brought against consequentialism. As this book is full of attempts to take option (1), here I will rather focus on 3, the claim that it is not permissible to intervene in *Bystander at the Switch*, and that therefore we don't need to answer the question that has come to be known as the Trolley Problem simply because there is no such problem – as we have argued in the previous chapter.

2 Thomson, Hauser and Huebner

Thomson herself (2008) has recently argued that the Trolley Problem is not actually a problem because it is not permissible to divert the trolley to kill the one workman in *Bystander at the Switch*. Thomson introduces a new scenario in which the bystander has also the possibility of sacrificing herself to save the five workmen. Here is Thomson's new *Bystander's Three Options*:

  i   do nothing, letting five die, or
  ii   throw the switch to the right, killing one, or
  iii   throw the switch to the left, killing himself. (2008: 364)

Thomson thinks that in this scenario choosing (ii) would not be right: 'I hope you will agree that choosing (ii) would be unacceptable on the bystander's part. If he *can* throw the switch to the left and turn the trolley onto himself, how dare he throw the switch to the right and turn the trolley onto the one workman?' (2008: 364). More importantly, Thomson thinks that the new scenario also illustrates why the bystander may not kill the one in the traditional *Bystander at the Switch*: 'Since he wouldn't himself pay the cost of his good deed if he could pay it, there is no way in which he can decently regard himself as entitled to make someone else pay it' (2008: 366). Thomson claims, then, that if the bystander would not be willing to sacrifice herself to save the five, then she may not sacrifice someone else.

Thomson's is, then, an argument about the traditional *Bystander at the Switch*: her new scenario is just the hypothetical question that, according to Thomson, the bystander should ask herself in deciding whether she may intervene. And Thomson claims that if the bystander cannot answer to the hypothetical question that she would indeed sacrifice herself, then she may not intervene.

Bryce Huebner and Marc Hauser have put Thomson's new trilemma to the experimental test. They have asked participants to the online Moral Sense Test the following question:

Jesse is standing near the railroad tracks and notices an empty boxcar coming down the tracks, moving fast enough to kill anyone that it hits. If Jesse does nothing, the boxcar will continue along the main track, killing five people who are walking down the main track. There is a switch nearby that Jesse can use to divert the boxcar onto either of two side tracks that split off from the main track in opposite directions. There is one person walking along the right-side track. So, if Jesse flips the switch to the right, the boxcar will hit and kill this person. Jesse's foot is stuck in the track on the left-side track. So if Jesse flips the switch to the left, he will be hit and killed by the trolley himself. What should Jesse do? (2011: 9[2])

The answers were as follows:

- 43 per cent judged that Jesse should flip the switch to the right;

- 38 per cent judged that Jesse should sacrifice herself;

- 18.7 per cent judged that Jesse should allow the trolley to proceed along the main track.

In a second version, the same question was put to respondents with the only variant that 'Jesse' was replaced with the pronoun 'you'. The outcome was very similar: 48 per cent judged that they should flip the switch to the right; 33.7 per cent judged that they should sacrifice themselves; and 18.2 per cent judged that they should do nothing.

Huebner and Hauser think that their numbers speak against Thomson's hypothesis:

The data reported in the previous section minimally suggests that Thomson's intuition is radically at odds with the commonsense intuition of what a person should do when she is faced with a difficult moral trilemma such as the three-track bystander case. If Thomson were right, we would expect it to be far more *transparent* that it is immoral to turn the trolley, and this increased transparency should be reflected, at least to some extent, in the folk-moral judgments that are offered in response to this case. Even if not everyone was sensitive to the hypocrisy of turning the trolley, we would expect a striking increase in the proportion of people who judge that one should just let the trolley go in such a case. In stark contrast to this hypothesis, we found no such pattern in folk-moral judgments about the three-track bystander case. Across both conditions in which altruistic self-sacrifice was at issue, only a small minority of participants (approximately 18%) judged that they should let the trolley go, suggesting that even when people are explicitly presented with the option of altruistic self-sacrifice, the inclination to save the five people on the main track continues to dominate their intuitive judgments. (2011: 13–14)

I think that this is a reasonable interpretation of the numbers: here I don't wish to deny the significance of those numbers nor do I want to offer alternative interpretations of those numbers. I would rather like to point out that Huebner and Hauser have not, even by their own standards, asked the right question; or, at least, that there was, even by their standard, a better question to ask. There was a much more significant question to ask, and this emerges quite clearly from their own discussion:

> Thomson's philosophical intuition is that considering the option of altruistic self-sacrifice makes the negative duty not to harm another person more salient. If this is the case, then perhaps the introduction of such an option will also have a significant effect on the proportion of people who will judge that it is permissible to flip the switch in a trolley case. (2011: 8)

Huebner and Hauser correctly identify the dialectic of Thomson's argument: her new scenario is only significant insofar as it illustrates (or makes more salient, to use their expression) something about the traditional trolley problem. But, then, why did Huebner and Hauser not ask participants who took the trilemma about the traditional trolley problem? If what Huebner and Hauser wanted to test Thomson's argument on was whether, as she claims, the trilemma has an effect on the traditional trolley problem, why not ask indeed about the traditional trolley problem?

> Thomson assumes, based on her own intuitions, that the introduction of altruistic self-sacrifice should lead others to see the hypocrisy inherent in sacrificing the person on the side track and to judge that the bystander should let the trolley continue along the main track. (2011: 7)

This is exactly what Thomson claims; and, importantly, she does so not just in the case of the new trilemma, but also in the case of the traditional trolley problem. But then the only way of testing Thomson's claim is to ask participants about the traditional trolley problem.

3 My own study

This is exactly what I did, finding that the trilemma significantly influences answers to the traditional dilemma. In December 2011, 152 subjects took an online survey that I designed by combining Thomson's trilemma (in the very wording of Huebner and Hauser's version) and the traditional *Bystander at the Switch*. Participants were randomly presented either with

- Thomson's trilemma and *then* the traditional dilemma; or with

- the traditional dilemma and *then* Thomson's trilemma; or with

- a trilemma not involving self-sacrifice (also modelled on one presented by Huebner and Hauser) and *then* the traditional dilemma.

Participants did not have access to the second question while answering the first, and they could not change their answer to the first question after having looked at or answered the second question. For the trilemma, I used Huebner and Hauser's Condition 2 question, where the pronoun 'you' replaces 'Jesse': I did so on the grounds of the principle of charity, as with 'you' the third option of doing nothing (the one that supposedly would have supported Thomson's argument) had even worse numbers than in Condition 1 with 'Jesse': 18.2 per cent instead of 18.7 per cent.

The trilemma question read as follows:

1) You are standing near the railroad tracks and notice an empty boxcar coming down the tracks, moving fast enough to kill anyone that it hits. If you do nothing, the boxcar will continue along the main track, killing five people who are walking down the main track. There is a switch nearby that you can use to divert the boxcar onto either of two side tracks that split off from the main track in opposite directions. There is one person walking along the right-side track. So, if you flip the switch to the right, the boxcar will hit and kill this person. Your foot is stuck in the track on the left-side track. So if you flip the switch to the left, you will be hit and killed by the trolley yourself. What should you do?

The three possible answers, whose order of presentation to the respondent was randomized, were:

- *I do nothing*
- *I flip the switch to the right*
- *I flip the switch to the left*

The traditional dilemma question was designed to replicate the *Bystander at the Switch* scenario while at the same time maintaining the wording of the trilemma question. It read as follows:

2) You are standing near the railroad tracks and notice an empty boxcar coming down the tracks, moving fast enough to kill anyone that it hits. If you do nothing, the boxcar will continue along the main track, killing five people who are walking down the main track. There is a switch nearby that you can use to divert the boxcar onto a side-track where one person is walking. So, if you flip the switch, the boxcar will hit and kill this person. What should you do?

The possible answers, whose order of presentation to the respondent was randomized, were:

- *I do nothing*
- *I flip the switch*

The third condition, designed in order to control for the specific effect of self-sacrifice and not just for the effect of any trilemma preceding the traditional dilemma, read as follows:

3) You are standing near the railroad tracks and notice an empty boxcar coming down the tracks, moving fast enough to kill anyone that it hits. If you do nothing, the boxcar will continue along the main track, killing five people who are walking down the main track. There is a switch nearby that you can use to divert the boxcar onto either of two side tracks that split off from the main track in opposite directions. There is one person walking along the right-side track. So, if you flip the switch to the right, the boxcar will hit and kill this person. There is another person walking along the left-side track. So if you flip the switch to the left, the boxcar will hit and kill this person. What should you do?

The three possible answers, whose order of presentation to the respondent was randomized, were:

- *I do nothing*
- *I flip the switch to the right*
- *I flip the switch to the left*

The three different questions were combined to form three conditions:

a 1, then 2
b 2, then 1
c 3, then 2

Conditions (a) and (b) tested the effect of the trilemma on the traditional dilemma; condition (c) tested the specific effect of self-sacrifice as opposed to the general effect of a trilemma before answering the traditional dilemma. One hundred and fifty-two subjects participated: 75 answered condition (a); 45 answered condition (b); 32 answered condition (c).

The answers to the dilemma question in the three conditions were as follows[3]:

- Condition (a): flip the switch 38.66 per cent; not flip the switch 61.34 per cent[4]
- Condition (b): flip the switch 66.67 per cent; not flip the switch 33.33 per cent[5]
- Condition (c): flip the switch 56.25 per cent; not flip the switch 43.75 per cent.[6]

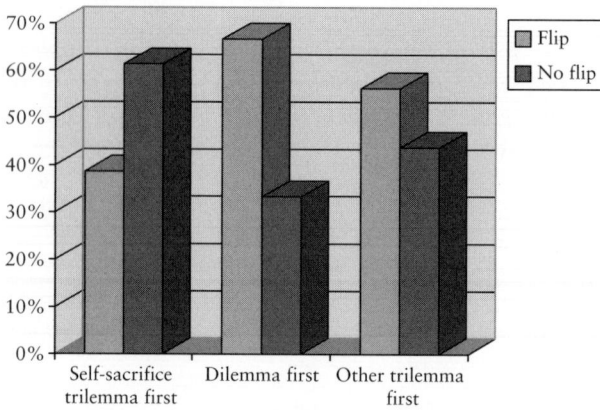

FIGURE 5.1 *The self-sacrifice trilemma.*

4 Discussion

The difference between the results of *Bystander at the Switch* when answered in isolation and *Bystander at the Switch* when answered after having answered Thomson's trilemma is impressive.[7] In the former case, a significant majority answer that intervening is permissible (confirming previous studies). In the latter case, the intuition that intervening is permissible disappears, with just over a third of respondents sharing it. Importantly, my study suggests that they reach such conclusion only after having been subjected to the self-sacrifice trilemma, just as Thomson argued: when answering the traditional dilemma only after having answered a trilemma that did not involve self-sacrifice, the majority still have the intuition that flipping the switch is permissible.

Recall the words of Huebner and Hauser: 'Thomson's philosophical intuition is that considering the option of altruistic self-sacrifice makes the negative duty not to harm another person more salient. If this is the case, then perhaps the introduction of such an option will also have a significant effect on the proportion of people who will judge that it is permissible to flip the switch in a trolley case' (2011: 8).

In my study, the introduction of such an option did indeed have a significant effect on the proportion of people who judge that it is permissible to flip the switch in a trolley case: those people drastically dropped from 66.67 per cent down to 38.66 per cent. And this is a direct result of considering the option of altruistic self-sacrifice, exactly as Thomson had predicted in her theoretical argument.

It may be objected that more needs to be done to prove that these results support Thomson's argument; my results only show, it may be argued, that the relevant moral intuitions are very unstable. I have already mentioned this issue in the previous chapter, and now that I have presented the data in detail, I can say that I think that the dialectic of Thomson's argument is such that my results do support it, because her argument is about the effect of the new case on the old one (and Huebner and Hauser seem to think that too). Also, condition (c) controls exactly against just any order effect: it isn't simply the introduction of *a* question before the traditional dilemma; and it isn't even the introduction of *a* trilemma before the traditional dilemma; it is the introduction of the option of self-sacrifice.[8]

Let me say something in the way of explaining the results of my experiment: why are the answers to the traditional Trolley Problem affected by engaging with the self-sacrifice trilemma? Here there are at least two alternative ways of thinking: (1) one may take it that having looked at the trilemma shifts the attention of the respondent, when thinking afterwards about the traditional dilemma, to the similarity between the one workman and oneself. The idea would be that the trilemma helps to let the respondent identify with the one workman: they are both, after all, on a side-track towards which a threat may be redirected.

This idea of a shift of perspective enabled or facilitated by the trilemma may indeed explain the results, but would it also support the normative conclusion that killing the one in the traditional Trolley Problem is indeed impermissible? Alternatively, (2) it may be argued that engaging with the trilemma does not just shift the agent's perspective, but actually allows the agent to *see* the morally relevant features which make intervening in the traditional Trolley Problem impermissible. It is only by comparing the one workman with ourselves that we realize the true nature of the workman's situation: namely that we are asking him to die for the sake of strangers.

Let me emphasize that the significance of my experiment does not depend on being able to defend the normative value of the effect that I have identified. Even if one wants to dispute the effect of the trilemma on the dilemma, our results would still show, in line with Swain et al. (2008), that the *Bystander* intuition is unstable and that it depends on the order of presentation so heavily that it disappears when the bystander is first introduced after Thomson's new self-sacrifice case. This latter outcome is anyhow more important than supporting Thomson's argument, because it is significantly more general in two different respects:

1 We must distinguish between the claim that killing the one in *Bystander at the Switch* is not permissible and arguments, such as Thomson's, for such claim that killing the one is not permissible. My results are relevant to the claim that killing the one is not permissible whether or not they support Thomson's argument. This is because my results defuse the supposed overwhelming intuition that it is permissible to kill the one.

2 As we have seen in the last chapter, Thomson's argument is that if you are not willing to sacrifice yourself you may not sacrifice someone else, then this argument – in such a form – does not have anything to say about those who are willing to sacrifice themselves. Indeed, one would suppose that, given Thomson's reasoning, those who are willing to sacrifice themselves would be then allowed to sacrifice the one.[9] This brings us back to the one workman and dying for the sake of strangers. As I have already dealt with this in the previous chapter, here I will only summarize my position.

As we saw in Chapter 4, Thomson tries to argue that even those who would be willing to sacrifice themselves may not kill the one. Thomson argues on two grounds: (a) she says that 'altruism that rises to this level is not morally attractive. Quite to the contrary. A willingness to give up one's life *simply* on learning that five others will live if and only if one dies is a sign of a serious moral defect in a person. "They're my children," "They're my friends," "They stand for things that matter to me," "They're young, whereas I haven't much longer to live," "I've committed myself to doing what I can for them": these and their ilk would make sacrificing one's life to save five morally intelligible. Consider, by contrast, the man who learns that five strangers will live if and only if they get the organs they need, and that his are the only ones that are available in time, and who therefore straightway volunteers. No reputable surgeon would perform the operation, and no hospital would allow it to be performed under its auspices. I would certainly not feel proud of my children if I learned that they value their own lives as little as that man values his' (2008: 366–7); (b) Thomson says that 'It remains the case that the altruistic bystander is not entitled to assume that the one workman is equally altruistic, and would therefore consent' (2008: 367).

We have already seen that Thomson's second point is quickly shown to be problematic: one cannot appeal to consent in arguments about the permissibility of intervening in the Trolley Problem quite simply because what is at stake is that intervention is permissible even in the absence of consent (again, see Chapter 4 on this). So this approach will not do, even though it may be interesting to enquire whether those that do think that intervening is permissible may take the one to be obliged to consent (so-called 'normative consent') or to implicitly give her consent given the circumstances (so-called 'tacit consent' – I have written on consent elsewhere, see Di Nucci (forthcoming g)).

What about Thomson's other approach, the idea that radical altruism is not attractive? This approach may be more promising, but it has to be supplemented with the claim that the kind of radical altruism involved in dying for the sake of five strangers is not morally valuable. If it were not morally valuable, then that would mean that someone who would be willing to sacrifice herself for the sake of five strangers would have to appeal to liberty – and since liberty as a justification would not apply to the case of killing the one, then we would have an argument for the claim that killing the one in *Bystander at the Switch* is not permissible on the grounds that radical altruism is not morally valuable (again, see Chapter 4 for more details on this).

5 Conclusion

This is, admittedly, a radical moral stance to uphold; but, importantly, I do not need to defend it here: the point here was only to empirically test Thomson's hypothesis that the trilemma would have an effect on the traditional *Bystander at the Switch* dilemma. The results are overwhelming: when answering the traditional Trolley Problem only after having answered Thomson's self-sacrifice trilemma, a large majority respond that it is not permissible to kill the one.

CHAPTER SIX

A theoretical problem with double effect: Closeness

Abstract *The distinction between intending and merely foreseeing harm which is at the heart of the Doctrine of Double Effect has been traditionally challenged by the so-called 'problem of closeness', according to which this distinction is so arbitrary that one can argue in all the relevant cases that the harm is not intended but rather merely foreseen, thereby undermining the Doctrine by preventing it from ruling against a wide range of intuitive impermissible cases. Attempts at solving the problem of closeness have therefore taken up a large part of the recent debate on double effect. In this chapter, I look at ten such attempts, finding them all wanting: in the order in which they are discussed; Michael Bratman's, T. A. Cavanaugh's, Jonathan Bennett's, William FitzPatrick's, Alison Hills's, Neil Delaney's, Ralph Wedgwood's, Lawrence Masek's, Alexander Pruss's and Warren Quinn's.*

1 Introduction

According to the common non-consequentialist constraint which is at the heart of the Doctrine of Double Effect, to bring about harm that one intends is sometimes morally worse than to bring about the same amount of harm if one merely foresees it. Over the years, this non-consequentialist constraint has found wide application. Only to mention the most common cases that feature in this book: collateral damage, palliative care, abortion, self-defence, self-sacrifice, stem cell research, the so-called *Trolley Problem* and what has recently come to be known as the *Knobe Effect*.[1]

So far in the book we have only dealt with cases that were obviously morally relevant. So this time to illustrate the generality of this non-consequentialist constraint, let us take a scenario that is not directly moral: take the head coaches of mediocre sports teams which, according to themselves and their own staff, competitors and also independent experts, have no chance of competing for the title this season. Those same insiders also think that there may be a reasonable chance to be in the mix next year if the teams improve. Coach1 decides that the best strategy is to give more minutes to the younger and less experienced players: that will have the negative consequence of compromising this season but will also have the positive consequence of having a much improved team next year.

We may say that Coach1 does not intend to lose games even though she foresees that her strategy will lead to lose more games: her intended means to the end of improving the team for the next season is to let the young ones mature, but this does have the side effect, which Coach1 acknowledges, that the team will lose more games this season. Coach2, on the other hand, decides that the best strategy is to lose games (by diminishing the minutes of her best players) in order to increase the team's chances in the coming draft: a high pick will considerably improve the team for next year. That will have the negative consequence of compromising this season but will also have the positive consequence of having a much improved team next year. We may say that Coach2 does intend to lose games: that is her intended means to the end of improving the team for next season. To be sure: Coach1 isn't stupid and has also thought about the consequences of her plan for the draft, but that is not part of her strategy – she is relying on the improvement of her young

players. Similarly, Coach2 has also thought about the consequences
of her own plan for the younger and less experienced players, but
that is not part of her strategy – she is relying on success in the
coming draft lottery.[2]

The non-consequentialist constraint according to which to bring
about harm that one intends is sometimes morally worse than to
bring about the same harm that one merely foresees can be analysed
as comprising of two parts: (1) a distinction between intending and
merely foreseeing, and (2) a claim about the respective moral value
of intending and merely foreseeing. (1) and (2) also respectively
identify two different streams in the double effect debate: action-
theoretical discussions about the intending/foreseeing distinction
and ethical discussions about the moral relevance of this distinction.
Here I only focus on a particular challenge to (1) which has taken
up most of the recent discussion of double effect: this is sometimes
referred to as 'the problem of closeness', going back to Philippa
Foot's original formulation of it (1967).

> Consider the story, well known to philosophers, of the fat man
> stuck in the mouth of the cave. A party of pot-holers have
> imprudently allowed the fat man to lead them as they make
> their way out of the cave, and he gets stuck, trapping the others
> behind him. Obviously the right thing to do is to sit down
> and wait until the fat man grows thin; but philosophers have
> arranged that flood waters should be rising within the cave.
> Luckily (luckily?) the trapped party have with them a stick of
> dynamite with which they can blast the fat man out of the mouth
> of the cave. Either they use the dynamite or they drown. In one
> version the fat man, whose head is in the cave, will drown with
> them; in the other he will be rescued in due course. Problem:
> may they use the dynamite or not? [The example is introduced
> in part] because it will serve to show how ridiculous one version
> of the doctrine of the double effect would be. For suppose that
> the trapped explorers were to argue that the death of the fat man
> might be taken as a merely foreseen consequence of the act of
> blowing him up. ("We didn't want to kill him . . . only to blow
> him into small pieces" or even ". . . only to blast him out of the
> cave.") I believe that those who use the doctrine of the double
> effect would rightly reject such a suggestion, although they will,
> of course, have considerable difficulty in explaining where the

line is to be drawn. What is to be the criterion of "closeness" if we say that anything very close to what we are literally aiming at counts as if part of our aim? (145–6)

Foot herself does not go on to offer such a criterion for closeness and her following paragraph starts with: 'Let us leave this difficulty aside and return too . . .' (1967: 146). This is a potentially devastating challenge to the intending/foreseeing distinction, according to which the distinction is so arbitrary that it can be also applied to all the cases that the Doctrine of Double Effect would want to forbid.

After Foot, many have tried to offer criteria for closeness, and here I discuss and reject a large number of representative attempts. But offering criteria for closeness is only one of various possible dialectical moves here, and before I discuss this one influential move, it helps to map it onto alternative strategies. One obvious move is to reject the intending/foreseen distinction or the whole Doctrine (those are two different options as the former is, at best, only a part of the latter; but as in this particular context the latter option would be motivated by the former, we can group them together).[3]

Another influential alternative move was Warren Quinn's, who was so compelled by the problem of closeness that he offered a reformulation of double effect in order to avoid that difficulty: Quinn distinguishes between 'agency in which harm comes to some victims, at least in part, from the agent's deliberately involving them in something in order to further his purpose precisely by way of their being so involved . . . and agency in which either nothing is in that way intended for the victims or what is so intended does not contribute to their harm' (1989: 343). As we shall see later on in this chapter, Quinn's reformulation in terms of deliberate involvement does not actually avoid the original difficulty – but it is important to set Quinn apart as his attempt did not consist in trying to offer criteria for closeness.

There is a further alternative to either abandoning or reformulating the Doctrine of Double Effect on the one hand and offering criteria for closeness on the other: questioning the intuitiveness of the cases that are supposed to motivate double effect. I have explored this option in Chapter 4, but it is important to mention it here at the outset to stress an important dialectical point: some authors who have tried to offer criteria for closeness write as if that were the only possibility, but a lot of recent work in moral psychology has shown that the distinctive judgements and intuitions at play in the classic double effect cases (where, normally, one of a pair of consequentialistically identical cases is judged as morally permissible while the other is judged as impermissible) can no longer be considered a *datum* against which to measure the different theories.

Having now mapped the problem of closeness onto the wider debate around the Doctrine of Double Effect, the rest of this chapter will only deal with the issue of closeness itself: I discuss and reject the accounts of (in the order in which those accounts are discussed here rather than in chronological order): Bratman (1984 and 1987), Cavanaugh (2006), Bennett (1980 and 1995), FitzPatrick (2003, 2006, 2012), Hills (2003 and 2007), Delaney (2007 and 2008), Wedgwood (2011a and 2011b), Masek (2010), Pruss (forthcoming) and Quinn (1989).

2 Bratman's three roles of intention

Let me start by saying that it won't do to ignore the problem of closeness on the grounds that Foot's cave story and related scenarios are just fanciful thought-experiments. There are well-documented historical cases which pose the very same problem. Here is a representative one, from World War II orders to the *RAF Bomber Command*:

> The ultimate aim of the attack on a town area is to break the morale of the population which occupies it. To ensure this we must achieve two things: first, we must make the town physically uninhabitable and, secondly, we must make the people conscious of constant personal danger. The immediate aim, is therefore, twofold, namely, to produce (i) destruction, and (ii) the fear of death. (*1941 British Air Ministry directif* – Harris 1995: 7)

The phrasing of this document could be considered a pretty accurate historical illustration of the problem of closeness, because this document strikingly omits from the list of 'immediate aims' the killing of the civilian population; indeed, it omits to mention killing altogether! Rather, the immediate aims of those bombing missions on town areas were *only* to produce destruction and fear of death. Only fear of death rather than death itself. To put this in the language of the closeness debate, then, one could say that Bomber Command intended to produce destruction and intended to produce fear of death; and that they may have only foreseen but not intended any deaths. Bomber Command may well argue, just like Foot's trapped explorers, that, in sending its planes to bomb town areas at night, it didn't intend to kill anybody: the point of dropping a bomb onto an inhabited house wasn't to kill the inhabitants, but only to destroy said house and to make the inhabitants fearful of death. This is, I submit, just as ridiculous as the explorers' hypothetical argument: indeed, all the more ridiculous because the British Air Ministry document is no philosophical disquisition (more on terror bombing in Chapter 8).

Let us now begin our analysis of different proposed solutions to the problem of closeness with Bratman's influential conception of intention. According to Bratman's planning theory, intention has three roles (1987: 140–3):

  i 'posing problems for further reasoning';

  ii 'constraining other intentions'; and

  iii 'issuing in corresponding endeavouring'.

The idea is that an attitude should count as an intention if and only if it satisfies all three of these roles. In order to see how the three roles of intention are supposed to distinguish between intending and merely foreseeing some consequence, we need to introduce the scenario of Terror Bomber and Strategic Bomber, as presented by Bratman himself:

> Both Terror Bomber and Strategic Bomber have the goal of promoting the war effort against Enemy. Each intends to pursue this goal by weakening Enemy, and each intends to do that by dropping bombs. Terror Bomber's plan is to bomb the school in Enemy's territory, thereby killing children of Enemy and terrorizing Enemy's population. Strategic Bomber's plan is different. He plans to bomb Enemy's munitions plant, thereby undermining Enemy's war effort. Strategic Bomber also knows, however, that next to the munitions plant is a school, and that

when he bombs the plant he will also destroy the school, killing the children inside. Strategic Bomber has not ignored this fact. Indeed, he has worried a lot about it. Still, he has concluded that this cost, though significant, is outweighed by the contribution that would be made to the war effort by the destruction of the munitions plant. Now, Terror Bomber intends all of the features of his action just noted: he intends to drop the bombs, kill the children, terrorize the population, and thereby weaken Enemy. In contrast, it seems that Strategic Bomber only intends to drop the bombs, destroy the munitions plant, and weaken Enemy. Although he knows that by bombing the plant he will be killing the children, he does not, it seems, intend to kill them. Whereas killing the children is, for Terror Bomber, an intended means to his end of victory, it is, for Strategic Bomber, only something he knows he will do by bombing the munitions plant. Though Strategic Bomber has taken the deaths of the children quite seriously into account in his deliberation, these deaths are for him only an expected side effect; they are not – in contrast with Terror Bomber's position – intended as a means. . . . In saying this I do not deny that Strategic Bomber kills the children intentionally. (1987: 139–40)

As the three roles of intention are applied to Terror Bomber's intention, Bratman says that Terror Bomber's intention will (i) pose the problem of how he is going to kill the children: 'Terror Bomber must figure out, for example, what time of day to attack and what sorts of bombs to use' (1987: 141). (ii) Terror Bomber's intention will also be incompatible with other possible strategies. Terror Bomber may not, for example, implement a plan to deploy some troops if this deployment would result in the enemy evacuating the children: 'So Terror Bomber's prior intention to kill the children stands in the way of his forming a new intention to order the troop movement' (1987: 141). (iii) Terror Bomber will also guide his conduct so as to cause the death of the children: 'If in midair he learns they have moved to a different school, he will try to keep track of them and take his bombs there' (1987: 141–2).

Bratman claims that these three roles are not true of Strategic Bomber's attitude towards killing the children: Strategic Bomber will not engage in practical reasoning about how to kill the children;

if further intentions of Strategic Bomber should be incompatible with killing the children, that will not be a prima facie reason to disregard them; and, to put Bratman's point crudely, if the children move, Strategic Bomber will not follow them.

Here I am not particularly interested in discussing the thought-experiment of Terror Bomber and Strategic Bomber (for that, please see Chapters 8 and 9), but only in whether Bratman's three roles of intention can be deployed to solve the problem of closeness. I say this because it has been suggested that the thought-experiment involving Terror Bomber and Strategic Bomber may deserve to be treated independently (FitzPatrick 2006: 590). Let us briefly look at this issue and then return to the application of the three roles of intention to Foot's cave.

Bennett (1980: 111–13 and 1995: 210–12) has argued that in such a case all the Terror Bomber needs is for the civilians to look dead for as long as it will take for the enemy to capitulate; and that therefore Terror Bomber may claim, just like Foot's explorers, that death was only foreseen but not intended.[4] FitzPatrick (2006: 589–91) has argued that this case of Bennett can be easily solved even without having to offer conditions for closeness by just pointing out that Terror Bomber's means to make the civilians seem dead is just to kill them – and that therefore killing civilians is in this case an intended means of Terror Bomber even if she kills them only in order for them to appear dead.

But, as FitzPatrick himself recognizes, this reply doesn't go very far, as it is itself subject to Foot's explorers' kind of problem:

> In fact, however, this is too hasty: for there is one response open to the terror bomber that will in fact lead us right to the real problem of closeness that arises for other kinds of case as well, so that a complete answer even to this sort of case will require an account of excessive closeness. The problem is that the terror bomber might reply to the above argument by saying that his more proximate intended means of making the civilians appear dead is not killing them per se, but only impacting them sufficiently with the bombs to put them in a condition of appearing dead. He doesn't deny the intention of that proximate means, but only denies that their death or even their harm as such is intended as a means, though he admits it is foreseen as a side effect of the intended means. (2006: 591)

So the Terror Bomber case does not stand alone but is rather subject, just like the other cases, to the challenge of identifying criteria for closeness.

Let us now go back to trying to use Bratman's three roles of intention for Foot's cave. The test, remember, is whether the attitude has the three roles in question: if, for example, the trapped explorers do intend to kill the fat guy, then their attitude will, first, pose the problem of how they are going to kill him. But the explorers will not deliberate or engage in practical reasoning regarding the question of how to kill the fat guy or how best to ensure that the fat guy dies. They will rather only deliberate or engage in practical reasoning over the question of how to free the cave's mouth. For example, any explosion that would kill the fat guy but not free the cave's mouth will be disregarded as an option, while they will not disregard explosions that may free the cave without killing the fat guy. Take, next, the third role: will the explorers guide their conduct so as to cause the death of the fat guy? Here, again, it seems that they will only guide their conduct so as to cause the freeing of the cave's mouth. Suppose that, to the explorers' surprise, the explosion frees the mouth of the cave while only cutting the fat guy in five pieces: the two arms, the two legs, and the rest. And that the fat guy doesn't die as a result of it. Now, the explorers will presumably go and call for help rather than organize a new detonation to finish the job.

Similar considerations apply to the second role of intention: suppose that one of the trapped explorers is a doctor who has had to deal with a lot because the party has been trapped and is now finally enjoying a well-deserved nap in a quiet corner of the cave. If the other explorers, while organizing themselves to free the mouth of the cave, intended to kill the fat guy, then that intention would constrain a further possible intention to wake up the doctor so that she can be there to assist the fat guy just in case. But the party is under no rational pressure not to wake the doctor up to assist the fat guy. Why? Because they do not intend to kill the fat guy.

Foot's cave, then, cannot be dealt with by the simple application of Bratman's three roles of intention. The very opposite indeed seems to be the case: Bratman's three roles of intention give the very absurd verdict they were supposed to rule out, namely that the trapped explorers do not intend to kill the fat guy in blowing him to little pieces in order to free the cave's mouth. And this poor result of Bratman's three roles of intention can be easily replicated across other scenarios that, in the debate on double effect, are supposed to be morally impermissible. Take, for example, the *Fat Man* scenario in the *Trolley Problem*.

Let us start with the first role, posing problems for further reasoning. I think we can here contrast the supposed intention to kill the fat guy with the intention to stop the trolley, and see that only the latter attitude has the role for further reasoning identified by Bratman, and that therefore only the latter attitude is an intention. The bystander will have to reason about whether the fat man is heavy enough, for example; because if the fat man is not heavy enough to stop the trolley, then it will not make any rational sense to throw him off the bridge. But the bystander will not have to reason about a way of throwing him off the bridge so as to increase the chances that the trolley will hit head on the fat guy's vital organs, so as to guarantee the fat guy's death.

The sort of further reasoning that the bystander will have to engage in has to do, then, only with how the fat guy will ensure that the trolley will be stopped; and not with the actual death of the fat guy. Similar points can be made about the other two roles of intention: if the trolley happens to stop, for example, before I have pushed the fat guy, then I will no longer endeavour to throw him off the bridge – just as, in Bratman's discussion, Strategic Bomber will not pursue the children in case they leave the school. But now *Fat Man* looks like Strategic Bomber and not like Terror Bomber, so that we would say that the bystander in *Fat Man* intends to stop the trolley but merely foresees the death of the fat guy. And that is, again, the opposite of the verdict that supporters of the Doctrine of Double Effect look for in the Trolley Problem.

Summing up, we have looked at an attempt to solve the problem of closeness by applying Bratman's influential conception of intention, and we have argued that Bratman's three roles of intention fail to deliver, in the crucial case of Foot's cave but also in another important case such as the Trolley Problem. In Section 3, I discuss Bennett's attempts at solving the problem of closeness; first, though, in the next sub-section I briefly discuss Cavanaugh's recent application of Bratman's planning theory of intention to the Doctrine of Double Effect.

2.1 Cavanaugh

Having shown why Bratman's three roles of intention do not solve the problem of closeness, I will not engage in detail with Cavanaugh's (2006) discussion, because his attempt at solving the problem of closeness is based exactly on Bratman's three roles of intention (See his Chapter 3, especially Section 3.4). Delaney (2007) has already done, I think, a very good job of showing why Cavanaugh's discussion of closeness does not bring us nearer to a solution:

> Basically Cavanaugh tries to solve the crucial problem of closeness by taking into account what *guides* the doctor in carrying out his objective. So, he thinks that the doctor is guided to crush the skull of the fetus so as to save the mother's life in craniotomy, whereas the doctor is in no way guided by the death of the fetus in hysterectomy. Of course this really accomplishes nothing; Hart et al will continue to insist that what the doctor in craniotomy is guided by is head modification, not killing at all, just as the doctor in hysterectomy is guided by removal of the uterus, not killing the fetus. To suggest that being guided in one's choice of surgical instruments by which are most likely to effectively crush the skull of the fetus is to be guided by evil, as Nagel might say, more specifically to be guided by what will promptly kill the fetus, is wholly question begging. The problem of closeness, I am afraid, rests right where it did before Cavanaugh attacked it with the planning theory of intention. (Delaney 2007)

So I will restrict myself to discussion of just one example – craniotomy – of how Cavanaugh's application of Bratman's planning theory of intention fails to solve the problem of closeness: this will serve the double purpose of showing the shortcomings of one of the recent attempts at solving the problem of closeness (Cavanaugh's) and of illustrating by example the overall argument of this section, namely that Bratman's three roles of intention are no solution to closeness. In discussing craniotomy, Cavanaugh describes the surgeon as follows (2006: 112):

> The intent to dismember the baby's cranium directs his action. For example, it leads him to ensure that the surgical instruments

he employs can cut and dismember the skull. If the physician were to use forceps that would not tear the baby's head apart, he would have to alter what he does in order to do what he intends. For he seeks to dismember the baby's skull. This intent causes him to deliberate about what surgical instruments to use and leads him to intend to use those deliberation discovers. The intent to destroy the baby's cranium solves the problem of how to preserve the mother's life.

This is, indeed, a very accurate application of Bratman's three roles of intention to the case of craniotomy. And in this respect it is also an accurate illustration of how the three roles of intention do not solve the problem of closeness: Cavanaugh's precise description of what the surgeon does is striking exactly because it does not mention the killing of the foetus. It mentions (a) the dismembering of the foetus' cranium; (b) the cutting of the foetus' skull; (c) the tearing apart of the foetus' head and (d) the destruction of the foetus' cranium. But the point of the problem of closeness is to show how any of these descriptions (either alone or taken together) could not be intended without also intending killing the foetus: what Cavanaugh ends up illustrating is that even a painfully precise description of the surgeon's aims and strategy need not involve 'killing the foetus'.

3 Bennett's tight binding

Jonathan Bennett is arguably the philosopher who has done the most work on the problem of closeness. Bennett rejects four different suggestions: (1) identity of events (1995: 205), (2) act-identity (1995: 207), (3) causal necessitation (1995: 209) and (4) entailment (1995: 209); and then concludes by sketching what he takes to be as good as a solution to the problem of closeness is going to get: (5) 'what the plain man would call inconceivable' (1995: 213):

> The best I can find is rather loose, but it may be the whole truth about our intended/foreseen distinction. Not only is there no chance of turning the ashes back into a building, or the smithereens back into people [TB], or of crushing the baby's head without killing it – these things are what the plain man

would call inconceivable. We can fairly easily imagine getting technology that would allow bombs to be aimed much more precisely, or would allow a fetus to be brought to term outside the mother's body; whereas the idea of destroying the head but not the baby, or of restoring a person who has been burnt to a cinder, is sheer fantasy. Without denying that it is conceptually possible, something God could do, we have not the faintest idea of what it might be like to have the means to bring it about. That, I suggest, is the 'tight binding' we have been looking for.

Bennett is right. This is rather loose: in fact, it is too loose. Whatever we make of the notion of the plain man's inconceivability (inconceivability *tout court* is already bad enough), it seems that it will both let in cases that the Doctrine of Double Effect wants to leave out and leave out cases that the Doctrine wants to let in. Inconceivability tout court will clearly not do the job because, as the debate shows, those scenarios are not inconceivable tout court. That's why Bennett introduces the notion of the *plain man's* inconceivability, which is another way of saying that some of these cases are pure philosophical fantasy. Here, a few different points are in order. First, we don't actually know what plain man's inconceivability is and therefore we have no idea even how to begin to use it in order to try to solve the problem of closeness (Delaney makes a similar point (2008: 351)).

Secondly, as our application of Bratman's three roles of intention to Foot's cave has shown, the plain man can very well conceive blowing the fat guy up away from killing the fat guy: we even offered a scenario that is not just conceivable but empirically accurate, where losing all four limbs does not cause death. And nobody will want to claim that the plain man is so plain that he could not conceive empirically possible scenarios. The case against plain man's conceivability is even stronger when we move to cases such as craniotomy (mentioned by Bennett himself; see also Hart 1967 and Foot 1967) or the Trolley Problem. And the same goes for the historical case of Bomber Command: indeed, the plain men that drew up the guidelines we discussed must have been able to conceive destruction and fear of death independently of killing, because they were able to write the guidelines without mentioning killing. So just about all the cases that the Doctrine of Double Effect wants to condemn are *plainly* conceivable and therefore would pass

Bennett's test. The test, then, is no use in drawing the distinction between intending harm and merely foreseeing the same harm.

There is a further point which illustrates just how loose Bennett's test is: we have just used it to show that it cannot rule any case out. But it could be as well used to rule out cases that the Doctrine of Double Effect wants to allow for: plain man's conceivability could be understood to mean that the plain man would react to it by shouting 'But that's just not possible!' That would rule out Foot's cave, as I'd imagine that most sensible people would react to the idea that the fat guy is blown to pieces without being killed with 'But that's just not possible!' But this criterion is too weak, because the same sensible people would react with 'But that's just not possible!' to *Bystander at the Switch*, once you have assured them – as the scenario does – that the worker on the side track has no chance of getting out of the way of the runaway trolley. In conclusion, Bennett's plain man's conceivability test is no help at all, which is what Bennett must have recognized by introducing it with 'The best I can find is rather loose' (1995: 213).

4 FitzPatrick on constitution

The next attempted solution of the problem of closeness that we look at is FitzPatrick's (2006: 593):

> The relation between the intended means and the harm in question is "too close" to allow for application of the intend/foresee distinction when the relation between the relevant states of affairs is a constitutive one rather than a merely causal one.

FitzPatrick (2006: 594) then goes on to describe *Bystander at the Switch* as a paradigmatic case of a relation which is 'merely causal' and not constitutive: the relation between 'the trolley being diverted onto the side track' and 'the one workman being killed'. On the other hand, FitzPatrick lists Foot's cave and craniotomy as cases of a constitutive relation between, for example, 'being blown to bits' and 'being killed'. FitzPatrick says hardly anything about what he means by 'constitution', but the following at least clarifies what constitution isn't: 'a man being blown to bits is not a cause of his being killed' (2006: 595).[5] This is a very ambitious proposal in at least three respects: (1) the aforementioned claim about causation; (2) the claim mentioned in 1 will have to apply to all the cases like Foot's cave that are not suitable for the Doctrine of Double Effect; (3) the claim mentioned in 1 should not apply to any of the cases that are suitable for the Doctrine of Double Effect.

Also, we should not take FitzPatrick's claim about constitution to be a claim about the relation between types of states of affairs. The idea clearly cannot be that states of affairs of the type 'being killed' require states of affairs of the type 'being blown to pieces' nor can it be that states of affairs of the latter type require states of affairs of the former type. The relation is supposed to be between the 'being blown to bits' token and the 'being killed' token in the individual case of Foot's cave (2006: 601).[6] So the idea is that, in the particular case of Foot's cave, the 'being blown to bits' token is not a cause of the 'being killed' token but rather the 'being blown to bits' token constitutes the 'being killed' token. I now move on to argue against FitzPatrick's proposal.[7]

The first problem with FitzPatrick's proposal is the very claim that 'a man being blown to bits is not a cause of his being killed' (2006: 595), which FitzPatrick clarifies by saying that 'the detonation of the dynamite is the cause of the man's being blown to bits and of his being killed, but *his being blown up* is *constitutive* of *his being killed*' (2006: 595). This is weird: if someone asked how the man was killed and was answered that the man was blown up, that would sound like a legitimate causal explanation.

The second problem is with the claim that, because the state of affairs of 'his being blown up' is a constitutive part of the state of affairs of 'his being killed', then there is no room for the intend/foresee distinction and we can therefore not claim that the agent intended the part without intending the whole which the intended part partly constitutes. First of all, that, as it must be assumed across all these cases, the agent foresaw the killing does not imply that the agent knew about the constitutive relation between the two states of affairs. But even if we extended what the agent foresaw also to the constitutive relation, then the claim that the agent cannot intend a part without also intending the corresponding whole is problematic.

Take the following case: I may intend to blow up the second floor of a 12-floor building to kill my enemy whose office is on the second floor and foresee that the whole building will come down as a result. That the second floor is a constitutive part of the 12-floor building doesn't make the intend/foresee distinction any less (or more, for that matter) plausible. Here one could object exactly by engaging in the usual debates on double effect and closeness: but that would just show, at best, that having introduced the relation of constitution hasn't allowed us to make any progress at all. A similar story can be told for body parts which are constitutive of the whole body and possibly the whole person: one can still intend to A a particular body part and only foresee the consequence of A for the whole body or person.

There are other problems with FitzPatrick's proposal that arise even if we would take it for a good way of dealing with, say, Foot's cave and craniotomy. Even if constitution were the way to go, for example, it wouldn't help us solve the Trolley Problem because both *Bystander* and *Fat Man* are cases of merely causal relations. And if we insisted that the state of affairs of the fat man being thrown off the bridge is a constitutive part of the state of affairs of the fat man being killed, even though those states of affairs are, for example, both spatially and temporally independent and also quite obviously causally related to each other, then we would water down the relation of constitution so much that it would prohibit those things that the employment of the intend/foresee distinction is supposed to enable the Doctrine of Double Effect to allow for: why say, for example, that there is a constitutive relation between the fat man being thrown off and the fat man being killed while there is no constitutive relation between, say, the bombs being dropped and the children being killed in the Strategic Bomber case? Here one could indeed start again with the usual arguments and attempted distinctions that characterize this debate: but that would again only show, at best, that the relation of constitution hasn't moved us forward.

5 Hills on actual intentions

We look next at Alison Hills's suggestion. Her suggestion is both different from and less ambitious than previous ones in that it concedes to begin with that 'we are compelled to give up the claim that the explorers and PSTB must intend to kill, given their other intentions. The second strategy cannot prove that, necessarily, these agents intend to kill; all that it can show is that, first, they have reason to intend to kill, and secondly, that we have reason to interpret them as intending to kill' (2007: 266 – PSTB is Philosophically Sophisticated Terror Bomber, namely Bennett's Terror Bomber who only intends for the civilians to appear dead).

Hills goes on to argue that, for Foot's cave, 'we have reason to judge that it is likely that the explorers intend to kill' (2007: 272). The idea is that only unusually callous and cruel explorers would 'choose a plan that might involve watching their victim die slowly and painfully as a result of injuries that they themselves had inflicted on him, when they could have chosen to kill him instantly. Given that we have no grounds for thinking that they are particularly unusual people, it is reasonable for us to assume that the explorers do not have these traits' (2007: 272).

This is an unusual attempt of solving the problem of closeness in that it appeals to normative assumptions. Those assumptions are normative in two different respects: there is moral normativity about the cruelty of injury without dead in Foot's cave; and there is psychological normativity about the attitudes of *normal* or usual people. Both are problematic: is death really better than serious and permanent disability in Foot's cave? The value of death, especially in relation to serious and permanent disability, is an hotly contested issue in bioethics; having to rely on a particular resolution of that issue for a resolution of the problem of closeness makes matters more rather than less difficult for a proposed solution of closeness. Furthermore, defenders of the Doctrine of Double Effect who are interested in a solution to the problem of closeness will, at least statistically, be very sceptical of the claim that killing is morally superior to serious and permanent injury.[8]

So having to assume that killing is morally preferable to causing serious injury is one important problem with Hills's proposal. The second is her assumption about normal people finding killing to be morally preferable to causing serious injury.[9] This is really an empirical point and I can't properly engage with it now, but it seems to me that it would be enough to look at current legislation across many different non-authoritarian regimes to establish that killing is still taken to be the ultimate transgression, whatever its actual moral value is.

There are other serious issues with Hills's proposal that have nothing to do with her questionable normative assumptions: first,

Hills's proposal is subject to the criticism that Thomson (1999), Rachels (1994) and Scanlon (2008) have famously brought against the Doctrine of Double Effect[10]: namely that whatever its role for justification, the Doctrine is no good at telling people what they are morally allowed to do because what they are morally allowed to do depends in turn on their attitudes about what they are deliberating whether or not to do (more on this in Chapter 11). If Hills concedes that the explorers must not intend to kill, then she concedes that they can take an attitude towards their escape from the cave such that they are allowed to do what it takes to escape from the cave, namely blowing the fat guy up. So Hills's solution to closeness would still not enable the Doctrine to tell the explorers that they ought not to blow up the fat guy.[11]

One more problem: Hills's solution can be easily shown to be *ad hoc* for Foot's cave. We certainly could not argue that, in the case of the Terror Bomber, we can reasonably attribute to Terror Bomber an intention to kill the children because having such an intention is morally better than not having such an intention and because normal people would have such an intention. That is just implausible! Admittedly, this point does not apply to the *Fat Man* scenario of the Trolley Problem, where one would imagine Hills indeed arguing that it would be better for the fat man to die – but all the other above arguments apply.

6 Delaney and intention consolidation

Neil Delaney suggests two principles of what he calls 'intention consolidation' as a solution to closeness:

1 'due to the closeness between detonation and killing an intention to detonate nuclear devices just is part of a limit complex intention to kill civilians and hence the action plan is morally impermissible under the Doctrine of Double Effect' (2008: 345);

2 'one may say that due to the closeness between detonation and killing a rational agent cannot but directly intend the deaths of civilians insofar as he pursues an action plan that makes use of nuclear detonations as a means, equally unacceptable according to the Doctrine of Double Effect'. (2008: 345)

Delaney prefers the latter principle; therefore we will focus on that. Delaney speculates, though, that Foot would probably rather go for the former. To be honest, I really can't see how the former principle is supposed to be a solution to the problem of closeness rather than just a re-statement of the problem of closeness. This, in fairness, may have to do with my interpreting Philippa Foot on closeness differently from Delaney – but whichever way one interprets Foot herself, I don't think that will make Delaney's first principle any more plausible. I take it that Foot, with the cave scenario, has presented a challenge for defenders of the Doctrine of Double Effect, namely to offer a plausible and principled way to account for the thought that some two descriptions can be too close to be divided by the intend/ foresee distinction.

I thereby interpret Foot has having identified a problem for the Doctrine of Double Effect. The fact that it is now common to talk about the 'problem of closeness' even among those sympathetic to double effect (see, for example, Cavanaugh 2006) suggests that my interpretation of Foot is at least widely shared. Delaney, on the other hand, appears to be interpreting Foot as having offered, by putting forward two descriptions that are too close, a solution to challenges to the intend/foresee distinction within double effect.

I am not interested in resolving this interpretative issue here (even though, as I mentioned, I have reason to think that my interpretation is at least widely shared across the double effect dividing lines): but this difference in interpretation explains, I am suggesting, both why Delaney attributes his first principle to Foot and also why Delaney takes his first principle to be a solution and not a statement of the problem. But it is hard to see it as any more than a statement of the problem of closeness: the idea is that detonation and killing are so close that an intention to detonate is part of a limit complex intention to kill. Once we have explained that an intention to detonate being part of a limit complex intention to kill means that the agent intends to [detonate and kill], where what is between the brackets is the content of the limit content intention, we are still at a loss as to how this suggestion is supposed to help: sure, if the agent has an intention with the above content [detonate and kill], then the agent intends to kill rather than just foreseeing killing. But the only reason Delaney's first principle offers for the claim that the agent has a limit complex intention to [detonate and kill] is the closeness (supposedly excessive) between the detonation and the killing. Obviously, though, in the absence of any criteria for closeness or excessive closeness, Delaney's first principle is nothing more than a stipulation or re-statement of the problem. We have, once again, made no progress at all.

What we needed all along, as Foot makes very explicit, is 'the criterion of "closeness"' (1967: 146). One suggestion for a possible criterion appears in Delaney's second and preferred principle, according to which x and y are too close if 'a rational agent cannot but directly intend' (2008: 345) y if she intends x. If this kind of criterion sounds familiar, you may be thinking of the following famous statement from Kant (1785/1993: 417): 'Whoever wills the end, wills (so far as reason has decisive influence on his actions) also the means that are indispensably necessary to his actions and that lie in his power'. But here Kant won't help Delaney because the whole point of the problem of closeness is to determine whether y is an 'indispensably necessary means' to x – stipulating as much won't do as a solution to the problem of closeness.[12]

Delaney's claim, then, is that it is irrational to intend to blow up the fat guy in order to free the cave's mouth without also intending to kill him; that it is irrational to intend to crush the foetus' skull in order to save the mother without also intending to kill the foetus; that it is irrational to intend to push the fat guy off the bridge in order to stop the trolley without also intending to kill the foetus. But why are those combined attitudes of intending to x and merely foreseeing y irrational? Delaney does not tell us. One may try to answer for him by looking at so-called rational constraints on intention which, as the name suggests, regulate when it is rational for agents to intend something. There are in the literature those who defend strong rational constraints on intention – according to which I can only intend to A if I believe that I will A (Grice 1971 is the most influential example); and there are those that defend weak rational constraints on intention – according to which I can only intend to A if I do not believe that I will not A (Bratman 1984 and 1987, for example). Whether one endorses strong rational constraints on intention or just weak rational constraints, that does not help Delaney's claim that not intending to y in the various double effect cases is irrational, as those are all cases in which I foresee (and that must take the form of a belief) y.

A different attempt at justifying Delaney's claim that not intending y is irrational would be to say that intending to y is necessary for the accomplishment of the agent's plans. But the point is quite obviously that only y but not the intention to y is necessary, because the agent can bring about y without having to intend to y. And so there is no rational pressure on the agent to intend to y. Similarly, it wouldn't do to suggest that not intending to y is irrational because the agent knows that it is impossible to achieve x without y, because again the point is the modality of intending to y and not the modality of y, and not intending to y is not impossible. Alternatively, one could take Delaney's claim about the irrationality of not intending to y as a claim about some conceptual connection between x and y; but as Delaney himself recognizes, Bennett has already shown this particular option to be unattractive (Delaney 2008: 349).

7 Wedgwood on trolleys

Next we look at a recent proposed solution to the problem of closeness which is distinctive in that it is applied to the Trolley Problem: Ralph Wedgwood's. This is interesting because we saw that many of the above proposals, even if they had been successful, would not have applied to the Trolley Problem. Here's Wedgwood's proposed solution.

> Suppose that you are a reasonably virtuous person, and you hear the news that someone has collided with a runaway trolley. You would presumably respond by thinking, "Oh no, how awful! That sounds terrible!" Now suppose that you hear the news that a runaway railway trolley was diverted onto a side track. You would naturally respond by thinking, "So what? That doesn't sound very interesting." In short, a person's colliding with a fast-moving railway trolley is in some way bad news, while a trolley's being diverted onto a side track is not bad news in the same way. When you take the person's colliding with the trolley to be bad news, it seems that you would somehow be being guided by your knowledge of a range of ceteris paribus moral generalizations – such as, for example, the generalization that other things equal, and under normal conditions, when a collision between a person and a runaway railway trolley occurs, the person suffers serious injury or even death as a result. (2011b: 8)

According to Wedgwood, the sort of ceteris paribus moral genera-lizations which guide the reasonably virtuous agent to judge a particular case as bad news take the form of 'other things equal, and under normal conditions, when a collision between a person and a runaway railway trolley occurs, the person suffers serious injury or even death as a result' (ibid.). This is why the virtuous person takes *Fat Man* to be bad news. And this account is supposed to explain why the virtuous person would not take *Bystander at the Switch* to be bad news, but rather no news at all: because, 'other things equal, and under normal conditions, when a trolley is diverted on a side-track, well, a trolley is just diverted on a side-track'. The content of the effect in *Fat Man* (collision between a person and a runway trolley) is, other things equal, and under normal conditions, more dangerous than the content of the effect in *Bystander at the Switch* (a trolley is diverted).

Wedgwood proposes two jointly sufficient conditions for a state of affairs to count as a bad state of affairs: 'first, a virtuous agent, guided by her knowledge of these true *ceteris paribus* moral generalizations, would form the kind of expectations about S that would lead her to view it as bad news in this way; and secondly, in this particular case, these expectations are borne out – that is, things turn out badly in more or less the very way in which S would lead such a virtuous agent to expect them to' (2011b: 8).

There are two independent ways of showing that this proposed solution will not do: first, that the expectations of a virtuous agent, based on ceteris paribus moral generalizations, are necessary for a state of affairs to count as a bad state of affairs, will have the unfortunate upshot that freaky accidents will not count as a bad state of affairs. I once achieved the remarkable feat of breaking my ankle while playing table-football (TABLE-football!). It is not clear whether freaky accidents like mine would meet the second condition but they would clearly not meet the first: the stipulation that 'things turn out badly in more or less the very way in which S would lead such a virtuous agent to expect them to' (ibid.) does not simply require that things turn out badly; they must turn out badly in accordance with the expectations; but the point of freaky accidents is that they defy expectations, so that they would not meet the first condition and probably not even the second depending on how strongly we interpret 'more or less the very way . . .' (ibid.).

No virtuous agent could have possibly had the expectation that I may break my ankle while playing table-football; if anybody had heard on the radio a news report about 'a young man playing table-football', they would have turned it off. If my own mother (the paradigmatic virtuous agent) would have warned me to look after my ankle upon hearing that I would play table-football, I would have booked her an appointment by a neurologist. That my freaky accident defied expectation didn't make it any better (as Wedgwood's account of a bad state of affairs implies); it clearly made it worse.

Here it may be objected that the account is not supposed to be general in the way in which freaky accidents would count as a counterexample to it, because it is just an account about agency or intentional agency. Apart from the fact that freaky accidents often involve agency (even if not under intentional descriptions, supposedly), this objection flies in the way of how Wedgwood introduces his conditions: 'I propose that for a state of affairs S to count as a bad state of affairs in the relevant way is for the following two conditions to be met' (ibid.); but the supposed generality of the account is not crucial here, because the account fails in another way, which is more specifically about the way in which it is supposed to defend the Doctrine from the problem of 'closeness'.

Wedgwood needs to give us plausible criteria why the descriptions should be cashed out as he does, otherwise he will have just offered two *ad hoc* descriptions of his choosing to emphasize the differences between the cases. Wedgwood identifies the contents of the two news items as 'someone has collided with a runaway trolley' and 'a runaway railway trolley was diverted onto a side track'. Why should we describe the former as Wedgwood proposes and not as 'there has been a collision involving an empty runaway trolley'? And why should we describe the latter as Wedgwood proposes and not as 'a runaway trolley was diverted onto a side track where a workman was stuck'? If we describe the former as 'there has been a collision involving an empty runaway trolley' and the latter as 'a runaway trolley was diverted onto a side track where a workman was stuck', then the reasonably virtuous person will show more concern for the latter than for the former. And this by Wedgwood's own criteria: other things equal, and under normal conditions, when a runaway trolley is diverted onto a side track where a workman is stuck, the person suffers serious injury or even death as a result.

The argument cannot work, then, without plausible criteria to identify the relevant contents as 'someone has collided with a runaway trolley' and 'a runaway railway trolley was diverted onto a side track' rather than, for example, 'there has been a collision involving a runaway trolley' and 'a runaway trolley was diverted onto a side track where a workman was stuck'. The crucial point is quite simple: Wedgwood identified the two contents by including the victim in *Fat Man* and excluding the victim in *Bystander at the Switch*. It is then no surprise that the virtuous person would express more concern for *Fat Man* than for *Bystander at the Switch*. Is there any plausible reason to include the victim in the description of *Fat Man* and exclude it from the description of *Bystander at the Switch*? What about that the victim is closer to the agent in *Fat Man* than he is in *Bystander*? Can we really believe that how far down the tracks the one workman is makes a moral difference? We can start to discuss differences between the two scenarios which may be suggested to warrant inclusion of the victim in one description and exclusion from the other; but the point is that then Wedgwood's proposal has brought us not one inch forward in the debate: we are still at the point of looking for morally relevant differences between the two scenarios, which is exactly where we were before.

Without criteria for the inclusion of the victim in one description and exclusion of the victim from the other description, we are back at the beginning. Sure, collisions between trolleys and people statistically cause more harm than diversions of trolleys. But that is not true of collisions involving trolleys or of diversions of trolleys onto side tracks where workmen are stuck. One could object that there are states of affairs that can be identified in a way which is not arbitrary to which Wedgwood's 'good news' and 'bad news' apply: in *Bystander*, the state of affairs of the trolley being diverted onto the side track is not bad news, while in *Fat Man* the state of affairs of the fat guy being pushed in front of the trolley is bad news. Why is it legitimate to pick exactly those states of affairs? It could be suggested that those states of affairs are what the agents in the two cases must minimally intend. Whether or not the agent in *Bystander* does intend killing, she must at least intend diverting the trolley. And whether or not the agent in *Fat Man* does intend killing, she must at least intend pushing the fat guy in front of the trolley. And between those states of affairs that agents must intend in the two cases there is a difference in terms of Wedgwood's 'bad news' criterion.

This reply will not do because it is subject to all the usual issues that normally come up with the problem of closeness: what if the agent in *Fat Man* only intended to push onto the tracks the only thing on the bridge that could have stopped the trolley and only foresaw thereby pushing down onto the tracks the fat man? Again, the issue is the inclusion in the description of the one state of affairs of the victim and the corresponding exclusion of the victim from the description of the other state of affairs (in *Bystander*).

There is another worry with the claim that, at least, Wedgwood's criteria allows one to say that the agent must have intended some bad news state of affairs which involves harm to the victim. Even if one had shown that the agent must have intended to throw the fat guy onto the tracks, one would still have the problem of showing that the agent must have intended killing the fat man – just the way in which in Foot's cave one has the problem of showing that the agent who intends to blow up the victim must also intend to kill her.[13]

Summing up, Wedgwood's solution does not work because it depends on stipulating the inclusion of the victim in one generalization and the exclusion of the victim from the other generalization; the criteria for exclusion and inclusion cannot just be given by stipulating what in particular cases must be intended means and what merely foreseen side effects: that would be question-begging as the distinction between intended means and merely foreseen side effects is exactly what's at stake. The criteria for inclusion and exclusion, which Wedgwood does not offer, are exactly what we have been looking for in the problem of closeness all along. So this attempt fails too.

8 Masek and the strict definition of intention

Lawrence Masek (2010) has recently defended double effect by putting forward what he refers to as a *strict* definition of intention (see also Marquis 1991), according to which 'an effect is intended (or part of the agent's plan) if and only if the agent A has the effect as an end or believes that it is a state of affairs in the causal sequence that will result in A's end. Any other effect is unintended' (2010: 569). This is not the place to discuss the strict definition of intention in general as a defence of the Doctrine of Double Effect: I only look at whether the strict definition of intention may be deployed to solve the problem of closeness and I argue that the strict definition of intention does not solve closeness.

Let us first of all stress that Masek himself concedes that, on the strict definition of intention, in both craniotomy and Foot's cave the agents do not intend to kill: 'I now maintain that they intend only to remove the fat man from the escape route, not to kill him. Likewise, the surgeon intends only to make the foetus' head smaller, not to cause death' (2010: 573). This is enough of a concession to conclude that the strict definition won't help with closeness, but there are other problems too. What is particularly problematic about the strict definition of intention put forward as both necessary and sufficient as Masek does is that there are counterexamples both against its necessity and its sufficiency. Craniotomy and Foot's cave are counterexamples against its necessity, as we have cases where we would like to say that the killing is intended but the strict definition of intention can't make that out.[14]

But there are also counterexamples against its sufficiency, where the strict definition would claim that an effect is intended which intuition would rather give as merely foreseen: take the Loop Variant of the trolley problem (Thomson 1985) where if the one worker is not hit the trolley will come around and hit the five from the other side; in this case the state of affairs of the one worker being killed is believed by the agent to be part of the causal sequence which will result in the end of saving the five being satisfied. On the other hand, it looks as though what the agent does in the Loop Variant is exactly the same as what she does in the original *Bystander* and that therefore we should say that the agent intends the end of saving the five and the means of diverting the trolley and merely foresees the side effect of killing the one.[15]

So the strict definition of intention is problematic: whether one puts it forward as only necessary, only sufficient, or necessary and sufficient (as Masek does), the strict definition is in each case subject to counterexamples. And whatever its problems, Masek himself concedes that the strict definition cannot give the outcomes (an intention to kill in Foot's cave and craniotomy, for example) which are presupposed by any solution to the problem of closeness. So the strict definition of intention does not solve the problem of closeness.[16]

9 Quinn's attempt to avoid the problem

Warren Quinn (1989) recognized the difficulty posed by the problem of closeness for the Doctrine of Double Effect and tried to avoid it by reformulating the Doctrine of Double Effect in terms of a Kantian prohibition against the deliberate harmful involvement of persons in our plans. Even though Quinn's proposal predates many of the attempts at solving the problem of closeness that I have discussed here, I discuss it only after discussing those attempts exactly because Quinn's proposal is distinctive in trying to avoid the problem of closeness rather than trying to solve it. As Quinn's proposal has been widely discussed and criticized elsewhere, here I don't mean to do justice to all of these discussions; I will focus on just one argument against Quinn to make the point that Quinn's attempt to circumnavigate closeness fails because his own account is subject to the problem of closeness.

Quinn distinguishes between:

DIRECT AGENCY: 'agency in which harm comes to some victims, at least in part, from the agent's deliberately involving them in something in order to further his purpose precisely by way of their being so involved' (1989: 343);

INDIRECT AGENCY: 'harmful agency in which either nothing is in that way intended for the victims or what is so intended does not contribute to their harm'. (1989: 343)

Let us take Terror Bomber and Strategic Bomber to illustrate how this distinction is supposed to work according to Quinn: 'In the former case, but not the latter, the bomber undeniably intends in the strictest sense that the civilians be involved in a certain explosion, which he produces, precisely because their involvement in it serves his goal. He may not, if Bennett is right, intend their deaths. But his purpose requires at least this-that they be violently impacted by the explosion of his bombs. . . . But [Strategic Bomber] can honestly deny that their involvement in the explosion is anything to his purpose' (1989: 342).

Quinn's proposal is subject to some counterexamples: 'Consider now Bomb Remover 3. Mary is in the library working at a table that is far removed from the valuable books. The books are scattered on another table at the other end of the library, and on that table is a black box containing the bomb. The bomb is on a timer and will blow up, we realize, in a matter of minutes. We grab the black box and carry it quickly to Mary's side of the library, where we gingerly place it on the table at which Mary is working. We run from the scene, leaving Mary to her fate and realizing that there is an extremely high probability of her death. The books are saved. Mary is killed when the bomb blows up. On Quinn's approach, this is deemed a case of indirect agency' (Fischer et al. 1993: 719). Harm comes to Mary in this case from the agent deliberately involving her, but harm does not come to Mary from the agent deliberately involving her in order to further his purpose precisely by way of her being so involved, so that the agent can honestly deny that her involvement in the explosion is anything to his purpose.

Woodward (1997) has criticized this and other cases put forward by Fischer et al on the grounds that these scenarios violate the fourth condition on the Doctrine of Double Effect, namely proportionality. But it is easy to generate alternative counterexamples that do not violate the proportionality condition and that, therefore, cannot be claimed to be impermissible on *that* ground. Just swap the books for our own five children in the above scenario. Harm still comes to Mary in this case from us deliberately involving her, but harm does not come to Mary from us deliberately involving her in order to further our purpose precisely by way of her being so involved, so that we can honestly deny that her involvement in the explosion is anything to our purpose: we only intended to save our children and merely foresaw that Mary would die as a result. Here one could object that you couldn't put a bomb which is just about to explode on someone's table without intending to blow this person up. But this objection would just bring us to the very place that Quinn wanted to avoid, namely the problem of closeness.[17]

10 Conclusion

Let us take stock: here I have looked at ten different attempts at dealing with the problem of closeness, arguably the most influential challenge to the Doctrine of Double Effect: I have argued that each of these ten proposals is problematic and that none solves the problem of closeness. The scope of this chapter was explicitly negative and it consisted, solely, in showing that all recent attempts at solving the problem of closeness fail, so as to defend closeness as a valid argument against the Doctrine of Double Effect.

CHAPTER SEVEN

Kamm, Kant and double effect

Abstract *I discuss Frances Kamm's distinction between 'in order to' means and 'because of' means, which is meant to deal with the Loop Variant of the Trolley Problem, a notorious hard case for defenders of the Doctrine of Double Effect. I find the following problems with Kamm's argument: her Party Case – meant to introduce the distinction between 'in order to' and 'because of' – is not analogous to the Loop Variant so that it cannot help in dealing with the Loop Variant. Further, Kamm's attempts to show that means can be unintended by appealing to Michael Bratman's three roles of intention are shown to be unsuccessful. Finally, I show that we cannot make coherent sense of the 'third' effect identified by Kamm as different from both traditional intended means and merely foreseen side effects. The present rejection of Kamm's unintended means is important far beyond discussions of double effect and trolley problems as Kamm claims that her new distinction shows that Kant's famous principle of instrumental rationality is false. I conclude with a defence of Kant's principle of instrumental rationality.*

1 Introduction

It is very common to distinguish between means and ends. Kant, for example, famously argued that 'Whoever wills the end, wills (so far as reason has decisive influence on his actions) also the means that are indispensably necessary to his actions and that lie in his power' (1785/1993: 417).

It is also common to distinguish between means and side effects. The *Doctrine of Double Effect*, for example, traditionally says that the same evil may sometimes be brought about as a side effect but never as a means or end. Many draw the distinction between means and side effects in terms of the difference between intending and merely foreseeing something: while means are necessarily intended (just like ends), side effects are merely foreseen.

Frances Kamm has recently denied this way of distinguishing between means and side effects by introducing a further distinction 'between doing something *in order* (or *intending*) *to* bring about something else and doing something *because* of something else that will thus be brought about' (2007: 92). Kamm's idea is that the latter does not imply the former: 'I claim that doing something because this will cause the hitting of an innocent bystander does not imply that one intends to cause the hitting or that one does anything in order to hit' (2007: 95).

According to Kamm this shows, among other things, that Kant's hypothetical imperative is false: 'a rational agent, insofar as he is rational, need not intend a means that he knows is necessary to an end that he continues to intend' (2007: 91–2). Another consequence of Kamm's distinction is, she says herself, that 'the idea (common since Elizabeth Anscombe's *Intention*) that if we find a reason why someone acted, we find what he intended is wrong' (2007: 95) – and this is indeed something that at least since Anscombe and Davidson has become standard in the philosophy of action.[1]

Kamm deploys the distinction between 'in order to' and 'because of' for what she calls the *Doctrine of Triple Effect*, 'which sometimes permits an agent to do something, when he does it because he will bring about an evil or involvement leading to evil (that he does not intend). It also permits an agent to do something that has a bad side effect when he does it because he will bring about a great good though he does not intend the good' (2007: 92–3).

The Doctrine of Triple Effect is meant to explain the Loop Variant of the Trolley Problem (Thomson 1985: 1402–3), where I divert the trolley away from the five onto a side track where one will be hit and killed (as in the traditional Trolley Problem), with the additional twist that the side track loops back onto the main track where the five are, so that if the trolley isn't stopped by the one on the side track, it will loop back and kill the five from the other side.

To illustrate her distinction between 'in order to' and 'because of', Kamm introduces the Party Case:

> I intend to give a party in order for me and my friends to have fun. However, I foresee that this will leave a big mess, and I don't want to have a party if I will be left to clean it up. I also foresee a further effect of the party: If my friends have fun, they will feel indebted to me and help me clean up. I assume that a feeling of indebtedness is something of a negative for a person to have. I give the party because I believe that my friends will feel indebted and (so) because I will not have a mess to clean up. These expectations are conditions of my action. I would not act unless I had them. The fact that they will feel indebted is a reason for my acting. But I do not give the party even in part in order to make my friends feel indebted nor in order to not have a mess. To be more precise, it is not a goal of my action of giving the party to do either of these things. I may have it as a background goal in my life not to have messes, but not producing a mess is not an aim of my giving the party. Further, if I see that my friends are feeling indebted, as a good host I may try to rescue them from these feelings (while expecting that I may not succeed). I might do this because I do not want to omit to help them only because I *intend* something negative for them, their feeling indebted. This would not be inconsistent with giving the party *because of* my belief that they will, as a side effect, feel indebted. (2007: 95)

Kamm's proposal, then, is important in at least three different respects:

1   It is an alternative to Kant's hypothetical imperative because it denies that means are necessarily intended; and given the

widespread influence of Kantian instrumental rationality, this is not only interesting from an historical perspective;

2   It is an alternative to the action-theoretical view made famous by Anscombe and Davidson according to which 'if we find a reason why someone acted, we find what he intended' (2007: 95);

3   It is, also, an alternative to the Doctrine of Double Effect because it can deal with the Loop Variant on the Trolley Problem, which is a challenge to the traditional Doctrine of Double Effect insofar as it is a case where one wants to say that killing the one is permissible *even though* killing the one would then be a means to the end of saving the five – which the Doctrine of Double Effect does not allow for.

We have, then, at least three different reasons why Kamm's proposal deserves careful critical attention. The first thing to notice is that while Kamm claims that the distinction between 'in order to' and 'because of' shows that means are not necessarily intended, in her discussion of Party Case Kamm talks only of side effects and not of means. This must mean, at least formally, that Party Case cannot, alone, support the claim that means are not necessarily intended because Party Case is not about means, at least if we don't assume that Kamm is using means and side effects interchangeably here – which she actually may be doing at least later on: 'I could have a goal, see that it would be wrong to intend the means to it, but act because I foresee that I will bring about my means as a side effect of doing something else that I have at least *some* (justifying) reason to do' (2007: 104).

How does Kamm's new distinction between 'in order to' and 'because of' map onto the traditional trio of ends – means – side effects? At least the following should be uncontroversial: ends are always 'in order to', while, according to Kamm, some means are 'in order to' and some means are 'because of'. Taking her example: 'having fun' is the end and it is 'in order to' have fun that I organize the party: so organizing the party is a means to the end of having fun and it is a 'in order to' kind of means. Organizing the party will have at least two relevant foreseen consequences: a mess and a feeling of indebtedness on the part of the friends who take part.

Kamm's idea is that the 'indebtedness' effect is a 'because of' means, in the sense that I 'only' organize the party because

I foresee that my organizing the party will bring about a feeling of indebtedness.[2] Should I not believe that organizing the party will bring about a feeling of indebtedness, I would not organize it. So the foreseen indebtedness on the part of my friends is a necessary condition to organizing the party, but not, according to Kamm, an intended condition – because I do not organize the party in order for my friends to feel indebted – just as I do not organize the party in order for there to be a mess.

The relationship between the two foreseen consequences 'indebtedness' and 'mess' suggests that Kamm would still want to distinguish between 'because of' means and mere side effects, where 'indebtedness' is a 'because of' means while the mess is a mere side effect: the mess is not a necessary condition, and I do not organize the party because of the foreseen resulting mess.

We have, then, identified the three effects that give The Doctrine of Triple Effect its name: the intended effect is the party; the unintended 'because of' effect is the feeling of indebtedness; and the unintended side effect is the mess. And there is also a further effect that does not enter the name of the principle, namely the fun which motivates the whole thing. Now we have, effectively, four categories that are identified through Kamm's Party Case:

1 **Ends:** *to have fun*
2 **IOT-Means** (In Order To-Means): *to organize the party*
3 **BO-Means** (Because Of-Means): *my friends' feeling of indebtedness*
4 **Side Effects:** *the mess that my friends will help clean up*

We see then that Kamm is actually adding an element to the traditional trio of ends – means – side effects by introducing two kinds of means without giving up on the idea that there is a difference (in terms of explanation, supposedly) between BO-Means and mere side effects: this is because *traditional* side effects are, differently from BO-Means, not effects *because of which* I do something but rather simply effects *despite of which* I do something. Obviously in order for Kamm to generate a genuine quartet out of the traditional trio she also needs to keep ends as conceptually separate from IOT-Means, which Party Case allows for: having fun can be considered to be the only value in itself while organizing the party is only valuable insofar as it serves the purpose of having fun; and in this respect, 'having fun' is an end while 'organizing the party' is a IOT-Means.

There are now three different questions:

i   The first question is whether Kamm has actually identified an interesting phenomenon which deserves the introduction of her quartet instead of the traditional trio (itself already controversial!);

ii The second question is whether Kamm's new distinction is morally relevant: the question here is whether there is a moral difference between intended (IOT)means and unintended (BO)means (this question is conceptually related to the one above in that a negative answer to the first question will imply a negative answer to this one too);

iii The third question is whether Kamm's Party Case and her Doctrine of Triple Effect do in fact challenge, as she claims, the three important philosophical principles (hypothetical imperative; reasons as intentions; double effect) which Kamm identifies as victims of her argument – and again this question is not independent from question (i).

Here I argue for a negative answer to each of these three questions raised by Kamm's distinction between IOT-means and BO-means.

2 'Because Of' means

Let us start from the supposed analogy between the Loop Variant and Kamm's Party Case. Even though Kamm herself admits that the analogy is not perfect, she fails to mention a difference between the structures of the two cases which challenges, I think, her very use of the Party Case. Recall the way we have identified Kamm's proposed new quartet within her Party Case: the end is to have fun, the IOT-means is to organize the party; the BO-means is that my friends will feel indebted; and the mere side effect is the mess which my friends (because of their feeling of indebtedness) will help clean up. How does this apply to the Loop Variant? The end is, supposedly, saving the five. The IOT-means is diverting the trolley; the BO-means is that the trolley will be stopped by the one on the side track; and the mere side effect is, well, what's the mere side effect of Kamm's quartet in the Loop Case?

Two possibilities: it seems plausible to suppose that the mere side effect – and therefore the equivalent of the mess – is the purely putative side effect that the five would be killed from the other direction; effect which will be avoided by the presence of the one on the side track. This is similar to the mess because the killing of the five from the other direction – if unavoidable – would stop me from diverting the trolley in the first place; the same way in which the mess, if unavoidable, would stop me from organizing the party in the first place. But there are also clear differences: the mess is actual (but I won't have to deal with it alone), while the killing of the five from the other direction is a mere possibility.

This difference can be easily avoided by re-describing the mess in terms of the mess which is left once my friends are gone without having helped to clean up, so that this is now also a mere possibility which, I am confident as I am planning, will be avoided; the same way in which as I plan to divert the trolley, I am confident that the killing of the five from the other direction will be avoided. So now one could indeed propose the following analogy between the two cases:

- **End:** having fun – saving the five

- **IOT-Means:** organizing the party – diverting the trolley

- **BO-Means:** feeling of indebtedness – trolley being stopped by the one

- **Side Effect:** having to clean up alone – the five being killed from the other direction

Now we have the analogy Kamm needs, but a crucial element is missing: that the one on the side track will be killed. And it is exactly this description that is the controversial one: everything turns on the status of the killing of the one on the side track, which therefore cannot be left out of the analysis. So we need to integrate the killing of the one without thereby losing the analogy between Party Case and the Loop Variant. And the killing of the one on the side track can, according to Kamm, only be a BO-means and therefore it can only be compared with my friends' feeling of indebtedness (this interpretation is supported by the fact that Kamm explicitly says that she assumes that the feeling of indebtedness is something negative: 'I assume that a feeling of indebtedness is something of a negative for a person to have' (2007: 95)). But that is where we get the relevant disanalogy between Party Case and the Loop Variant: while my friends' feeling of indebtedness is a necessary element of my decision to organize the party, the same need not be said of the killing of the one: what I need is that the trolley be stopped (by the one) so that it won't kill the five from the other side, but I don't actually need the one to be killed. But, as Kamm's story goes, I actually need my friends to feel indebted to me; otherwise, they won't help me clean up.

So Kamm's supposed analogy falls apart exactly at the crucial point – for the whole double effect debate – of the negative effect, as she claims that this is what the feeling of indebtedness is supposed to represent (see the quote in the paragraph above). Here we can easily see that what Kamm says in Party Case cannot be said of the Loop Variant: 'The fact that they will feel indebted is a reason for my acting. But I do not give the party even in part in order to make my friends feel indebted' (2007: 95). The negative effect – the indebtedness – is supposed to be a reason for my acting even though it is not supposed to be the case that I act even in part in order to bring about the negative effect. That is how Kamm wants to generate her so-called 'because of' (unintended) means.

The same cannot be said of the Loop Variant: the negative effect is that the one will be killed; but that the one will be killed is not a reason for my acting. We can say that I do not act in order for the one to be killed; but we cannot say – crucially for Kamm's analogy – that the killing of the one is a reason for my acting. What *is* a reason for my acting – and therefore what is analogous to Kamm's feeling of indebtedness in the Party Case – is only that the trolley will be stopped or that the one on the side track will stop the trolley and thereby prevent the trolley from hitting the five from the other side.

We have now identified a disanalogy between the Party Case and the Loop Variant: the next question is what consequences this disanalogy may have for Kamm's argument. Kamm's argument, remember, is that the Party Case shows that there is a yet undisclosed category of BO-means, that these means are unintended, and that this is the category that we should also use to analyse the Loop Variant, so that the killing of the one in the Loop Variant is a BO-means and it is therefore unintended. It may be, as we have argued so far, that the two cases are not analogous, but that does not show, of itself, that the killing of the one in the Loop Variant is not an unintended means.

There is an aspect of our argument which speaks *against* the claim that the killing of the one is an unintended means, but there is also an aspect of our argument that speaks *for* the claim that the killing of the one is an unintended means. What speaks against the claim that the killing of the one is an unintended means is that it is not the killing of the one which is an element without which I would not have acted: that is only that the trolley will be stopped and therefore prevented from killing the five from the other side. Therefore, it could be argued, the killing is not a means; and therefore, it cannot be an unintended means either just because it is no means at all.

On the one hand, what our argument against Kamm does speak for the claim that the killing of the one is an unintended means (Kamm's claim), is that – whether or not it is a means – the fact that the killing of the one is not an element of my action without which I would not have acted (because the necessary element is, again, only that the trolley be stopped) could be considered to be a consideration in favour of the claim that it is unintended. Why should I have intended to kill the one if the killing of the one is not even a 'because of' element of my plan? In this respect, one could claim that even if in Party Case the agent must have intended for her friends to feel indebted because the success of her plan depended on her friends feeling indebted, in the Loop Variant the agent must not have intended for the one to be killed because the success of her plan did not depend on the one being killed but rather only on the one stopping the trolley from killing the five from the other side.

So our argument may invalidate the role of Party Case in an argument about the Loop Variant but may also actually even be thought to substantiate the claim that the agent does not intend to kill the one in the Loop Variant. I am not sure we should jump to this conclusion, because there is an easier alternative: namely, once we have shown, as we did above, that Party Case is not analogous to the Loop Variant, it could simply be suggested that we return to the default position of considering killing the one in the Loop Variant a mere side effect, since we have shown that, differently from indebtedness, it is not a BO-means because it is not an element without which I would not act. But if killing the one in the Loop Variant is a mere side effect, then we are back at square one and Kamm's argument and her introduction of the Party Case and of the distinction between intended means and 'because of' means have made no progress at all.[3]

I would like to say one final thing about Party Case: if we slightly modify the case by just altering the temporal sequence of events so that the friends' help is necessary to organize the party rather than to clean up afterwards, we see how unstable the point about unintended means is. Call this new version **Party (organizing) Case:**

> I intend to give a party in order for me and my friends to have fun. However, I foresee that this will *be a lot of work*, and I don't want to have a party if I will be left to *do all the work*. I also foresee a further effect of *organizing the party: If I tell my friends about the plan, they will feel indebted to me and help me with all the tasks related to organizing it.*[4]

Now the friends' contribution really looks like an intended means of the agent: I need their gratitude; without their gratitude and consequent help, there will be no party; their gratitude and consequent help is a necessary part in the chain of events that will lead to the party, and I have considered this fact during my deliberations. Here I will not engage in a full blown comparative analysis of the two cases; I just mentioned this modified case to emphasize the point that the intuitive appeal of the original Party Case may only have to do with the temporal sequence of events, so that once we have moved the indebtedness to a point in time which is before the intended action of organizing the party, the negative effect suddenly looks like an intended means again.

3 Loop and intention

So far, we have mainly focused on Party Case. But, it may be argued, whatever the value of Party Case and its relation with the Loop Variant, it may still be the case that Kamm's 'because of' means can be applied to the Loop Case to show that hitting the one is an unintended 'because of' means which, according to the Doctrine of

Triple Effect, may be legitimate. So it is also with this part of Kamm's argument that we must engage. Kamm's argument, here, relies on Bratman's three roles of intention (1987; see also Bratman's earlier 1984 article; also, see the previous chapter for a detailed discussion of Bratman's three roles of intention as a possible solution to the problem of closeness, some of the same arguments apply here): Kamm argues that the bystander does not intend to hit the one because his hitting of the one does not meet Bratman's three roles of intention and does not thereby count as something the agent intended to do (even though this does not mean, at least according to Bratman, that the agent does not intentionally hit the one – but this fine point does not need to bother us here[5]).

Kamm argues that none of the three roles of intention identified by Bratman applies to the agents in the Loop Case:

1 *If we intend to bring about x, we seek means to accomplish the end of bringing it about.* But, in the Loop Case, we do not survey the field for any way to hit the one.

2 *If we intend to bring about x, we pursue x. That is, if one way fails to produce x, we adopt another way.* But if we act because we notice that our doing only what needs to be done in order to stop the trolley from hitting the five from the front will thereby also cause the one to be hit, we need not, as rational agents, be committed to hitting the one by other means if the hitting fails to come about.

3 *If we intend x, and our intentions should be consistent insofar as we are rational, then we will filter our intentions that conflict with intending x.* But, I believe, it is consistent for someone who redirects the trolley because he believes that it will hit the one to then try to rescue the one from being hit. (2007: 96–8)[6]

The first role discussed by Kamm is what Bratman refers to as 'posing problems for further reasoning'; Kamm says that we do not reason about how to hit the one; but that seems just false. What we may not reason about is how to kill the one, because we are not especially interested in killing the one, only in killing the one if that's the only way to save the five. But if the trolley hitting the one just is how the trolley comes to stop and therefore how the trolley comes to not kill the five from the other direction, then we *do* need to work out how the trolley is going to hit the one; otherwise, we will not achieve our goal of saving the five. To bring out this thought, imagine that there are various side tracks, each of which is sufficient to avoid the trolley killing the five from the front and each of which connects back to the main track in a loop. But there is a man that will stop the trolley only on one of these side tracks, so we reason about how to divert the trolley so that it will be diverted on the one side track that has someone on it rather than on the empty side tracks.[7]

The second role discussed by Kamm is what Bratman refers to as 'issuing in corresponding endeavouring': Kamm says that we need not be committed to hitting the one by other means if the hitting fails to come about. One could, again, try to run Kamm's argument for killing (but, on that, see the problem of closeness), but it seems hard to run it for hitting if the hitting has been stipulated to be what stops the trolley: should the trolley not hit the one and continue on its course, we are still committed to stop the trolley and, since we have already decided that we are willing to sacrifice the one in order to do that, we are still committed to hit the one if that is going to stop the trolley. Imagine a case in which, because of some sort of fluke, the trolley does not hit the one and continues its run, threatening to hit the five from the other side. Now imagine that there is, in this modified case, a side track to the side track and that once the trolley has missed the one we can still re-divert it on the side-side track, which will loop back onto the side track at a point before where the one is, so that the trolley will have to pass the point where the one is once again. It seems that if, as in this case, we have this second shot at stopping the trolley by hitting the one through this further diversion, then we are committed to do so and that we were from the beginning committed to the conditional according to which, in case because of some fluke the trolley misses the one and continues its course, we would divert it on to the side-side track to try to stop it again.[8]

The third role is what Bratman refers to as 'constraining other intentions': Kamm argues that it is consistent for someone to 'try to rescue the one from being hit' (2007: 98). I, again, disagree. It may be that it is consistent for someone who diverts the trolley because it will hit the one to (after the crash) phone an ambulance to try and help the one (as long as the hit has been powerful enough to stop the trolley), but redirecting the trolley is not consistent with the intention to 'try to rescue the one *from being hit*' (emphasis mine) on many instantiations of such an intention. An intention to shout as loud as possible 'Get off the tracks otherwise you will be hit' is an example of an intention which is constrained by my attitude towards hitting the one: it would be irrational to have such an intention because the success of my plan depends on the one not getting off the tracks. In short, it would be irrational to divert the trolley and then shout to the one to get off the tracks: indeed, once I have diverted the trolley, I am rationally committed to do what I can in order to avoid that the one gets off the track.

In sum, then, I do not think that Kamm's appeal to Bratman's three roles of intention shows that the bystander does not intend to hit the one: indeed, the bystander's attitude towards hitting the one – as we have just shown – fulfils all three of Bratman's roles of intention.

Here it could be objected that Kamm's analysis may not succeed for 'hitting the one' but that if it does succeed for 'killing the one', then someone on behalf of Kamm could argue that 'killing the one' is the unintended 'because of' means. Now, here I will ignore the whole issue of the problem of closeness and the relation between 'hitting the one' and 'killing the one' because even if one were to successfully argue that the three roles of intention cannot be applied to 'killing the one' that would not help Kamm's argument. This is because, as we have already mentioned, 'killing the one' is not a 'because of' means – the fact that the trolley will kill the one is not a reason why the bystander diverts it; the bystander diverts it in order to save the five and because she believes that it will hit the one and thereby stop.

What Kamm wanted, in short, was that the 'because of' effect be shown to be an unintended effect by Bratman's three roles of intention: since 'killing the one' is not the 'because of' effect, then its status is beside the point. And, Kamm's opponent will argue, it should be no surprise that the 'because of' element cannot be shown to be unintended: that only goes to show that the further – fourth – category that Kamm tries to introduce is a mere construct. There are no unintended 'because of' means, or at least the ones put forward by Kamm have been shown to be intended. And, even if one were to show that some other effect was indeed unintended – say, 'killing the one' in this case – that would be no surprise for

Kamm's opponent either: it would just go to vindicate the old trio of ends – means – side effects over Kamm's attempted novel quartet; the unintended effect would just be a mere side effect. So we are, indeed, back at the beginning: if it is a 'because of' effect, then it is an intended means; and if it is not a 'because of' effect, then it is an unintended side effect. We have shown that there is no room in between for Kamm's unintended means.

4 Different attitudes: In order to, because of and despite

I have argued so far that Kamm's attempted distinction between 'in order to' and 'because of' cannot be mapped onto the intended-foreseen distinction which dominates the double effect literature so as to show, as Kamm wishes, that means can be unintended (and that therefore the permissibility of the Loop Variant can be dealt with). But what should we make of Kamm's distinction in itself, independently of its relevance for attributions of intention? It would certainly be important, both in itself and for the double effect debate, if Kamm had identified a genuine new distinction.

What Kamm suggests is that we can have at least three different attitudes towards an effect of our action or plan:

i   The first attitude is one in which the plan is formulated or the action is performed *in order to* bring that effect about;

ii The second attitude is one in which the plan is formulated or the action is performed *because* it will bring about that effect but *not* in order to bring about that effect;

iii The third attitude is one in which the plan is formulated or the action is performed *despite* the fact (or likelihood) that it will bring about that effect.[9]

In Party Case, for example, we formulate the plan of organizing the party and perform the action of organizing the party in order to have fun (i); we formulate the plan of organizing the party and perform the action of organizing the party only because we believe that it will cause a feeling of indebtedness in our friends (ii); and finally we formulate the plan of organizing the party and perform the action of organizing the party despite the fact that this will cause a mess (iii). We believe the plan and action of party-organizing to have all these three properties: fun-causing; indebtedness-causing and mess-causing (obviously here nothing is supposed to depend on the relation being causal, so feel free to substitute 'causal' with whatever you see fit). Some of these properties count in favour of our plan (fun-causing and indebtedness-causing); some count against our plan (mess-causing)[10]; but none of these properties is enough to put us off the plan, at least given the combination with the other two (because mess-causing would be enough to put us off if it weren't for indebtedness-causing).

What is the difference between our attitudes towards these different properties of our plan and action? We have – one could argue – a positive attitude towards fun-causing and indebtedness-causing and a negative attitude towards mess-causing. Our attitude towards mess-causing is negative because the fact that the party will cause a mess does not in any way motivate us, it could be said: we would rather spare everybody the mess, but it is just not possible. This isn't the case, a defender of Kamm would argue, for the fact that the party will cause the indebtedness: that does motivate us insofar as we only act because we believe that the party will cause the indebtedness – that property is a necessary condition for our acting, would we not believe that our action had that property, we would not act.[11]

But why should one accept this point? Could we not rather argue that the attitude towards the indebtedness is just like the attitude towards the mess? Indebtedness is also unavoidable if we want to have fun, just like the mess; because without the indebtedness there will be no party and therefore no fun. But, just like one could say of the mess that we would rather spare everybody the mess but that is just not possible if we want to have fun, then we can say of the indebtedness that we would rather spare everybody the indebtedness but that this is just not possible if we want to have fun. So the agent's attitude towards both the indebtedness and the mess is a negative one in general, it could be said, but a positive one in particular (just like with Aristotle's *mixed actions*, unsurprisingly): namely under different circumstances, the agent would be more than happy to spare herself and her friends both the mess and the indebtedness; say the agent would be extremely rich and be able to afford enough staff which would take over all the organizing tasks and cleaning tasks and would do so with such promptness and efficiency that the agent and her friends could have just as much fun without any mess or indebtedness being produced. But under the present circumstances the agent is willing to cause both the indebtedness and the mess so as to have fun.

The mess, just like the indebtedness, is functional to the agent's plan: both are necessary, given the agent's preference for fun – both would and could be spared under different conditions. So, again, it looks like Kamm's further distinction between 'because of' means and mere side effects does not hold up to scrutiny, and that the problems with it – as this section shows – do not only have to do with the issues about intention that we discussed in the previous section. Here one could still be tempted to distinguish between 'functional' and 'necessary' in order to argue that while both the indebtedness and the mess are necessary (where that means that given the current situation we cannot do without either if we want to have fun), only the indebtedness is functional while the mess is merely necessary. This would be the case, supposedly, because the indebtedness is functional to avoiding that the agent will have to clean up the mess on its own, while the mess itself has no comparable function: it is just an unavoidable nuisance.

I think this is premature: the mess has its functions too. If it weren't for the mess, guests would have to restrain and constraint their fun by always washing up their glasses after use; by bringing out the trash regularly; limiting their use of chairs and other pieces of furniture; I could go on, and the circumstances would sound increasingly less like a party. In a slogan, there is no party without mess; and even though the mess may not be the point of the party, the mess is functional to the party being a party (or at least a successful and fun one anyway). Once the functionality of the mess has been put this way, the opponent, in order to insist that the mess is not functional, would have to appeal to the mess being the effect and not the cause in the above structure; and she would also have to appeal – and this does not necessarily need to be implied by the previous remark – to the mess taking place, temporally, after the events to which it is supposed to be functional. But, first of all, we ought not to forget that we are talking in intensional terms here: we are talking about the agent's deliberation about the causal structure of the world, not about the causal structure of the world itself. And in the agent's deliberation, things may not necessarily be ordered – temporally, say – the way in which they are ordered in the world the agent is deliberating about.

When we talk about some effect being an end, means or side effect, we are talking about the nature of that effect within the agent's deliberation: to illustrate this simple point, we may just imagine someone having a party in order to have a mess or in order to make her friends feel indebted. Indeed, parties do often fulfil social functions: people often organize parties not just to have fun, but to network, get favours, get to know useful people better, get invited to other parties and so on. And while the case of someone organizing a party in order to cause a mess is a bit less usual, it is not far-fetched: you can easily imagine a bitter teenager wanting to get one back on her parents; or you can imagine a slightly disturbed person who has come to have such problematic relationship with her cleaning lady that she organizes parties only to make more work for her cleaning lady and make her life less pleasant. This may be weird, but quite possible: it just goes to show the simple point that the mess being the effect rather than the cause and the mess being temporally after the party does not prevent its being an end in itself or a means to an end: what is decisive is its role within the agent's deliberation rather than the causal structure of the world.

Here it could be objected that my argument is arbitrary insofar as one could equally argue against the distinction between 'in order to' means and 'because of' means rather than against the distinction between 'because of' means and mere side effects. And indeed there is logical space for such an argument, where one could argue that they are actually both 'in order to' means: it could be pointed out, for example, that even though causing indebtedness is not the overall goal of organizing the party, it is one of its aims, and that organizing the party is dependent on this particular aim being achieved too: if the agent did not believe she could bring about that effect (indebtedness), she would not organize the party in the first place – that much is shared between Kamm and the critics.

Since the organization of the party is conditional on its causing indebtedness, the agent will be under rational pressure to organize the party in such a way as to guarantee indebtedness. The agent will not necessarily be under rational pressure to maximize indebtedness (and this could very well be what distinguishes this from an overall aim)[12]; but she will need to cause enough indebtedness to make sure that her friends help out with the mess afterwards. This may affect, say, which friends she will invite to the party – maybe if the numbers will have to be limited and she will have to make some tough calls (pun intended), then she will be under some rational pressure to invite the more grateful ones over the thankless ones – given that their reaction to the invite and the party is for the agent such a priority (this, by the way, may be thought to be one of Bratman's roles of intention: the one about constraining other intentions). Further, it may be that if the evening starts to develop in a certain way which may endanger the friends' feeling of indebtedness, our host will have to intervene, remedy and correct to make sure that the friends do feel indebted by the end of it.

Imagine the following development: during the party, someone asks out loud to our host how much money she has spent on booze and food (the plausibility of this scenario may be highly culture dependent, I will admit). Now, if our host thinks that a truthful answer here may be conducive to a feeling of indebtedness on the part of her friends (or if she thinks that talking down her expenses may endanger indebtedness), then it seems that our agent would be in this situation under rational pressure to act in order to bring about a feeling of indebtedness in her friends (this, again, reminds us of Bratman's roles of intention).

Having now considered the possibility that indebtedness is an 'in order to' means – after having considered the possibility that it is a mere side effect like the mess caused by the party – let me say that we don't need to take a definite position on this issue here. The point throughout has been, here, to show that Kamm's supposed novel distinction is unwarranted and does not move the debate on double effect and anti-consequentialist constraints in general forward. How we should properly interpret the cases that Kamm offers is a further issue that does not bear on the critique of her supposed novel distinction: indeed, we have here shown that there are multiple plausible alternative ways to interpret Kamm's cases rather than just a single alternative to Kamm's argument. And let me say one more thing about this issue: that one can plausibly argue both in favour of indebtedness being a mere side effect and in favour of indebtedness being an 'in order to' means only goes to show that it is not only Kamm's novel distinction between 'in order to' and 'because of' that is problematic, but also that the distinction between means and side effects is problematic too – and this should be no surprise for an opponent of double effect! On the contrary, it is one more argument against the distinction.

Let us take stock: so far we have argued against Kamm's suggested distinction between intended means, unintended 'because of' means and side effects (question i). As we anticipated in setting up the argument, a negative answer to question (i) implies also a negative answer to question (ii): quite simply, if there is no further distinction, then that non-existent distinction can also have no moral value because there would not be anything that such moral value could be attributed to. One question remains, though: what about the three principles – Kant's hypothetical imperative, Anscombe's intention–reason principle and the doctrine of double effect – that, according to Kamm, her new distinction would have challenged? Here, again, it can be said that this issue is also related to the first question so that if there is no distinction, then there is also no challenge for the three principles. But as Kamm discusses at least one of them – Kant's instrumental rationality principle – separately, I want to briefly take issue with that.[13]

5 Kant and Korsgaard

One would have thought that, since Kamm's argument against Kant's hypothetical imperative – 'Whoever wills the end, wills (so far as reason has decisive influence on his actions) also the means that are indispensably necessary to his actions and that lie in his power' (1785/1993: 417) – depends solely on her point about means being also unintended, then our arguments so far against unintended means would also suffice to defend Kant from Kamm. And this is, in principle, true. But, as it happens, Kamm discusses Kant's hypothetical imperative (and more precisely Korsgaard's (1997) influential work on it) by relying on one more thought-experiment which, she claims, provides further independent evidence that means need not be intended (2007: 108).

Specifically, Kamm develops a case meant to show that what she refers to as the *Claim* is false (I will spare the reader a detailed analysis of whether attributing the Claim to either Kant or Korsgaard is legitimate). The Claim, as formulated by Kamm, goes as follows:

It is commonly thought that if a rational agent intends an end and believes that his doing something is a means necessary to that end, then insofar as he is rational and does not abandon the end, it follows that he intends that means to his end. Call this the Claim. (Kamm 2007: 104)

Here is Kamm's counterexample to the Claim, the *House Case*:

> Suppose that I want to build a private home and I must create a hole in plot A in order to do this. However, creating the hole is too expensive just to build my house, so I must not aim to do it. However, I receive a contract to build an apartment complex on plot B, which is next to A. In order to clear the land for the apartment complex, I must use explosives that unavoidably make a hole in plot B but, as an unintended side effect, they also create a hole in plot A. The hole in plot A is an undesirable side effect from the point of view of building on B, since it makes it harder for me to move materials to B, but it is a tolerable cost relative to the goal of building on B. Given that I will produce the hold in plot A as a side effect, I can still pursue my goal of building my home. I do everything else (e.g., buying bricks) that I must do to build my house in order to build it. (2007: 109)

Kamm's claim is, here, that producing a hole in plot A is an unintended means. This is on the face of it weird, as Kamm explicitly says, in presenting the case, that the 'hole in plot A is an undesirable *side effect*' (109, emphasis mine). Is producing the hole in plot A then a means or a side effect? We have already seen that Kamm does distinguish (or at least wants to distinguish) between means and side effects (indebtedness and mess, for example), so that the answer here cannot be that there is no difference. I guess Kamm could mean that producing the hole in plot A is an undesirable side effect of producing the hole in plot B but a means to build my own home. Supposing that this is what Kamm has in mind, here I don't want to rule out the possibility of something being a means to x while at the same time being a side effect of y (even though I am not sure that every account of means and side effects could deal with that); but I do think that, if we want to relativize the question of whether something is a means or side effect as proposed above, then the fact that something is a side effect of y cannot count in favour of its being an unintended effect (but a means) to x.

These technicalities aside, what speaks against producing a hole in plot A being an *intended* means? Suppose that, once our builder has realized his luck (viz. that the explosive he needs for B will also do for A, and that the extra bother is tolerable relative to the goal of building on B – so that he can build both the apartments and his home), his partner phones with the good news that he has found online alternative offers for explosives: Brand1 is cheaper but will produce a hole in B and A too; Brand2 is cheaper (it costs just as much as Brand1) and will also produce the hole only in B; Brand3 costs the same as the one they had planned to use but will only produce the hole in B.

Now, for the partner this is a no brainer: they should order Brand2, which is cheaper and produces only the hole in B, so they save money and can move materials to B more easily. But what about our builder? He now faces a difficult decision: because given the tolerable costs involved in moving materials to B if there is a hole in A, our builder prefers Brand1. Our builder has a conflict of interests: his professional interests are the same as those of his partner, namely Brand2; but his private interests make Brand1 preferable. And given that Brand1 and Brand2 cost the same and that the costs involved in moving materials to B with a hole in plot A are tolerable anyway, our builder's overall preference – once both his professional and private interests have been taken into account – must be for Brand1, because he is under rational pressure – given his preferences – to prefer Brand1 over Brand2. And where is the pressure coming from? From his intention to produce a hole in plot A; had our builder not planned to produce a hole in A too, then his preferences would clearly be different. Were our builder indifferent to produce a hole in plot A, then his preferences would have been different. That our builder prefers Brand1 shows that producing a hole in A is not just a side effect: it is part of his overall plan which makes a difference to further decisions, planning and preferences. Indeed, we can easily imagine a builder of which one may say that she does indeed not intend to produce the hole in plot A: that is the builder who answers to her partner that she should clearly buy Brand2 and thereby sacrifices building his own home on the altar of professionalism.

In conclusion to this section, we have argued from two independent points of view against Kamm's criticism of Kant and Korsgaard: in the first place, our general rejection of Kamm's distinction between 'in order to' and 'because of' means takes away Kamm's first argument against Kant's hypothetical imperative. In second instance, we have shown that Kamm's further argument – her House Case thought-experiment – is no counterexample to the claim that means are necessarily intended.

6 Conclusion

In this chapter I have argued that there is no reason to complicate the debate on double effect by introducing – on top of the already controversial trio of ends/means/side effects – a further distinction between two kinds of means: 'in order to' means (which are intended) and 'because of' means (which are unintended). I have criticized Kamm's attempt to draw this further distinction by introducing her Party Case (and related thought-experiments) in order to deal with the Loop Variant of the Trolley Problem. I have shown that Party Case is not analogous to the Loop Variant so that it cannot be used in an argument for the permissibility of intervening in the Loop Variant. Further, I have shown that the putative distinction between 'in order to' and 'because of' means does not hold: causing the effect of indebtedness by organizing a party cannot be distinguished from causing the effect of a mess by organizing a party. My argument against Kamm has particular relevance to the debate on the Doctrine of Double Effect because Kamm's distinction was meant to be able to deal with the Loop Variant of the Trolley Problem, a notorious hard case for the Doctrine of Double Effect.

PART THREE
Double Effect in Practice

CHAPTER EIGHT

The classic application of double effect: Collateral damages

Abstract *I argue against the Doctrine of Double Effect's explanation of the moral difference between terror bombing and strategic bombing. I show that the standard thought-experiment of Terror Bomber and Strategic Bomber which dominates this debate is underdetermined in three crucial respects: (1) the non-psychological worlds of Terror Bomber and Strategic Bomber; (2) the psychologies of Terror Bomber and Strategic Bomber; and (3) the structure of the thought-experiment, especially in relation to its similarity with the Trolley Problem. (1) If the two worlds are not identical, then it may be these differences between the two worlds and not the Doctrine of Double Effect that explain the moral difference; (2a) if Terror Bomber and Strategic Bomber have the same causal beliefs, then why does Terror Bomber set out to kill the children? It may then be this unwarranted and immoral choice and not the Doctrine of Double Effect that* *explains the moral difference; (2b) if the two have different causal beliefs, then we can't rule out the counterfactual that, had Strategic Bomber had the same beliefs as Terror Bomber, she would have also acted as Terror Bomber did. Finally, (3) the Strategic Bomber scenario could also be constructed so as to be structurally equivalent to the* Fat Man *scenario in the Trolley Problem: but then the Doctrine of Double Effect would give different answers to two symmetrical cases.*

1 Introduction

Since even before World War II,[1] the discussion of the *Doctrine of Double Effect* has been intertwined with the discussion of *terror* bombing and *strategic* bombing.[2] The concepts of 'terror bombing' and 'strategic bombing' are, both in historical and philosophical context, quickly clarified by looking at how the British changed their directives to their pilots sometime in late 1940. Frankland writes that in June 1940 British authorities still 'specifically laid down that targets had to be identified and aimed at. Indiscriminate bombing was forbidden' (1970: 24[3]). Here indiscriminate bombing is what has come to be known in the literature as terror bombing. And it has presumably acquired that name because the British soon changed their fighting ways: already in November 1940 'Bomber Command was instructed simply to aim at the center of a city . . . the aiming points are to be the built-up areas, not, for instance, the dockyards or aircraft factories' (1970: 24).

'Built-up areas' here means residential areas, as the British did not care to hide: Churchill spoke in the Commons of the 'the systematic shattering of German cities' (July 1943[4]); 'the progressive destruction and dislocation of the German military, industrial and economic system and the undermining of the morale of the German people to the point where their capacity for armed resistance is fatally weakened' (joint British-American Casablanca conference); 'To the RAF fell the task of destroying Germany's great cities, of silencing the iron heart-beat of the Ruhr, of dispossessing the working population, of breaking the morale of the people'(*Target: Germany*, an RAF official publication of that period). Finally they ended up calling it 'terror' bombing themselves: 'Here, then, we have *terror* and devastation carried to the core of a warring nation' (Still from *Target: Germany* as quoted by Ford 1944: 294).

2 The thought-experiment

The British started with what in contemporary literature we refer to as strategic bombing and then turned to so-called terror bombing. As we have seen (Ford 1944), the connection between these practices and the Doctrine of Double Effect was drawn already at the time. In the post-war period, the distinction between terror bombing and strategic bombing has evolved into a philosophical thought-experiment widely used to illustrate (and often also to defend) the Doctrine of Double Effect.

An influential example is Jonathan Bennett's discussion in his *Tanner Lectures on Human Values*:

In this lecture I shall exhibit some difficulties about a certain distinction which is thought important by many moralists – namely that between what you intend to come about as a means to your end and what you do not intend although you foresee that it will come about as a by-product of your means to your end. This has a role in most defences of the Doctrine of Double Effect, and is one source for the view that terror bombing is never permissible though tactical bombing may sometimes be – i.e., that it is never right to kill civilians as a means to demoralizing the enemy country, though it may sometimes be right to destroy a munitions factory as a means to reducing the enemy's military strength, knowing that the raid will also kill civilians. In the former case – so the story goes – the civilian deaths are intended as a means; in the latter they are not intended but merely foreseen as an inevitable by-product of the means; and that is supposed to make a moral difference, even if the probabilities are the same, the number of civilian deaths the same, and so on. (1980: 95)

The similarity between Bennett's characterization of terror bombing and the British directives from World War II is striking: 'to kill civilians as a means to demoralizing the enemy country' is offered as an example of terror bombing; strategic bombing is described as 'to destroy a munitions factory as a means to reducing the enemy's military strength, knowing that the raid will also kill civilians'. The case we are asked to imagine is, supposedly, one in which a pilot is ordered to bomb a munitions factory, so as to reduce the enemy's military strength; she is also informed that there is a very high probability of civilian casualties as a result of the bombing of the munitions factory. The day after, the same pilot is ordered to bomb civilians as a means to demoralize the enemy; she is informed that there is a very high probability (the same very high probability as yesterday) that the numbers of civilian deaths will be the same as yesterday.[5] Now the idea that the Doctrine of Double Effect is supposed to defend is that it is permissible on the first day but not on the second day for the pilot to drop her bombs.

Michael Bratman – as we have already seen – develops this very scenario as follows:

> Both Terror Bomber and Strategic Bomber have the goal of promoting the war effort against Enemy. Each intends to pursue this goal by weakening Enemy, and each intends to do that by dropping bombs. Terror Bomber's plan is to bomb the school in Enemy's territory, thereby killing children of Enemy and terrorizing Enemy's population. Strategic Bomber's plan is different. He plans to bomb Enemy's munitions plant, thereby undermining Enemy's war effort. Strategic Bomber also knows, however, that next to the munitions plant is a school, and that when he bombs the plant he will also destroy the school, killing the children inside. Strategic Bomber has not ignored this fact. Indeed, he has worried a lot about it. Still, he has concluded that this cost, though significant, is outweighed by the contribution that would be made to the war effort by the destruction of the munitions plant. Now, Terror Bomber intends all of the features of his action just noted: he intends to drop the bombs, kill the children, terrorize the population, and thereby weaken Enemy. In contrast, it seems that Strategic Bomber only intends to drop the bombs, destroy the munitions plant, and weaken Enemy. Although he knows that by bombing the plant he will be killing the children, he does not, it seems, intend to kill them. Whereas killing the children is, for Terror Bomber, an intended means to

his end of victory, it is, for Strategic Bomber, only something he knows he will do by bombing the munitions plant. Though Strategic Bomber has taken the deaths of the children quite seriously into account in his deliberation, these deaths are for him only an expected side effect; they are not – in contrast with Terror Bomber's position – intended as a means. . . . In saying this I do not deny that Strategic Bomber kills the children intentionally. (1987: 139–40)[6]

The philosophical discussion of terror bombing and strategic bombing starts with the intuition that there is a moral difference between them; indeed, the Doctrine of Double Effect is normally offered as an explanation of the moral difference between Terror Bomber and Strategic Bomber. I have looked at this supposed moral intuition experimentally and found no evidence for it – see the next chapter for details on my experiments on moral intuitions on collateral damage cases. Here I concentrate on theoretical consi-derations and offer three arguments against the Doctrine of Double Effect's explanation of the thought-experiment. I show that, once the thought-experiment of terror bombing and strategic bombing is properly analysed, it should really be no surprise that there is no intuitive moral difference between Terror Bomber and Strategic Bomber: depending on how some crucial underdetermined aspects of the thought-experiment are interpreted, either the relevant differences around which the thought-experiment is constructed (such as intending/merely foreseeing and means/side effects) do not explain the supposed moral differences or there are, indeed, no such moral differences – as the evidence from intuition suggests.

3 Bratman and different options

Reading Bratman's version of the thought-experiment, one may think that we are in a twin thought-experiment, where everything is identical apart from the plans of the two pilots. But what Bratman writes after a few pages indicates that this is not what he meant:

. . . this does not tell us whether or not Strategic Bomber would also go ahead and bomb if his bombing option were precisely that of Terror Bomber's. The difference between Strategic Bomber and

Terror Bomber in the original case lies in the options with which they are presented; it need not involve a difference in inclination to plump for terror-bombing if that is the only bombing option available. (1987: 161)

Bratman's though-experiment, then, is not only different in the psychology of the two pilots; it is also different in the options available to them, which means, supposedly, that the difference between the Terror scenario and the Strategic scenario goes beyond psychological differences between Terror Bomber and Strategic Bomber. From the way both Bennett and Bratman describe the though-experiment, it would have been legitimate to suppose, for example, that the consequences of the bombings would be identical: both Terror Bomber and Strategic Bomber destroy the munitions factory, both kill the same number of children. But actually there is no munitions factory in the world of Terror Bomber; otherwise, we could not make sense of the above remark that 'this does not tell us whether or not Strategic Bomber would also go ahead and bomb if his bombing option were precisely that of Terror Bomber's'.

That the difference between Terror Bomber and Strategic Bomber need not involve 'a difference in inclination to plump for terror-bombing if that is the only bombing option available' suggests that the Doctrine of Double Effect may have to argue for the permissibility of what Strategic Bomber does even in the case in which Strategic Bomber would have behaved exactly as Terror Bomber had he been faced with the options that Terror Bomber was faced with.[7] We will see in Section 5 that this is a problematic position to defend.

Let us take stock: we have identified the classic terror–strategic thought-experiment as being underdetermined in a first important respect: the options with which Terror Bomber and Strategic Bomber may be presented need not be identical, as long as they kill the same number of children (or some such). This is left open to the extent that Bratman, for example, allows for the possible counterfactual in which Strategic Bomber would admit that, had she been presented with the options Terror Bomber was presented with, she would have done just what Terror Bomber has done. This first point, then, can be summarized by saying that the thought-experiment is underdetermined as to the non-psychological differences between the two scenarios.

There is also an important underdetermination as to the psychological differences between the two agents, which I discuss in the next two sections: it may be that Terror Bomber and Strategic Bomber have the same causal beliefs, or it may be that they have different causal beliefs. Let us begin with discussing the variant in which the two pilots have the same causal beliefs.

4 Same causal beliefs

Let us suppose that the two agents, Terror Bomber and Strategic Bomber, have the same causal beliefs[8]: of the sixteen possible permutations resulting from combining the two agents with the two beliefs 'killing children will weaken enemy' and 'destroying munitions will weaken enemy' (and their respective negations), twelve involve at least one of the two agents in some form of irrationality – I will therefore disregard those even though some of them are such that the two agents have the same causal beliefs.[9] Of the remaining four, three are such that the two agents have different causal beliefs. So there is only one permutation such that neither of the agents is irrational and the two agents have the same causal beliefs, which are the following:

- Terror Bomber believes that killing children will weaken enemy *and* she believes that destroying munitions will weaken enemy.

- Strategic Bomber believes that destroying munitions will weaken enemy *and* she believes that killing children will weaken enemy.

Here there is both a cognitive problem and a normative problem. In brief, the cognitive problem is how we get a difference in intention out of the same motivation and the same causal beliefs.[10] The normative problem is why Terror Bomber sets out to kill the children. Both Terror Bomber and Strategic Bomber believe that killing the children will weaken enemy. Both Terror Bomber and Strategic Bomber believe that destroying munitions will weaken enemy. Their instrumental beliefs are the same, then. And their motivation is the same too: they both want to promote the war effort by weakening enemy. That is, they have the same motivating reasons or, if you will, pro-attitudes. And the same beliefs too: they both believe that 'killing children' will satisfy their pro-attitude towards 'weakening enemy', and they both believe that 'destroying munitions' will satisfy their pro-attitude towards 'weakening enemy'. They also both know that they cannot destroy munitions without killing children (and that they cannot kill children without destroying munitions). Where does the difference in intention come from?

What we have, here, is a kind of Buridan case: both 'killing children' and 'destroying munitions' satisfy the agent's pro-attitude, and the agent does not seem to have distinctive reasons to do one over the other. Still, the agent has overwhelming reasons to do one, and therefore we may suppose that she just picks one because of her overwhelming reasons to do one of the two things. But here we may think that from the motivating perspective this may be like a Buridan case, but from the normative perspective, it is outrageous to talk about *picking* between 'killing children' and 'destroying munitions'.

There are strong normative reasons to *choose* 'destroying munitions' over 'killing children'. And since there are no instrumental reasons to choose 'killing children' over 'destroying munitions' or to not choose 'destroying munitions' over 'killing children', then the agent ought to choose 'destroying munitions' over 'killing children'. And so we have already come to the normative problem: starting from a cognitive identity, we get a duty (or at least moral reasons) to choose 'destroying munitions' over 'killing children'. And Terror Bomber violates this duty to choose 'destroying munitions' over 'killing children'. But then, and this is the crucial point here, it is not double effect, but Terror Bomber's violation of her duty to choose 'destroying munitions' over 'killing children' – duty which Strategic Bomber has not violated – which explains the moral difference between Terror Bomber and Strategic Bomber.

The following plausible moral principle may be what is implicitly doing the work here: if you believe that both A and B satisfy your legitimate goal C, and you believe that A involves the death of no one while you believe that B involves the death of many children, then other things being equal you have a duty not to choose or do B. It is this very plausible moral principle, and not double effect, that may justify the distinction between Terror Bomber and Strategic Bomber if the two have the same causal beliefs.

Here it may be objected that this principle does not apply here because both agents choose or do both A and B: but whether or not one wants to talk about 'choosings' or 'doings' in cases of merely foreseen side effects (see next paragraph), the point stands: given that there is an obvious moral difference between A and B such that B is morally much worse than A, why does Terror Bomber settle on B instead of A when she believes that A would be just as effective in satisfying her goals? She may be ignorant of the obvious moral difference between A and B, but then, given that Terror Bomber knows all too well what A and B are, her ignorance about their relative moral value would be itself a serious moral shortcoming on the part of Terror Bomber – and that moral shortcoming would be able to distinguish, morally, between what Terror Bomber does and what Strategic Bomber does. On the other hand, Terror Bomber may not be ignorant of the moral difference between A and B but just indifferent to it – but that's as serious a moral shortcoming as the previous one.

It could still be objected that my critique depends on being able to say that Terror Bomber 'settles' on B or 'chooses' B or 'does' B but does not do A, and that, in turn, we need double effect to be able to distinguish between Terror Bomber's attitude towards A and B. Two things here: first, the above objection could be taken to be saying that there is no difference between the agent's relation to A and the agent's relation to B. Whatever the merit of this point, it is not open to defenders of double effect, because the Doctrine depends on there being some difference – so that I am allowed, dialectically, to talk about 'settle' or the like.

Secondly, the Doctrine of Double Effect contains a distinction between intended means and merely foreseen side effects which could be applied to distinguish between Terror Bomber's attitudes towards A and B. But, crucially, that distinction need not exhaust the difference between Terror Bomber's attitude to A and her attitude to B; and, more importantly, the Doctrine of Double Effect claims that it is the distinction between intended means and merely foreseen side effects which is, itself, morally relevant; while here we have shown that the moral work is being done by other considerations. Notice, also, the advantage of my solution over the solution offered by the Doctrine of Double Effect: the Doctrine requires an is-ought gap in that it claims that a theoretical distinction in the psychology of the agent makes a moral difference, while my solution only appeals to normative distinctions, which are in themselves *basic* – as the simple moral principle I put forward.

Alternatively, it may be objected that we should not understand this interpretation of the thought-experiment as a Buridan case because the two agents may have different motivations despite having the same causal beliefs. The two agents may indeed be taken to have different moral motives in that they may be following different moral principles: but then, as in the argument already offered, it is the difference in the moral principles they are following and not the Doctrine of Double Effect that is doing the normative work: namely, nothing would depend on the difference between intended means and merely foreseen side effects.

We have just shown that if we understand the thought-experiment in terms of same causal beliefs, then we can show why this thought-experiment does not support the Doctrine of Double Effect – and this without even beginning to get into the usual arguments on double effect that dominate the literature and that we have covered in previous chapters. This, it may be argued, is a reason to think that we should not understand the thought-experiment in terms of Terror Bomber and Strategic Bomber having the same causal beliefs – even though such an understanding is compatible with the standard versions of the thought-experiment (as those by Bennett and Bratman that we have been following here): in the next section, I discuss the alternative interpretation of the agents' psychologies according to which the two agents have different causal beliefs.

5 Different causal beliefs

Let us then look at the interpretations on which Terror Bomber and Strategic Bomber do not have the same causal beliefs. There are three permutations which do not involve either of the two agents in criticizable irrationality where the two agents do not have the same causal beliefs:

A Terror Bomber believes that killing children will weaken enemy *and* she believes that destroying munitions will weaken enemy.

Strategic Bomber believes that destroying munitions will weaken enemy *and* she does not believe that killing children will weaken enemy.

B Terror Bomber believes that killing children will weaken enemy *and* she does not believe that destroying munitions will weaken enemy.

Strategic Bomber believes that destroying munitions will weaken enemy *and* she believes that killing children will weaken enemy.

C Terror Bomber believes that killing children will weaken enemy *and* she does not believe that destroying munitions will weaken enemy.

Strategic Bomber believes that destroying munitions will weaken enemy *and* she does not believe that killing children will weaken enemy.

Readings (A) and (B) share a problem with the interpretation on which Terror Bomber and Strategic Bomber have the same causal beliefs: namely, on (A) it is not clear why Terror Bomber chooses 'killing children' over 'destroying munitions', and on (B) it is not clear why Strategic Bomber chooses 'destroying munitions' over 'killing children'. The problem with (A) we have already discussed. The problem with (B) is symmetric, and may have a symmetric effect on morally preferring Strategic Bomber over Terror Bomber. Namely, we may morally prefer Strategic Bomber because, in the absence of instrumental reasons to choose between 'killing children' and 'destroying munitions', we assume that she must have had some moral reasons to prefer the morally superior alternative, namely 'destroying munitions'. But this need not be the case: maybe, in the spirit of Buridan, Strategic Bomber flipped a coin; and then it would be difficult to morally prefer Strategic Bomber over Terror Bomber, after such a show of indifference towards the moral difference between 'destroying munitions' and 'killing children'.

Let us then leave (A) and (B) aside and focus on (C), which has clear advantages over the interpretation on which Terror Bomber and Strategic Bomber have the same causal beliefs. (C) explains, namely, why Terror Bomber sets out to kill children and not to destroy munitions. And (C) explains, also, why Strategic Bomber sets out to destroy munitions and not to kill children. Terror Bomber opts for the plan of killing children over the plan of destroying munitions because she believes that killing children will weaken enemy and she does not believe that destroying munitions will weaken enemy. And Strategic Bomber opts for the plan of destroying munitions over the plan of killing children because she believes that destroying munitions will weaken enemy and she does not believe that killing children will weaken enemy. And this leaves open the crucial possibility that, had Strategic Bomber had the same beliefs as Terror Bomber, she would have also chosen as Terror Bomber (and *vice versa*). This counterfactual is importantly different from the counterfactual – mentioned also by Bratman – about what Strategic Bomber would have done had she been presented with the same options as Terror Bomber. That counterfactual was about non-psychological options; this counterfactual is about the beliefs of Terror Bomber and Strategic Bomber, not the strategic options offered by their worlds. Still, both counterfactuals generate similar problems for double effect.

Reading (C) leaves open both the possibility that Terror Bomber, had she had Strategic Bomber's beliefs, would have acted as Strategic Bomber did; and the possibility that Strategic Bomber, had she had Terror Bomber's beliefs, would have acted as Terror Bomber did. And one may think that this is going to be a problem for those who want to offer different moral judgements for what Terror Bomber and Strategic Bomber did. On the other hand, it may be objected, what is at issue are moral judgements over actions (e.g. the permissibility of killing the children in the case of Strategic Bomber) and not moral judgements over agents, and suggest that therefore not being able to distinguish, morally, between the two agents does not imply that we will not be able to distinguish, morally, between the two actions.

The symmetrically opposite position is often put forward as a softer version or last resort of the Doctrine of Double Effect: namely, that in the impossibility of distinguishing, morally, between the two actions, we may at least distinguish, morally, between the two agents – for example, talk about differences in character between the two agents; or talk about 'the way the agent went about deciding what to do' (Scanlon 2008: 36). Without discussing the merits of this position (I talk again about this position in Chapter 12), it illustrates the difficulties of its symmetrical opposite: if we can't even find moral differences in the agents, where are the moral differences in the actions going to come from, given that what actually happens in the world is identical in both cases? So interpreting the thought-experiment as supposing that Terror Bomber and Strategic Bomber have different causal beliefs is problematic because then we can't even distinguish, morally, between Terror Bomber and Strategic Bomber as we do not have any reason to think that Strategic Bomber would have acted differently from Terror Bomber had she had her beliefs. There is another problem with tracing back the moral difference to a difference of belief, which I shall just mention here briefly: it exposes the normative judgement to too much luck, and agents should be judged for their actions and inclinations, and not for their causal beliefs.

Let us take stock: we have here analysed another way in which the thought-experiment is underdetermined, namely the beliefs of the two agents. We have shown that there are important differences between interpreting the two agents as having the same causal beliefs and interpreting the two agents as having different causal beliefs. In both cases, although for different reasons, the thought-experiment is shown not to support the Doctrine of Double Effect: in the former case because there is a much more basic moral principle which explains the moral difference; in the latter case because there is no moral difference – which was also the problem with Bratman's allowing for the two pilots being confronted with different options.

6 Structural similarity with the Trolley Problem

There is another, important, variable: the relation between the collateral damages cases discussed in this chapter and the trolley cases discussed in Chapter 4. The Doctrine of Double Effect – as we have seen – is often used to argue that in *Bystander at the Switch* it is morally permissible to intervene because the killing of the one workman is just a side effect of saving the five, while in *Fat Man* it is not morally permissible to intervene because the killing of the fat man is a means to save the five. Roughly, then, *Bystander at the Switch* should be paired with Strategic Bomber and *Fat Man* should be paired with Terror Bomber. There are some obvious differences between the Trolley thought-experiment and the Terror–Strategic thought-experiment: in the Trolley Problem, there are definite non-psychological differences between the two scenarios. In *Fat Man* there is a bridge, and in *Bystander at the Switch* there is no bridge, for example. Secondly, in the Trolley Problem there is no talk of intentions; we rather talk of 'means' and 'side effects'. This suggests that, borrowing respectively from the other thought-experiment, we could analyse the Trolley Problem and the Terror–Strategic thought-experiment as follows: we can say that Terror Bomber kills the children as a means to weakening enemy, while Strategic Bomber's killing of the children is just a side effect of weakening enemy. Similarly, we can say that, in *Bystander at the switch*, the bystander does not intend to kill the one workman; and we will say that on the other hand in *Fat Man* the bystander does intend to kill the fat guy.

I mention the Trolley Problem because the thought-experiment of Strategic Bomber and Terror Bomber is underdetermined also with respect to its structural similarity with the Trolley Problem. Suppose that the munitions are kept under the school's ground[11]; that is, supposedly, why we cannot destroy the munitions without killing the children. That the munitions be geographically located under the school is compatible with the way in which the thought-experiment is normally told (see Bennett and Bratman as quoted at the beginning of this chapter, for example) and it presents a structural similarity with *Fat Man* as opposed to *Bystander at the Switch*, as the children are now physically between the bombs and the munitions just as the poor fat guy will find himself physically between the trolley and the five workmen. The bombs will hit the school and then, and only then, hit the munitions, in the same way in which the trolley will hit the fat guy and then, and only then, stop, while in *Bystander at the Switch* we may say that the five are saved before the trolley kills the one, as it is enough that the trolley is deviated on the side track.

Now we know where the munitions and the school are located, but nothing is supposed to hinge on this. We will still say that Terror Bomber's plan is to kill the children in order to weaken the enemy, and that she knows that in killing the children she will also destroy the munitions. Similarly, we will say that Strategic Bomber's plan is to destroy the munitions in order to weaken the enemy, and that she knows that she will also kill children. The proposed analysis is

that Terror Bomber intends to kill children and merely foresees that
she will destroy munitions; and that Strategic Bomber intends to
destroy munitions and merely foresees that she will kill children.[12]

We can see that the above structure is supposed to make no
difference to Bratman's analysis of Terror Bomber's intention to
kill the children, which Strategic Bomber lacks. The three roles of
intention individuated by Bratman (1987: 140–3) are: (i) 'posing
problems for further reasoning', (ii) 'constraining other intentions'
and (iii) 'issuing in corresponding endeavouring'. As these roles
are applied to Terror Bomber's intention, Bratman says that Terror
Bomber's intention will (i) pose the problem of how he is going to
kill the children: 'Terror Bomber must figure out, for example, what
time of day to attack and what sorts of bombs to use' (1987: 141).
(ii) Terror Bomber's intention will also be incompatible with other
possible strategies. Terror Bomber may not, for example, implement
a plan to deploy some troops if this deployment would result in the
enemy evacuating the children: 'So Terror Bomber's prior intention
to kill the children stands in the way of his forming a new intention
to order the troop movement' (1987: 141). (iii) Terror Bomber will
also guide his conduct so as to cause the death of the children: 'If in
midair he learns they have moved to a different school, he will try to
keep track of them and take his bombs there' (1987: 141–2).

Bratman claims that these three roles are not true of Strategic
Bomber's attitude towards killing the children: Strategic Bomber
will not engage in practical reasoning about how to kill the children;
if further intentions of Strategic Bomber should be incompatible
with killing the children, that will not be a prima facie reason to
disregard them; and, to put Bratman's point crudely, if the children
move, Strategic Bomber will not follow them. These three claims are
independent of the three underdetermined elements that we have so
far identified: (a) whether or not there is a munitions factory in the
world of Terror Bomber, his attitude towards killing the children will
have these three roles and Strategic Bomber's attitude will not have
these three roles; (b) whether Terror Bomber and Strategic Bomber
have the same causal beliefs (for example, about the efficacy of
killing children to weaken the enemy) will not alter the three roles
of Terror Bomber's attitude towards killing the children. And the
same goes (c) for the structure of the scenario, so that even if the
munitions are hidden under the school, then it will still be the case
that Strategic Bomber will have to engage in practical reasoning

which has to do with, say, the sorts of bombs that will penetrate deep enough in the ground while that element will not play a role in Terror Bomber's reasoning.

The problem for the Doctrine of Double Effect is that, apparently, borrowing the structure of *Fat Man* from the Trolley Problem does not make any difference to the attribution of the relevant intention to Strategic Bomber. But then we have two structurally similar scenarios, *Fat Man* and Strategic Bomber, to which the Doctrine gives different answers, as it says that it is not morally permissible to kill the fat guy in *Fat Man* while it says that it is morally permissible to kill the children in Strategic Bomber: and this latter claim seems in turn less plausible if the munitions are hidden under the children – think of the case of human shields.

7 The three roles of intention and the Trolley Problem

What happens if we apply Bratman's analysis of the three roles of intention to the Trolley Problem? As we said, the comparison between the Trolley Problem and the Terror–Strategic thought-experiment is complicated by the use of different terminologies in discussing the two cases: for the Trolley Problem, the talk is of side effects as opposed to means; for the Terror–Strategic thought-experiment, the talk is of intended as opposed to merely foreseen. But if both thought-experiments are to be explained by the Doctrine of Double Effect, then there must be an available common reading.

There are, in fact, two common readings: we can either talk in both cases of side effects and means, or we can talk in both cases of intended and merely foreseen. The outcome is that we would say, of *Bystander at the Switch*, that the bystander does not intend to kill the one workman and that the killing of the one workman is just a side effect of the bystander's rescue of the five. Of *Fat Man*, we would, on the other hand, say that the bystander does intend to kill the fat guy and that the bystander's killing of the fat guy is a means to the bystander's end of saving the five. Of Terror Bomber, we will say that she intends to kill the children and that killing the children is a means to Terror Bomber's end of weakening the enemy. Finally, we will say of Strategic Bomber that she merely foresees the killing of the children without intending it, and that killing the children is, for Strategic Bomber, merely a side effect of her destruction of the munitions factory.

With this common understanding in place, we can test Bratman's three roles of intention on the attribution of the relevant intentions to the Trolley scenarios. Let us, for example, take the bystander's intention, in *Fat Man*, to kill the fat guy. This can be compared to the bystander's intention to stop the Trolley. As we have seen in Chapter 6, defenders of double effect have, traditionally, difficulties in explaining why in these cases we may not just say that the agent only intended to stop the trolley but did not intend to kill the fat guy. We can look in the *Fat Man* scenario for the three roles identified by Bratman: (i) posing problems for further reasoning; (ii) constraining other intentions; and (iii) issuing in corresponding endeavouring. Does the bystander's attitude towards killing the fat guy have the following three roles? If it does not have these three roles, it is no intention, and then we cannot say, at least on Bratman's understanding of intention, that the bystander intended to kill the fat guy. And this would be particularly damaging for the Doctrine of Double Effect, as Bratman's understanding – as we have seen – is meant to be sympathetic to double effect.

Let us start with the first role, posing problems for further reasoning. I think we can here contrast the supposed intention to kill the fat guy with the intention to stop the trolley, and see that only the latter attitude has the role for further reasoning identified by Bratman, and that therefore only the latter attitude is an intention. The bystander will have to reason about whether the fat man is heavy enough, for example; because if the fat man is not heavy enough to stop the trolley, then it will not make any rational sense to throw him off the bridge. But the bystander will not have to reason about a way of throwing him off the bridge so as to increase the chances that the trolley will hit head on the fat guy's vital organs, so as to guarantee the fat guy's death. The sort of further reasoning that the bystander will have to engage in has to do, then, only with how the fat guy will ensure that the trolley will be stopped, and not with the actual death of the fat guy.

Similar points can be made about the other two roles of intention: if the trolley happens to stop, for example, before I have pushed the fat guy, then I will no longer endeavour to throw him off the bridge – just as, in Bratman's discussion, Strategic Bomber will not pursue the children in case they leave the school. But now *Fat Man* looks like Strategic Bomber and not like Terror Bomber, so that we would say that the bystander in *Fat Man* intends to stop the trolley but merely foresees the death of the fat guy (or, in the other terminology, that the killing of the fat guy is a side effect of the bystander's stopping of the trolley, which is in turn a means to his end of saving the five).

8 Historical closeness

I want to discuss one further aspect of the problem of closeness, which brings us back where we started, namely to the explicit character of the directives and language of the British Bomber Command in World War II. We have seen how, in the course of 1940, the British went from explicitly forbidding indiscriminate bombing ('specifically laid down that targets had to be identified and aimed at. Indiscriminate bombing was forbidden' (1970: 24)) through ordering that bombs be directed at inhabited areas ('Bomber Command was instructed simply to aim at the center of a city . . . the aiming points are to be the built-up areas, not, for instance, the dockyards or aircraft factories' (1970: 24)) to, finally, referring themselves to their own operations as *terror* ('Here, then, we have *terror and devastation* carried to the core of a warring nation' (as quoted by Ford 1944: 294)). This is interesting because it gives a very clear historical context to the Terror–Strategic thought-experiment that we have been examining throughout. But there is a further element of interest in the directives and language of the British: they never actually explicitly talk about killing civilians.

The following Air Ministry directif and Air Staff paper from 1941 are illustrative (cited by Harris):

> to focus attacks on the morale of the enemy civil population, and, in particular, of the industrial workers. (1995: 7)
> The ultimate aim of the attack on a town area is to break the morale of the population which occupies it. To ensure this we must achieve two things: first, we must make the town physically uninhabitable and, secondly, we must make the people conscious

of constant personal danger. The immediate aim, is therefore, twofold, namely, to produce (i) destruction, and (ii) the fear of death. (1995: 7)

Let me first note that the civil servants of the time appear to have read Bentham, when they talk of the *immediate* aim of the operation.[13] More importantly, they explicitly talk about destruction, about fear of death and of making German cities 'physically uninhabitable'. It could not be any clearer that the targets are no longer only military or industrial sites; but, interestingly, the British stop short of writing down the obvious, in their orders: namely that the immediate aim is to terrorize civilians ('constant personal danger' and 'fear of death') by killing as many of them as possible. That is, the order of killing civilians is nowhere explicitly formulated. And this shows a surprising sensibility of the British authorities to the problem of closeness: we only intend to scare them; we only intend to destroy their houses and workplaces; but we do not intend to actually kill them. As we bomb their houses at night while they sleep in them, we only intend to destroy the houses, not to kill those sleeping inside. Yeah, right!

Here I am not making an historical point: first, for all I know, it may be that there are documents that talk about the explicit killing of the civilian population; secondly, I am not even claiming that the killing of the civilian population was deliberately left implicit in the formulation of orders.[14] All I am saying is that we can find in those historical documents all the argumentative force of the problem of closeness, as the challenge for the Doctrine of Double Effect is exactly to spell out why an agent who intentionally bombs houses she knows to be full of people cannot be said to merely intend to destroy the houses without also intending to kill the inhabitants.[15]

9 Conclusion

Summarizing, we have here identified three different ways in which the terror–strategic thought-experiment is underdetermined, all of which are crucial to its support of the Doctrine of Double Effect: (1) the thought-experiment is underdetermined as to whether the non-psychological worlds of Terror Bomber and Strategic Bomber are identical: but if the two worlds are not identical, then it may be those differences and not double effect which explain the supposed moral difference between Terror Bomber and Strategic Bomber. The thought-experiment is also underdetermined as to (2) whether the psychologies of Terror Bomber and Strategic Bomber are identical: we have shown that, whether or not we interpret Terror Bomber and Strategic Bomber as having the same causal beliefs, the Doctrine has a problem: if the two agents have the same causal beliefs, then why does Terror Bomber choose killing the children over destroying munitions? Terror Bomber's choice is morally problematic in the absence of a difference in causal beliefs; but then it may be Terror Bomber's dubious moral choice, and not double effect, that explains the moral difference between Terror Bomber and Strategic Bomber. And if the two have different causal beliefs, then we can't rule out the counterfactual that, had Strategic Bomber had the same beliefs as Terror Bomber, she would have also acted as the Terror Bomber did. But then how are we to morally distinguish between the two? And if we can't distinguish, morally, between the two agents, and the two worlds are identical, then where is the moral difference going to come from? Finally, the thought-experiment is also underdetermined as to (3) its structural similarity with the *Fat Man* scenario of the Trolley Problem: what if, namely, the munitions were kept under the school? Here the Doctrine of Double Effect would give different answers to two structurally symmetrical cases, Strategic Bomber and *Fat Man*.

CHAPTER NINE

An experimental approach to the distinction between intending and merely foreseeing

Abstract *Here I present and discuss a study of intuitions on Terror Bomber and Strategic Bomber. The study has two interesting results for discussions of double effect and collateral damage: (a) participants distinguish between the agents' attitudes, attributing an intention to kill the children only to the pilot in Terror Bomber – so participants seem to catch onto the distinction between intending and merely foreseeing; but, crucially, (b) participants do not distinguish morally between what agents in the two cases do.*

1 Introduction

We have seen so far in this book that cases, whether they are imaginary or historical, play an important role in the double effect debate: they function both as *illustrations of* double effect and as *motivation for* double effect. Those cases normally take the form of two consequentialistically identical scenarios whose apparent moral difference can be traced back to a difference in what the agents in the two cases intended. Cases that motivate and illustrate double effect have, then, three distinct characteristics:

1 they are consequentialistically equivalent;
2 they are intuitively morally different; and
3 there is a difference in the intentions of the agents.

All three of these characteristics are essential: without (1), one could argue that the difference between the cases was a matter of consequences; without (2), one could argue that there is no intuitive moral difference between the cases so that there is nothing for the Doctrine to explain; without (3), one could not apply the Doctrine of Double Effect in order to distinguish between the cases.

(1) can often be at issue in determining whether an historical case is appropriate for application of double effect, but it is typically a non-issue when it comes to thought-experiments in the double effect literature, where the consequentialist equivalence between the scenarios is simply stipulated. (3) has traditionally received the most attention within discussions of double effect – see previous chapters. Here – as I did in Chapter 5 for trolley cases – I rather concentrate on (2).

As we have seen in the last chapter, arguably the most influential case in the double effect literature is collateral damage in war, formalized by the thought-experiment of Terror Bomber and Strategic Bomber, where the case of a pilot who intends to bomb a school to demoralize the enemy is confronted with the parallel case of a pilot who intends to destroy a munitions factory to demoralize the enemy and foresees that she will also thereby kill children in the nearby school. This case is supposed to have all three of the characteristics we mentioned: (1) the amount of harm is equal (imagine that the same number of children is killed in both air strikes); (3) the two agents have different intentions: Terror Bomber intends to kill the children, says Bratman, while Strategic Bomber 'does not, it seems, intend to kill them' (1987: 140). And the two cases are supposed to be morally different (2): one thing is deliberately targeting children in order to demoralize the enemy; an altogether different thing, it could be argued, it to accept the risk of killing children within an otherwise legitimate military operation.

The dialectic of this issue is clear: if there were no moral difference between Terror Bomber and Strategic Bomber, then it would no longer be clear that the case in question had anything interesting to say about double effect: one could no longer use the case to illustrate double effect, because one would need a case where there is a genuine moral difference between the two scenarios and not just a morally irrelevant intend/foresee difference; and one could also no longer use such cases of collateral damage to motivate the Doctrine of Double Effect – not ones where there is no genuine moral difference anyway.

As we have already mentioned, one should distinguish between a theoretical and a normative issue in the double effect debate: there is the action-theoretical issue of the distinction between intending and merely foreseeing, and there is the ethical issue of the moral relevance of the distinction between intending and merely foreseeing. But double effect, as a moral principle, needs the latter as much as the former. Intuitions have a long tradition in philosophy as a standard for principles, and moral intuitions are no exception. Recently, though, what counts as a stable intuition in philosophy has slightly changed, as philosophers have started asking lay people for their intuitions. In line with this new wave, that has come to be known as 'experimental philosophy', here I report on a study of moral intuitions on collateral damage and the case of Terror Bomber and Strategic Bomber in particular.

2 My experiment

In November 2012, 299 arts and humanities students at my local university took an online survey about the thought-experiment of Terror Bomber and Strategic Bomber. Participants were randomly assigned to either the Terror Bomber scenario (133 participants) or to the Strategic Bomber scenario (166 participants).

Terror Bomber (TB) was put to them as follows:

A bomber pilot plans to bomb an enemy school because she thinks that the death of many children will force the enemy to a quick capitulation. The pilot knows that it won't be possible to effectively bomb the school without also destroying a nearby munitions factory. As planned, the pilot bombs the school and kills many children. As expected, the munitions factory is also destroyed.

Strategic Bomber (SB) was put to them as follows:

A bomber pilot plans to bomb an enemy munitions factory because she thinks that the destruction of the munitions factory will force the enemy to a quick capitulation. The pilot knows that it won't be possible to effectively bomb the munitions factory without also killing many children in a nearby school. As planned, the pilot destroys the munitions factory. As expected, many children in the nearby school also die.

Those presented with TB had to answer one of the following three questions:

1   *Does the bomber pilot intend to kill the children?*
2   *Did the bomber pilot destroy the munitions factory intentionally?*
3   *Is what the bomber pilot does morally wrong?*

Those presented with SB had to answer one of the following three questions:

1   *Does the bomber pilot intend to kill the children?*
2   *Did the bomber pilot kill the children intentionally?*
3   *Is what the bomber pilot does morally wrong?*[1]

Answers were as follows:

Condition	Yes	No	Percentage value Yes/No
TB1	59	8	88.1/11.9
TB2	20	10	66.7/33.3
TB3	31	5	86.1/13.9
SB1	9	20	31/69
SB2	33	23	58.9/41.1
SB3	68	13	84/16

3 Discussion

Two things emerge from the results: participants distinguish between TB and SB in action-theoretical terms[2]; but participants do not distinguish between TB and SB in moral terms.[3] Participants attribute the intention to kill the children only to TB:

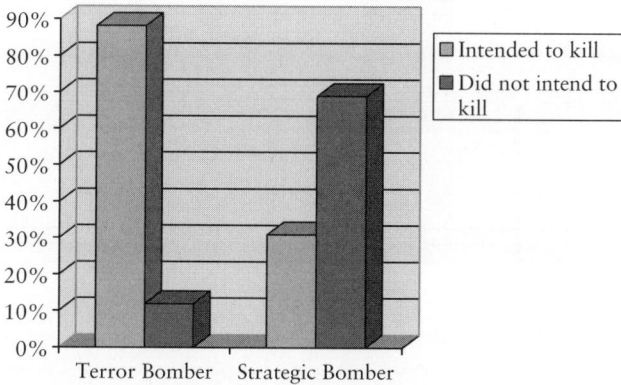

FIGURE 9.1 *Action-theoretical question.*

While participants offer opposing action-theoretical judgements for TB and SB, they offer the same moral judgement for both TB and SB:

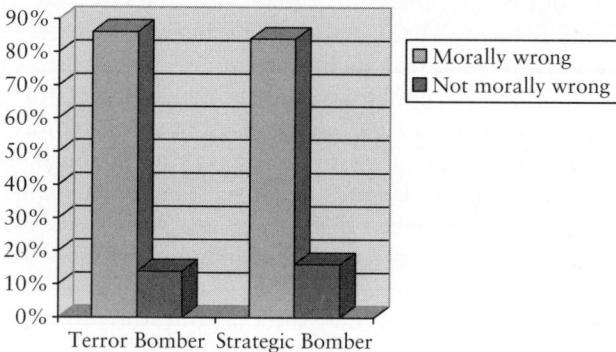

FIGURE 9.2 *Ethical question.*

It also emerges that participants do not equate 'intended to A' with 'A-ed intentionally' (see Chapter 2 on the so-called Simple View of intentional action), as they overwhelmingly characterize SB as not having intended to kill the children while nonetheless having killed the children intentionally.[4]

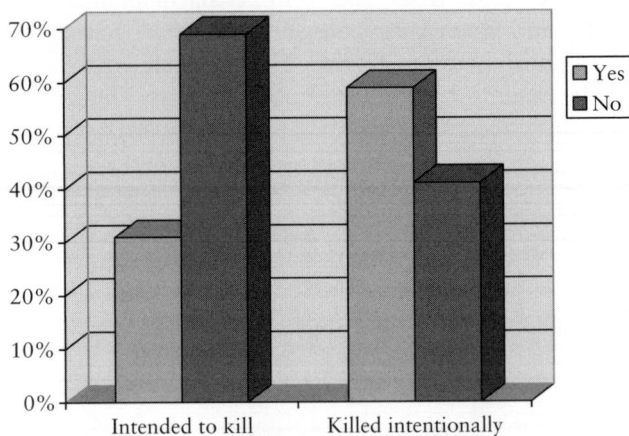

FIGURE 9.3 *Intentionality question.*

So participants appear to have refined enough action-theoretical concepts both to reject the Simple View of intentional action by distinguishing between what is intended and what is done intentionally and to pick up on the distinction between intending and merely foreseeing that, according to the Doctrine of Double Effect, is morally relevant. Unfortunately for the Doctrine, though, participants distinguish between intending and merely foreseeing, but do not appear to think that such distinction is morally relevant.

These results, one could argue, are a mixed bag for double effect: there is some positive from the point of view of double effect to be drawn from one part of the results (the action-theoretical distinction) and there is some negative (that participants don't distinguish morally between the two cases). But I think that even this would be too optimistic a conclusion to draw for a defender of double effect: indeed, I think that the bag is worse than mixed here. Clearly there could have been a better set of results for a defender of double effect (results containing some evidence that participants do distinguish morally between the two cases). But could there have been a worse set of results for a defender of double effect? According to the above mixed bag interpretation, one would say that still worse for double effect would have been if participants had failed to draw even the action-theoretical distinction. That part of the results must support double effect, then.

Imagine that participants hadn't drawn the action-theoretical distinction either. Then, a defender of double effect could have at least argued that the results would then have not been relevant for double effect at all, but only for this particular thought-experiment: the idea being that since the Doctrine of Double Effect is a principle about the moral relevance of a particular action-theoretical distinction, in the absence of such distinction one could not draw any conclusions about the moral relevance of an absent distinction. The experiment may still have had something to say about the TB/SB thought-experiment, but not necessarily about double effect. But the actual results make the relevance to double effect clear by showing that participants do make the distinction that, according to double effect, is morally relevant. They simply don't think that the distinction *is* morally relevant.

Before drawing some conclusions about what these data tell us, there is still one set of results that I have not discussed, namely TB2 and SB2: my hypothesis was that the attribution of intentionality may vary according to the perceived moral value of the action (as has been already overwhelmingly demonstrated to be the case across a wide variety of cases following Knobe 2003), but there is no perceptible difference in the attribution of intentionality to the merely foreseen consequences between TB and SB.[5]

Now, this could be taken to be an exception to what has come to be known as the Knobe Effect, but there is a much simpler explanation that emerges from the rest of the data: as participants do not distinguish morally between TB and SB, then it would have been surprising if we had found a Knobe Effect. In the absence of a moral difference between TB and SB, then, not finding any evidence of the Knobe Effect is exactly what one would have expected – indeed, this further finding could even be said to corroborate the point that there is no moral difference between TB and SB.

4 Moral intuitions and double effect

What can we say about the Doctrine of Double Effect on the basis of these data? What we can certainly not say is that these data show that the Doctrine of Double Effect is false. But that could have never been the point of this study, as no set of data could show that the Doctrine, or any other moral principle, is false.

What we can say is the following: the Doctrine of Double Effect is supposed to be able to explain the intuitive moral difference between cases that are consequentialistically equal by holding that there is a moral difference between intending harm and merely foreseeing harm. An important part of the argument in favour of the Doctrine is constituted by pairs of consequentialistically equal cases that are intuitively morally different. We have looked at arguably the most influential such case in the literature, the thought-experiment involving TB and SB, and surveyed moral intuitions about this case.

We have found no evidence that the layman distinguishes morally between the 'intending' bomber pilot and the 'merely foreseeing' bomber pilot. This, again, should not be overestimated: it neither shows, as we said, the falsity of the Doctrine; nor does it even show that there is no moral difference between TB and SB – quite clearly, there could be a genuine moral difference that the layman does not pick up on. What it does show, though, is that even if there is such a difference, it is not an intuitive moral difference that can be used to motivate the Doctrine: but then the further argument needed to argue for the moral difference may end up making the Doctrine redundant – we have seen such an example in the previous chapter.

Let us stress that last point because I think it is important: what is crucial about the intuitiveness of the moral difference between scenarios such as TB and SB is that the Doctrine could then be offered as a way of analysing an intuitive moral difference. If one needs a further argument to distinguish morally between TB and SB, then who needs the Doctrine anymore? Here there is a dialectical way out, but it is not a promising one for the Doctrine of Double Effect: it could be that there is a moral difference between cases such as TB and SB; that such moral difference is not intuitive; but that such moral difference will not be cashed out by any other moral argument than the Doctrine itself; and that some other independent argument can be brought in favour of the Doctrine of Double Effect. So far, so good: the problem with this option is only that cases like TB and SB then no longer speak in favour of the Doctrine. So whichever way the defender of the Doctrine chooses to go, these data do speak against it.

One important caveat to the above argument needs to be discussed: I have defended the claim that these data speak against the intuitive moral difference between TB and SB and argued that this is a problem for defenders of double effect. It will be objected, though, that the survey was formulated in terms of moral permissibility, and that two morally impermissible cases can still be morally different. That's true, and it would be interesting to test for possible alternative moral differences apart from permissibility. But the Doctrine of Double Effect is a justification principle about moral permissibility: both traditionally and in the contemporary debate (as we have seen in Chapter 2).

One can reformulate the Doctrine – and many attempts have been made to that effect. But one thing is to reformulate the Doctrine of Double Effect as to its conditions; a different thing is to reformulate the Doctrine as to its role, whether justificatory or otherwise. Then, we are no longer talking about the Doctrine of Double Effect but rather about some watered-down criterion for, say, excuse or mitigation. I think there is a lot to be said against a criterion for excuse based on the intend/foresee distinction; and there is also much to be said against a criterion for mitigation based on the intend/foresee distinction. But those would really be altogether different principles from the Doctrine, so that their discussion does not belong here (see Chapter 12 on this issue).

One could, alternatively, accept my point about permissibility but deny that these results say anything interesting about the Doctrine as a permissibility principle on the grounds that there may be other things that explain why the overwhelming majority thinks that both TB and SB act impermissibly: respondents may have been absolute pacifists; or they may have been some sort of children-absolutists who draw the line in war at violence against children; or they may have been neither pacifists nor particularly bothered by the welfare of children in war but would have required more details about the advantages of a shortening of the war to justify so much violence: how much shorter? How many lives would thereby be saved? Those are all plausible possibilities, but they are not particularly damaging to the significance of these data because they apply across the board to any application of the Doctrine to TB and SB.

Take as illustration the case of absolute pacifism: absolute pacifists will supposedly judge both cases as impermissible independently of any double effect-related considerations. But that does not speak against the data presented here: it rather speaks against there being a moral difference between TB and SB in terms of permissibility which double effect can explain. The point of this study was exactly to look at possible evidence of moral intuition which would be favourable to double effect in collateral damage cases: what may explain the absence of such double effect-friendly intuitions does not speak against this study but rather makes the findings of this study more plausible.

I have discussed in the last chapter how I think the TB/SB thought-experiment should be dealt with independently of double effect, so here I will just briefly discuss the plausibility of the answers given by respondents. One important consideration is that in this study participants were confronted with properly symmetric sets of consequences: one should at least note, for example, that the destruction of the munitions factory is mentioned in TB too, while in most discussions of the thought-experiment one normally gets a SB scenario containing both the school and the factory and a TB scenario containing only the school (see previous chapter).

This is important in two respects: (a) whatever one thinks of the moral value of the factory, even if the destruction of the factory is not a morally relevant consequence, having scenarios that are different in their non-moral consequences may bias intuitions. Also, (b), the following may explain why participants distinguished TB and SB action-theoretically but not morally: maybe TB set out to attack the school because she didn't believe that attacking the munitions factory would demoralize the enemy and shorten the war; or (inclusive disjunctive) maybe SB set out to attack the munitions factory because she didn't believe that attacking the school would demoralize the enemy and shorten the war. These considerations point to the following counterfactuals: (1) had TB believed that attacking the factory would have demoralized the enemy, she would have not targeted the school; (2) had SB believed that attacking the school would have demoralized enemy, she would have not targeted the factory.

One may think, and maybe that is something like what participants thought, that any combination of these two counterfactuals apart from the negation of both of them (so three different combinations: $[1 \wedge 2]$; $[1 \wedge \neg 2]$; and $[\neg 1 \wedge 2]$) would motivate thinking that, given the identity of morally relevant consequences, there was not enough ground to distinguish, morally, between what the two agents did.

This solution, importantly, would be alternative to double effect, but it would not be a consequentialist solution, as it would take into account something other than just the moral consequences, namely the above counterfactuals. Alternatively, it may indeed be that what explains the participants' judgement are consequentialist considerations. And there are possibly other explanations too: here I just meant to give some theoretical background to the participants' judgement, and I meant to show that their judgements *need not* be interpreted consequentialistically.

5 Conclusion

In conclusion, here I have presented a study of intuitions on collateral damages in war where participants were presented with the philosophical thought-experiment of Terror Bomber and Strategic Bomber which has played such a dominant role in recent discussions of the Doctrine of Double Effect: the study's results indicate that participants are able to distinguish theoretically between intending harm and merely foreseeing harm but do not distinguish, morally, between what the Terror Bomber does and what the Strategic Bomber does.

CHAPTER TEN

Bioethical applications: The example of embryo loss and stem cell research

Abstract *I defend the argument that if embryo loss in stem cell research is morally problematic, then embryo loss in in vivo conception is similarly morally problematic. According to a recent challenge to this argument, we can distinguish between in vivo embryo loss and the in vitro embryo loss of stem cell research by appealing to the Doctrine of Double Effect. I argue that this challenge fails to show that in vivo embryo loss is a mere unintended side effect while in vitro embryo loss is an intended means and that, even if we refine the challenge by appealing to Michael Bratman's three roles of intention, the distinction is still unwarranted.*

1 Introduction

Bioethics has historically been a very fertile ground for the Doctrine of Double Effect. Even though, if one accepts the standard attribution to Aquinas's discussion of self-defence (which I have challenged in Chapter 3), double effect cannot be said to have been born out of bioethical debates, it has been classically used by the Catholic Church to allow for some forms of abortion, and that has generated huge interest and debate around the Doctrine (for academic standards, anyway). We have already seen in Chapter 6 the difficulties in using double effect to claim that some forms of therapeutical abortions could possibly be justified while others must still be forbidden – so I will not replicate those arguments here.

Abortion is only one example from bioethics and medical ethics. It may not even be the most famous one, if we think about death-inducing pain alleviation and the attempts to distinguish such therapeutical interventions from euthanasia through appeals to the Doctrine of Double Effect. As we mentioned in Chapter 3 already, those kinds of arguments are misplaced since there is overwhelming medical evidence that the sort of dosages of opioid drugs which are effective against pain do not actually hasten death (Sykes and Thorns 2003).

Since this book is a purely theoretical discussion of double effect, I have chosen not to apply my arguments against double effect neither to all possible bioethical applications nor to all the famous ones, but just to pick one example which I find particularly interesting and which should serve as illustration of how double effect has been used and can be used in bioethics and medical ethics. Before discussing the stem cell case, let me say why I have chosen this particular one: it is because I find it more promising – in two different respects – than the other classic applications. On the one hand, as I have argued in Chapter 6, I find the abortion cases particularly bad illustrations of double effect. On the other hand, as I said in Chapter 3 and repeated here, I think that the discussions of double effect in relation to death-inducing pain alleviation have to be considered purely academic in the pejorative sense, namely that they do not have any application for known medication – at least if you believe the medical evidence I cite above. This is why I chose to deal – in this chapter – with the topic of stem cell research.

Stem cell research is sometimes criticized on the grounds that the embryo loss that it causes is morally problematic (Finnis 1995; Holm 2003). A standard reply to this charge is to point out that embryo loss is also involved in the mundane practice of trying to conceive and conceiving children through sexual intercourse (Brock 2006; Harris 2007; Sparrow 2009). According to this argument, if stem cell research is ethically problematic because of its embryo loss, then trying to conceive and conceiving children through sexual intercourse is similarly ethically problematic; but since trying to conceive and conceiving children is obviously not ethically problematic – or so this argument goes – stem cell research is also not ethically problematic.

Recently the disjunctive premise of this argument in defence of stem cell research has been challenged by application of the Doctrine of Double Effect (Murphy forthcoming). According to this challenge, by appealing to double effect one can distinguish between the embryo loss involved in stem cell research and the embryo loss involved in the mundane practice of trying to conceive and conceiving children through sexual intercourse. The Doctrine of Double Effect could then be used to morally justify the latter but not the former. The idea is, in short, the following: both in vivo conception and stem cell research involve embryo loss. But embryo loss is an intended means of stem cell research while embryo loss is only a merely foreseen unintended side effect in the case of in vivo conception.

The Doctrine of Double Effect says that, in pursuing the good, we may sometimes bring about some evil as long as such evil is not intended and as long as such evil is not out of proportion with the good we are pursuing. So merely foreseen unintended evil can, under certain conditions, be morally justifiable, while intended evil can never be morally justifiable. If embryo loss is intended evil in stem cell research, then, according to the Doctrine, it cannot be morally justifiable. And if embryo loss is a merely foreseen unintended side effect in in vivo conception, then it can be morally justifiable as long as the evil involved in embryo loss is proportional to the good involved in the conception of children. Murphy argues exactly along these lines that embryo loss in in vivo conception is not an intended means; that in vivo conception is driven by the good intention to procreate; and that the embryo loss involved is proportional to the good represented by procreation.

2 Murphy's argument

Here I argue against this appeal to double effect in two steps: I first show the failings of Murphy's particular argument, and then I offer a more general critique of appeals to the Doctrine of Double Effect in line with the arguments of the rest of the book. I leave Murphy's discussion of IVF to the side, as it has already been criticized elsewhere (Devolder forthcoming). Murphy's discussion is divided into three parts, reflecting three classic elements of DDE: the value of the intention and action in itself; the intended means as opposed to merely foreseen side effects distinction; and proportionality. Here I argue that his discussion of each of these three elements is defective.

A. First of all, I take issue with Murphy's claim that 'The intention to have children is not, therefore, morally disqualified in itself' (forthcoming) on the grounds that 'for most of human history, the scope of zygote and embryo loss would have been unknowable to people trying to have children. Earlier human beings would not have even been able to link the two effects into a single motive' (forthcoming). This talk of action in itself and intention in itself (which is characteristic of double effect, see Mangan's already quoted first condition requiring 'that the action in itself from its very object be good or at least indifferent' (Mangan 1949)) is too permissive: that a morally questionable effect of an action (in this case, embryo loss) has been previously unknown cannot be a justification for the 'action in itself' or 'intention in itself' even after the morally questionable effect has been established. After we found out that Thalidomide caused very serious physical malformations, then the act or intention of prescribing Thalidomide was morally disqualified in itself. This suggests that we should abandon this part of the Doctrine and focus only on the distinction between intended and merely foreseen and on the issue of proportionality – and this move has indeed become standard among contemporary commentators (see Chapter 2).

B. Murphy claims that 'the death of some embryos is not inherently a condition of success for conception in vivo that results in children, so that we cannot treat efforts to achieve conception in vivo as involving a necessary evil used as the means to a good end' (forthcoming); this is because 'Some conception, implantation and gestation occur without loss of zygotes, embryos or fetuses' (forthcoming). This is a misunderstanding of the conception of 'means' in the double effect debate. Whether or not something counts as an intended means is not a mind-independent matter of extensional necessity: it is a purely intensional matter. Being extensionally necessary is neither necessary nor sufficient to being an intended means. It can't be sufficient, quite obviously, because that something is extensionally necessary does not imply that it is intended. And it isn't necessary either: take one of the classic cases of impermissible intended means in the double effect debate, Terror Bomber (see Chapter 8). Terror Bomber intends to kill the school children in order to demoralize the enemy. Killing the school children is Terror Bomber's intended means to her end of demoralizing the enemy. But that does not mean that killing school children is necessary to demoralizing the enemy (even though it may be sufficient): there are plenty of alternative ways of demoralizing the enemy which do not involve killing school children. All the same, killing school children is an intended means even if it is not extensionally necessary.

Also, extensional necessity cannot be the right criterion because it does not distinguish between intended means and merely foreseen side effects. In both scenarios of the Trolley Problem, *Bystander at the Switch* and *Fat Man*, the death of the one is extensionally necessary. But that is not taken to mean that in both cases the death of the one is an intended means, as the Trolley Problem was developed exactly to illustrate the distinction between intended means and merely foreseen side effects that the Doctrine is found on.

To further illustrate how implausible Murphy's proposal is, imagine that we could finally effectively conduct stem cell research without destroying embryos but that some scientists deliberately continued to destroy embryos. Murphy's conception would here deliver the weird outcome that those scientists would *now* be allowed to destroy embryos because the embryo loss would no longer be extensionally necessary while they would have been previously not allowed – namely the very opposite verdict that one would have reasonably expected even from Murphy's own point of view.

C. As we said, for a defence of in vivo embryo loss through double effect, one needs the bad effect (embryo loss) to be proportional to the good effect (procreation). And indeed Murphy argues that the bad of embryo loss is not out of proportion with the good of having children. This, indeed, does not sound implausible on the face of it. But rather than considering this point at face value, we should see that the defence of in vivo embryo loss through double effect is a step in an argument against embryo loss in stem cell research. And that wider argument is funded on the premise that embryos are either persons or potential persons or anyway near enough to persons to be deserving of some moral status. This premise is very clear in Murphy's argument too: 'In the discussion that follows, I will treat all conceived human organisms as persons' (forthcoming).

So embryos, at least for the sake of the argument under discussion, are persons. But if embryos are indeed persons, then it is not at all clear that the proportionality condition will be met. Murphy cites two different estimates on in vivo embryo loss, and according to both the number of embryos who die in the course of in vivo conception is greater than the number of children who are born (Brock 2006). If embryos are persons (and babies too), then according to these estimates in vivo conception kills more persons than it gives birth too. This is obviously still different from the claim that in vivo conception kills more persons than it creates – as that claim is necessarily false if all are thought to be persons. Still, the sacrifice of persons involved in in vivo conception is, on this argument, very great: this practice kills more persons than it does not kill, for example.[1] It will not do, here, to propose that one drop the premise according to which embryos are persons. Because once that premise is dropped, then the argument against stem cell research that the Doctrine is supposed to defend no longer holds – at least in the form under discussion.[2]

3 Double effect and embryo loss

So far I have only argued that Murphy's particular appeal to double effect is problematic. That does not mean, it will be objected, that one cannot appeal to double effect at all. In the rest of this chapter, I look at alternative possible appeals to double effect, arguing that the problem is the Doctrine itself and not simply its application to embryo loss. We have shown the problems with Murphy's attempt to argue that the embryo loss involved in in vivo conception is not intended while the embryo loss involved in stem cell research is intended: his appeal to extensional necessity misrepresents double effect. What could we rather appeal to in order to distinguish between intended means and merely foreseen side effects?

Let us try to use Bratman's already discussed three roles of intention: (i) 'posing problems for further reasoning', (ii) 'constraining other intentions' and (iii) 'issuing in corresponding endeavouring'. Terror Bomber's intention will (i) pose the problem of how he is going to kill the children: 'Terror Bomber must figure out, for example, what time of day to attack and what sorts of bombs to use' (1987: 141). (ii) Terror Bomber's intention will also be incompatible with other possible strategies. Terror Bomber may not, for example, implement a plan to deploy some troops if this deployment would result in the enemy evacuating the children: 'So Terror Bomber's prior intention to kill the children stands in the way of his forming a new intention to order the troop movement' (1987: 141). (iii) Terror Bomber will also guide his conduct so as to cause the death of the children: 'If in midair he learns they have moved to a different school, he will try to keep track of them and take his bombs there' (1987: 141).

Those roles, on the other hand, do not apply, according to Bratman, to Strategic Bomber's attitude towards killing the children: Strategic Bomber will not engage in practical reasoning about how to kill the children; if further intentions of Strategic Bomber should be incompatible with killing the children, that will not be a prima facie reason to disregard them; and, to put the point crudely, if the children move, Strategic Bomber will not follow them.

Similarly, a couple trying to conceive through sexual intercourse will not engage in practical reasoning about how to kill embryos; if their further intentions should be incompatible with killing embryos, that will be no reason to disregard those intentions; and, finally, if for some reason the embryos appear to be surviving, the couple has no reason to react to this turn of events. Indeed, the couple will normally not be in a position to monitor whether or not there is embryo loss; and the fact that this state of affairs makes no difference to the couple suggests that indeed they are indifferent to embryo loss and therefore that they do not intend embryo loss.

The problem is that we can say the same of the stem cell researcher: should embryos somehow survive her research intact, she will not 'go after them'. Similarly, the researcher will have no reason to disregard intentions which are incompatible with killing embryos; and the researcher will not engage in practical reasoning about how to kill embryos. So this analysis of intention does not warrant the claim that in vivo conception does not involve the intention to kill embryos while stem cell research does.

Here it could be objected that the latter claims misrepresent the empirical facts about how stem cell research is conducted, and that because of the way in which stem cell research is conducted a stem cell researcher does indeed need to, for example, engage in practical reasoning about how to kill embryos. So let us then look in some more detail at how stem cell research works:

> HESCs are derived *in vitro* around the fifth day of the embryo's development. A typical day-5 human embryo consists of 200–250 cells, most of which comprise the trophoblast, which is the outermost layer of the blastocyst. HESCs are harvested from the inner cell mass of the blastocyst, which consists of 30–34 cells. The derivation of HESC cultures requires the removal of the trophoblast. This process of disaggregating the blastocyst's cells eliminates its potential for further development. (*Ethics of Stem Cell Research* entry of the Stanford Encyclopaedia of Philosophy[3])

Let us remember that we are assuming that embryos are persons. On that assumption, an opponent to stem cell research could compare the above procedure to removing vital organs from an adult human being in order to save the life of many other adult human beings and then ask whether it would be at all plausible, in this alternative case, to claim that the surgeon who removes the vital organs did not intend the death of the adult human being in question. The idea being that it is preposterous to claim that the surgeon did not intend to kill the person from which she is removing vital organs. But let us put that to the test of the three roles of intention: does the surgeon need to engage in practical reasoning about how to kill the adult human being in question? No, she only needs to deliberate about how to remove the required organs. Will the surgeon kill the adult human being in case the patient would miraculously survive the successful removal of the required organs? No she wouldn't because she is only interested in the organs. Yes, but the surgeon knows that the patient will die.

That's true, but let us not forget that this epistemic condition does not distinguish the two cases: we know that there will be embryo loss in in vivo conception too.[4] Indeed, the in vivo conception case seems to be even worse, like if our surgeon would have to perform lethal surgery on various different people before she got the one whose organs will do the job. Similarly, a couple will have to cause the loss of various embryos before one develops into a foetus and then a child. Indeed, there is another disanalogy between in vivo conception and the original surgeon which, again, does not reflect well on in vivo conception. Not all embryo loss caused by in vivo conception will ultimately result in a baby (couples may give up, split up, die, etc.): this is as if the surgeon would perform the lethal surgery many times without even being sure that she will finally get the passing organs.

It may be objected that showing that we can't effectively distinguish between in vivo conception and stem cell research by appeal to double effect is not enough, because there may be other ways, independent of the Doctrine of Double Effect, to draw that distinction. This point would bring us too far from the topic of this paper, but I want to briefly discuss at least the most important alternative, the distinction between actions and omissions and the related distinction between killing and letting die. On this interpretation, one would argue that only the stem cell researcher kills embryos while a couple trying to have children does not *kill* embryos – merely letting embryos die. But I really can't see how one could defend this position in this particular case, whatever one thinks about its general merits: the couple freely and actively engages in an activity that she knows will cause the death of embryos the same way in which the researcher freely and actively engages in an activity that she knows will cause the death of embryos. Both are clear cases of action rather than omission.

4 Conclusion

In conclusion, I have defended the argument that if the embryo loss involved in stem cell research is morally problematic, then the embryo loss involved in in vivo conception is similarly morally problematic. I have argued that appeals to the Doctrine of Double Effect fail to make a case for a morally relevant distinction between embryo losses in the two cases because one cannot make sense of the distinction between intended embryo loss in stem cell research and merely foreseen embryo loss in in vivo conception. Importantly, here I have presented a challenge to the distinction between intended harm and merely foreseen harm in general (in line with my arguments in the whole book) and not only a challenge to its particular application to this one case.

CHAPTER ELEVEN

What shall i do? The Doctrine cannot tell us how we may permissibly act

Abstract *It is sometimes held against the Doctrine of Double Effect that it cannot tell agents what they should (or may) do: Jonathan Bennett, Thomas Scanlon and Judith Jarvis Thomson are prominent examples of this sort of challenge. Ralph Wedgwood has recently argued against this particular challenge to the Doctrine of Double Effect on the grounds that we should understand the Doctrine as applying to thick act-types or plans; and that the Doctrine can actually distinguish, morally, between different thick act-types or plans; and that therefore it can tell agents which thick act-types or plans they may choose. Here I argue against this defence of the Doctrine, showing that it is subject to well-known problems that we have already dealt with in this book. The Doctrine of Double Effect, then, can't even tell agents what they should do, so that it fails to fulfil a basic function of normative principles.*

1 Introduction

Normative ethics answers questions of the following two sorts[1]:

1 What may/ought/shall I (to) do?
2 How may/ought/shall I (to) judge others?[2]

Normative theories offer the same general answer to both sorts of questions, so that utilitarianism for example suggests maximizing utility as the criterion for both the first and the second sort of question (similarly, the categorical imperative – to mention another famous example – is a criterion that can answer both sorts of questions).

It is sometimes held against the Doctrine of Double Effect that it cannot answer questions of the first sort.[3] Here is Thomson:

> Suppose a pilot comes to us with a request for advice: "See, we're at war with a villainous country called Bad, and my superiors have ordered me to drop some bombs at Placetown in Bad. Now there's a munitions factory at Placetown, but there's a children's hospital there too. Is it permissible for me to drop the bombs?" And suppose we make the following reply: "Well, it all depends on what your intentions would be in dropping the bombs. If you would be intending to destroy the munitions factory and thereby win the war, merely foreseeing, though not intending, the deaths of the children, then yes, you may drop the bombs. On the other hand, if you would be intending to destroy the children and thereby terrorize the Bads and thereby win the war, merely foreseeing, though not intending, the destruction of the munitions factory, then no, you may not drop the bombs." What a queer performance this would be! (1991: 293)[4]

Scanlon has a similar case, explicitly inspired by Thomson's[5]:

> Suppose you were prime minister, and the commander of the air force described to you a planned air raid that would be expected to destroy a munitions plant and also kill a certain number of civilians, thereby probably undermining [the enemy's] public support for the war. If he asked whether you thought this was

morally permissible, you would not say, "Well, that depends on what your intentions would be in carrying it out. Would you be intending to kill the civilians, or would their deaths be merely an unintended but foreseeable (albeit beneficial) side effect of the destruction of the plant?" (2008: 19–20)

Those thought-experiments are in turn indebted to Bennett's remarks:

[The Doctrine of Double Effect] is a much odder position than is commonly recognized As a rule, if it is worse to intend to bring about X than to intend to bring about Y, that is because X is worse than Y; but here the moral difference is supposed to be introduced by the intention, rather than existing at the intention level only because of a difference at the level of events in the world . . . it is a mistake to think of first-order morality – morality for the guidance of deliberating agents – as making any use of the concept of the deliberator's future intentions. The morality I consult as a guide to my conduct does also guide my intentions, but not by telling me what I may or may not intend. It speaks to me of what I may or may not do, and of what are or are not good reasons for various kinds of action; and in that way it guides my intentions without speaking to me about them. The concept of intention has a role in second-order morality, i.e., in guiding judgments on people in respect of past actions. How much I blame someone depends in part on his intentions in acting; and if it is I who am in the dock then it is my intentions that I must consider. But they are my past intentions, and I treat them as external objects of judgment like anyone else's. Nothing in this is remotely like consulting a moral rule which forbids me to have such and such an intention. (1980: 96–7)

We can now illustrate the difference between moral questions of the first kind and moral questions of the second kind in relation to the Doctrine of Double Effect: on the one hand, morality must answer the pilot who wants to know what she may/ought/shall (to) do, should she drop the bombs or should she not drop the bombs – that is the pilot's moral dilemma. And the critics' contention is that the Doctrine of Double Effect has simply no answer to the pilot's legitimate moral questioning.[6]

Once the bombing has taken place, then the Doctrine may, on the other hand, be able to offer guidance as to the moral value of what has taken place: it may indeed distinguish between two different ways in which events could have developed, and conclude that, in one case, what the pilot of Strategic Bomber does is permissible while in the other case what the pilot of Terror Bomber does is not permissible.

2 Thick act-types

Ralph Wedgwood has defended the Doctrine from the charge that it cannot answer questions of the first kind:

What the DDE says about this case is that there are stronger reasons against the thick act-type dropping the bombs with the intention of killing civilians than against the thick act-type dropping the bombs with the intention of destroying the munitions plant. So the DDE supports the conclusion that the former act-type is impermissible, while the latter is permissible. But this conclusion does not imply that what the bomber should do is determined by any purely psychological facts about the intentions that he would have if he dropped the bombs. It simply implies that he ought not to drop the bombs with the intention of killing the civilians. It is irrelevant if he has the property that if he were to drop the bombs, he would do it with the intention of killing the civilians – after all, that is presumably a property that he ought not to have. So you should respond to the bomber as follows: "You may drop the bombs, but only with the aim of destroying the munitions plant. You may not drop the bombs with the aim of killing the civilians; that would be wrong." If the bomber retorts, "Actually, I hate the enemy so much that were I to drop the bombs, I would be doing it with the intention of killing their civilians", then you should reply: "For the purposes of answering your question, I am not interested in your despicable attitudes towards enemy civilians. I am telling you what plan you may adopt. You may adopt the plan of destroying the munitions plant by means of dropping the bombs, and you may not adopt the plan of killing the civilians by means of dropping those bombs: the plan that you may adopt would still be carried out if your dropping the bombs somehow destroyed the munitions plant without killing the civilians; it would not be carried out if your dropping the bombs killed the civilians without destroying the munitions plant." (2011a: 4–5)

The Doctrine, claims Wedgwood, does answer the pilot: the pilot is morally permitted to 'drop bombs without the intention to kill children' but she is not morally permitted to 'drop bombs with the intention to kill children' (or at least, but that's not the controversial issue here: the latter thick act-type is morally worse than the former thick act-type).[7]

One could propose the following here. If the question had been asked by Terror Bomber, then she would have had an answer: she may *not* drop the bombs because her plan is to drop the bombs with the intention to kill the children, and she may not adopt that plan nor 'drop bombs with the intention to kill children'. And if the question had been asked by Strategic Bomber, then she would have had an answer too: she *may* drop the bombs because her plan is to drop bombs with the intention of destroying the munitions factory and without the intention to kill children, and she may adopt that plan (she may, viz. 'drop bombs without the intention to kill children'). So the pilot gets an answer to the question of whether she may drop the bombs both in the case of Terror Bomber and in the case of Strategic Bomber.

Obviously, though, the success of this solution cannot just depend on whether the pilot has already *adopted* a certain plan or formed certain intentions; it cannot depend on actual plans and intentions because, first, the pilot may consult moral council before she has set on any plans or intentions exactly in order to work out what sort of plans or intentions she should settle on; and, secondly, because the pilot who has already settled on a certain plan or intention is not supposed to be able to answer: 'Well, I will just drop my intention, then, and go through with it'.

It may be objected, here, that agents cannot just *drop* their intentions. But that won't do, as whichever view of intention one takes, the issue here cannot depend on *actual* intentions. If intentions were indeed droppable – maybe because one would adopt an agential view of intentions according to which they are a bit like decisions and decisions are in turn a bit like actions which can be avoided, inhibited and reversed – then the problem would be the one illustrated above, namely that someone who were to be said that she may 'drop bombs without the intention to kill children' would simply go ahead as before without the intention (either because she has dropped it in the case in which she had already settled on a plan or because she never forms it in the first place in order to be morally permitted to bring about the relevant effect).

Obviously, one could deny the above view of intentions and hold that a pilot who were to be said that she may 'drop bombs without the intention to kill children' would not be able to simply drop her previously formed intentions: intentions don't work like that; we cannot control them as easily as that objection presupposes. But this case won't do either, because then we would make the moral permissibility of something depend on something else which is not controllable and we would thereby violate 'ought implies can'. In short, then, whichever view of intention one takes, the issue here cannot be *actual* intentions.

The problem, then, must be whether some effect *can* be brought about without intending it, so that in telling us that we may 'drop bombs without the intention to kill children', the Doctrine is telling us that we may only bring about bad effects which can be brought about unintended. If – in the relevant scenario – dropping bombs can be carried out without the intention to kill children, then go ahead and drop bombs; if it cannot be carried out without the intention to kill children, then stop: this seems to be Wedgwood's defence of double effect. Whatever the agent's *actual* intention, then, double effect's answer is that if the children can be killed without the intention to kill them (and other conditions are met, obviously, but that's not the point here), then the pilot may go ahead (or at least, if we are not talking about permissibility, then the pilot's behaviour should be judged more leniently than her actions in the case in which the children cannot be killed without the intention to kill them).

This point has already been made in defence of the Doctrine of Double Effect by FitzPatrick: in replying to Thomson, he says that 'none of this constitutes a real objection to the DDE, because the DDE does not in fact link the moral permissibility of an act with the token intentions with which a given agent would be acting. Rather, it links the permissibility of a certain type of act with the existence of a justification in terms of a sufficiently worthy end that can be pursued through so acting without intending anything illicit as a means' (2003: 319).

In applying his argument against actual intentions to terror bombing, FitzPatrick writes:

> But while a particular pilot sent to bomb a munitions plant may harbour such an intention, the fact remains that there exists a sufficient justification for bombing the munitions plant simply in terms of its military significance, such that one could so act for the justifying end without intending the deaths of innocents. This is sufficient to declare the act morally permissible as far as intention is concerned, and this permissibility is not further affected by the actual intentions of particular agents. (2003: 320)

Let us clarify how this position should not be misunderstood with an extensional interpretation of double effect. In Chapter 2, we have seen how double effect is normally interpreted intensionally and how problematic it would be to interpret it extensionally – so I will not repeat those arguments here. But one should not understand the kind of defence of double effect at play here as an extensional interpretation of double effect: the point is not, for example, whether killing the children is a necessary extensional means to destroy the munitions factory.[8]

Applying the point about actual and possible intentions to Wedgwood, then, what distinguishes the thick act-type 'dropping bombs with the intention to kill children' from the thick act-types 'dropping bombs without the intention to kill children' and 'dropping bombs with only the intention to destroy munitions' are not the actual attitudes of the agents involved but whether the relevant plans would necessarily involve an intention to kill children. And this is clear from Wedgwood's own text, when he writes:

> If the bomber retorts, "Actually, I hate the enemy so much that were I to drop the bombs, I would be doing it with the intention of killing their civilians", then you should reply: "For the purposes of answering your question, I am not interested in your despicable attitudes towards enemy civilians. I am telling you what plan you may adopt. You may adopt the plan of destroying the munitions plant by means of dropping the bombs, and you

may not adopt the plan of killing the civilians by means of dropping those bombs: the plan that you may adopt would still be carried out if your dropping the bombs somehow destroyed the munitions plant without killing the civilians; it would not be carried out if your dropping the bombs killed the civilians without destroying the munitions plant." (2011a: 5)[9]

3 Closeness and thick act-types

There is, then, only one question left to settle the issue between critics such as Thomson, Scanlon and Bennett and supporters such as Wedgwood and FitzPatrick: how do we determine whether the relevant plan can be possibly carried out without the incriminated intention?[10]

First of all, let us see why Wedgwood's proposed solution will not do. The pilot comes asking whether she may drop the bombs. She is told that she may adopt the plan of dropping the bombs to destroy the munitions factory but not the plan of dropping bombs to kill the children. So the permissibility of dropping bombs depends on which plan the pilot adopts. The pilot may reply that her plan is to drop the bombs in order to weaken enemy, and that she believes that dropping the bombs will cause both the destruction of the munitions factory and the killing of the children. At that point, the moral council asks the question which is supposed to be the decisive one according to Wedgwood: would your plan still be carried out if your dropping the bombs somehow destroyed the munitions plant without killing the civilians? Would it be carried out if your dropping the bombs killed the civilians without destroying the munitions plant?

The answers must be YES to the former question and NO to the latter question: in that case, you may go ahead. The problem for Wedgwood – and it is a familiar one from previous chapters – is that the pilot may truthfully reply the following: to the question of whether the plan would still be carried out even if the bombs somehow destroyed the munitions without killing the children, the pilot may reply that, as long as the enemy has been weakened, her plan would still be carried out even if the children were to be spared somehow. And to the question of whether the plan would still be carried out even if the bombs somehow killed the children without destroying munitions the pilot would also reply that, as long as the enemy has been weakened, her plan would still be carried out even if the munitions were to be spared somehow.[11]

Let us now return to the question of how to determine whether some plan can be possibly carried out without the incriminated intention. Since the discussion is now general and no longer just about Wedgwood's defence of double effect, we should also say that here nothing should hang on the talk of plans, so that the question can also be formulated in terms of whether some bad effect can be possibly brought about without intending to bring it about. And the reader will have probably already noticed that this is, now that it has been explicitly formulated, a question which has already been addressed in this book.

Take the classic example again: 'Am I allowed to detonate the explosives in order to free us?'; the answer will depend – we have seen in this chapter – on whether I can free us without thereby having to necessarily intend to kill the fat guy who is blocking the cave's mouth. And we have argued in Chapter 6 that attempts at dealing with the problem of closeness fail to show that I cannot free us without thereby intending to kill the fat guy. But if I am allowed to do that, then what on earth I am still not allowed to do?

Here we don't need to replicate any of the arguments already presented in this book. The issue is that we will have serious difficulties – as illustrated especially in Chapter 6 – to distinguish those effects that can be brought about without intending to bring them about from those effects that cannot be brought about without intending to bring them about. So that if the Doctrine's answer to the question 'Am I allowed to do that?' will depend on whether we can do the thing in question without intending to bring about the negative effect, and we cannot offer the conditions under which an effect cannot be brought about without intending to bring it about, then the Doctrine will have to allow for everything that meets the other conditions of the Doctrine and always answer in the positive when the other conditions are met.

And even if here one wanted to argue that the burden of proof is misplaced so that the Doctrine would have to always answer in the negative rather than the positive, the point clearly is that the Doctrine is not able to distinguish between the effects that can be brought about without necessarily intending to bring them about and the effects that cannot be brought about without necessarily intending to bring them about – so that its answer to the question 'Am I allowed to do that?' will either have to be always negative or always positive and therefore useless.

I shall put this point also explicitly in Wedgwood's terms to show that we have not departed from the content of his defence of double effect: Wedgwood's idea is that the Doctrine can rule against thick act-types which contain intentions to bring about negative effects such as the thick act-type 'dropping bombs with the intention to kill children'; here we have not said that the Doctrine cannot rule against such thick act-types (viz. we have not engaged in the normative arguments), but we have shown that – given that what makes out a thick act-type containing a certain intention is not whether or not the agent actually has that intention but whether that intention is necessary for the agent's plan – agents never have to perform such thick act-types (see Foot's cave) and so the prohibition against those is empty.

Let me also say that since we have established early on in this book (Chapter 2) that only one other of the Doctrine's classic conditions is non-redundant – namely proportionality – then the Doctrine's answer to the question 'Am I allowed to do that?' will have to depend on the proportionality condition alone: and then the normative justification of the proportionality condition (Kantian, Utilitarian or whatever takes one's fancy) will be all that is left to the Doctrine's answer to the question 'Am I allowed to do that?'

4 Conclusion

In conclusion, here I have shown that the Doctrine of Double Effect has a further problem: it cannot tell agents how they may permissibly act and it is therefore useless as an action-guiding normative principle. Even though this chapter has dealt with a claim that had not been discussed in the rest of the book, the arguments that I have brought to bear to justify the claim that the Doctrine of Double Effect cannot tell us what we may permissibly do are familiar ones from previous chapters.

CHAPTER TWELVE

Concluding remarks: Responsibility, character and *Mends*

Abstract *In this final chapter, I look at what is left of double effect at the end of a book full of arguments against it: I explore the hypothesis that even though double effect may not make sense as a principle of moral justification, its founding distinction between intended means and merely foreseen side effects may still make a difference to an agent's responsibility. I argue – against Antony Duff and the evidence from the Knobe Effect – that the distinction between intended means and merely foreseen side effects makes no difference to responsibility either. I propose a different way of looking at this normative issue – what I call the moral correlate of sentencing. Also, I conclude by putting forward an alternative understanding of reasoning in double effect cases, where I distinguish between Ends, Mends and Means.*

1 Introduction

Throughout this book, I have been arguing against the Doctrine of Double Effect as a principle of moral justification. If you have made it this far, you probably won't have found my arguments completely implausible; at the same time, if you have made it this far, you probably won't have found my thesis totally obvious either. Now, whichever place in the scale between not completely implausible and almost totally obvious you happen to occupy, you may wonder what – at the end of a book full of arguments against it – we should make of the Doctrine of Double Effect. And even if you thought, like I do, that the answer to this question is rather simple – namely that we should abandon once and for all the Doctrine as a principle of moral justification – you may consider one of the following two issues still worth talking about: first, if the Doctrine is flawed and should therefore be abandoned, why have so many clever and illustrious people down the centuries found it so compelling?

Secondly, once we have abandoned the Doctrine of Double Effect as a principle of moral justification, is there any job left for it? Ok, maybe it can't do moral justification, but can it really not do anything at all? Those two questions are, unsurprisingly, related to each other: if there was something more or less closely related to moral justification that the Doctrine or something close enough to it turned out to be able to deal with, then maybe that would also explain the Doctrine's appeal through the ages.

In this concluding chapter, I look at this very possibility: the hypothesis being that even though the Doctrine can't do moral justification, it (or something related to it, anyway) may be able to do other normative work – and that this is what has made it so compelling through the centuries (even though this latter issue won't concern me here, in keeping with the theoretical focus of the rest of the book). I will pursue the above hypothesis by looking at two moral concepts which are related to but independent from moral justification (well, the 'independent' bit does turn out to depend on your moral theory, but that's unimportant here): character and responsibility. Let us start from the latter and make our way towards the former. In the final section, then, I offer an alternative understanding of double effect reasoning by distinguishing among Ends, *Mends* and Means.

What does double effect have to do with responsibility? After all, you would think that nobody would want to endorse the absurdly weak account of responsibility according to which we are only responsible for those things that we intended to do. Similarly, you may think that nobody would want to deny that, in double effect cases, agents are not only responsible for their intended means and ends but also for their *foreseen* side effects. Since the side effects were both foreseen and avoidable, a plausible theory of responsibility will want to include them within the things that the agent is responsible for having brought about. This would indeed be a quick way of dismissing the whole issue of responsibility.[1]

To take an example, whatever the moral worth of the relevant actions, it is just obvious – it could be argued – that Strategic Bomber is responsible for killing the school children: Strategic Bomber foresaw the death of the school children and decided to proceed anyway and Strategic Bomber could have avoided the death of the school children by deciding to not proceed with her plan. Similar considerations would apply across the board to all the standard cases of double effect that we have discussed throughout this book, you would have thought.

This appears to be what H. L. A. Hart had in mind when he wrote[2]:

> ... both the case of direct intention and that of oblique intention share one feature which any system of assigning responsibility for conduct must always regard as of crucial importance. This can be seen if we compare the actual facts of the Desmond case [where "Barrett dynamited the prison wall outside the area where he mistakenly believed they would be at exercise. Though the plot failed, the explosion killed some persons living nearby" (1968: 119)] with a case of direct intention. Suppose Barrett shot the prison guard in order to obtain from them the keys to release the prisoners. Both in the actual Desmond case and in this imaginary variant, so far as Barrett had control over the alternative between the victims' dying or living, his choice tipped the balance; in both cases he had control over and may be considered to have chosen the outcome, since he consciously opted for the course leading to the victims' death. Whether he sought to achieve this as an end or a means to his end, or merely

foresaw it as an unwelcome consequence of his intervention, is irrelevant at the stage of conviction where the question of control is crucial. (1968: 121–2)

There are, however, those who take exception to what one would have thought is a rather obvious view of responsibility. One way to argue that Strategic Bomber is not responsible for killing the school children is to simply point out that – if the Doctrine of Double Effect finds application to the specific case and Strategic Bomber's actions turn out to be morally justified[3] – then Strategic Bomber was morally justified in killing the children and she is therefore not to blame; which just means, it could be argued, that Strategic Bomber is not morally responsible for killing the children.

According to this view of responsibility, then, we are only responsible for our wrongs[4]: whenever our actions are morally justified, then we are not responsible for them. But it is easy to show that there is at least a sense in which this account of responsibility is absurd: should we not be praised for our morally justifiable or (inclusive disjunctive) good actions? But we can only be praised if we were responsible – so that we must be responsible for more than just our wrong actions in order to make sense of moral praise. And here it will not do to object that we ought not to be praised for our morally permissible actions but only for the morally good ones, because both of those categories represent exceptions to morally wrong actions: so that it is enough that we need to praise agents for their morally good actions in order to show that agents must be responsible for more than simply their unjustified actions.

That we should be held responsible for more than just our unjustified actions should be no surprise: after all, in double effect cases the epistemic considerations that often make attributions of intentionality unwarranted do not apply: so that double effect cases are different from standard cases of unintentional action. It is not as if Strategic Bomber would mistake the school for the factory; Strategic Bomber knows perfectly well that her bombs will fall onto the school – there is no epistemic gap, no ignorance, and no mistake or false belief.

In this respect, the case of Strategic Bomber is completely different from the one made famous by Davidson where someone wanting to fly to London, England, boards a plane marked for 'London' which is actually heading to London, Ontario (1978). That is a case where the agent thought that the plane marked 'London' was heading to London, England (or at least a case where the agent did not realize that it was heading to London, Ontario; so either a false belief or just ignorance of some relevant fact). Now, whatever you think about responsibility for these cases of unintentional action – this issue won't concern us here[5] – my point is that one cannot appeal to these sorts of considerations in cases of double effect: the second effect is, in all cases of double effect, accepted to be known and avoidable by everyone independently of which side of the double effect debate they stand on.

To appreciate this point, let us remember that even Michael Bratman, whose planning theory of intention – as we saw in previous chapters, especially Chapter 6 and Chapter 8 – is meant to show that the side effect in double effect cases is not intended by the agent, accepts that the agent in double effect cases brings about the side effect intentionally:

> Though Strategic Bomber has taken the deaths of the children quite seriously into account in his deliberation, these deaths are for him only an expected side effect; they are not – in contrast with Terror Bomber's position – intended as a means. . . . *In saying this I do not deny that Strategic Bomber kills the children intentionally.* (1987: 139–40 – my emphasis)

2 Duff on responsibility

Within the context of the double effect debate, Antony Duff has suggested a way to deny responsibility for at least a sub-class of double effect cases which he identifies as those where the agent 'regards y as irrelevant to his action: it plays no part in his practical reasoning as a reason either for or against doing X' (1982: 2).

Duff distinguishes this kind of attitude (or lack thereof) towards an effect from two other alternative attitudes towards an effect:

1 He acts with the intention of bringing y about: y's expected occurrence forms at least part of this reason for doing X; if y does not occur he will have failed, at least in part, in his intended enterprise. . . .

2   He sees y as a reason against doing X which is outweighed
by stronger reasons in favour of doing X. (1982: 1–2)

Duff suggests that for the case where the agent herself regards y
as irrelevant to her action, there is an important sense in which,
according to Duff, y is not part of the agent's intentional agency and
therefore the agent is not responsible for y:

> I noted earlier that ascriptions of intended and intentional
> agency belong with ascriptions of responsibility and demands
> for justification. To say that A brings y about intentionally is
> to say that he is responsible for its occurrence and may have
> to justify his action under the description "bringing y about".
> But in a context in which y has no significance there is no
> sense in such a demand for justification or such an ascription
> of responsibility: there is thus in such a context no sense in
> an ascription of intentional agency. The criteria of intentional
> agency as to a given effect are also the criteria of responsibility
> for that effect; and they involve not just the agent's knowledge
> of and control over that effect, but the significance of that effect
> in the context of his action as providing a reason for or against
> the action. (1982: 4)

Duff goes on to note that we may not share the agent's perspective
on things and that, for that reason, we may still hold the agent's
responsible for the effect that she regarded as irrelevant:

> If we agree with A's view of y's relevance and significance our
> description of his action and our judgements of his responsibility
> for y will again match his own. But we may disagree with A: in
> particular, we may regard y as significant, as providing a reason
> against doing X, while A regards y as insignificant and irrelevant
> in the context of his action. We may not think that A is wrong
> to do X; we may believe that there are stronger reasons in X's
> favour: but we disagree with him about y's *relevance* as providing
> at least a reason against his action. . . . To ascribe responsibility
> to an agent for an effect is to claim, not that he does see it as
> relevant to his action or hold himself to be answerable for it, but
> that he should see it as relevant, as providing a reason against his
> action, and that he should be answerable for it. (1982: 5–6)

When Duff says that we may take the agent's own view of things and that then, in agreeing with the agent, we would not hold her responsible, then his view starts to sound a lot like the one we already discussed according to which, as long as the agent's action is permissible, then we would not hold them responsible for their actions. I have already said why I find this view less than plausible and Duff himself acknowledges something similar in a nearby endnote (1982: 6, endnote number 9). Still, there is something appealing to the thought that agents should not be held responsible for effects that they themselves regarded as irrelevant to their motivation.[6]

To illustrate this point, take the two scenarios made famous by the Knobe Effect, where in one condition a company's CEO does not care about a new project harming the environment and in the other condition the CEO does not care about a new project helping the environment.

> The vice-president of a company went to the chairman of the board and said, "We are thinking of starting a new program. It will help us increase profits, but it will also harm the environment." The chairman of the board answered, "I don't care at all about harming the environment. I just want to make as much profit as I can. Let's start the new program." They started the new program. Sure enough, the environment was harmed.
>
> The vice-president of a company went to the chairman of the board and said, "We are thinking of starting a new program. It will help us increase profits, and it will also help the environment." The chairman of the board answered, "I don't care at all about helping the environment. I just want to make as much profit as I can. Let's start the new program." They started the new program. Sure enough, the environment was helped. (Knobe 2003: 190–1)

These may be taken to be cases of the kind identified by Duff, where harming/helping the environment is not a means or end and it is also not a consideration outweighed by the goal of profit: it is, rather, simply irrelevant ('I don't care at all').[7] This seems to be at least a plausible way to interpret the chairman's attitude: the environment does not enter the chairman's deliberation at all; it isn't – from the chairman's point of view – a reason in either direction. Following Duff, we would then have to say that the chairman is not responsible for harming/helping the environment and that harming/helping the environment is not part of the chairman's intentional agency (at least in the cases in which we agree with the chairman's view of things, anyway).

Now take the help condition: the fact that the chairman is not responsible for helping the environment could be taken to mean that the chairman should not be praised for having helped the environment. And this, I want to suggest, seems right. We should not praise the chairman for helping the environment because helping the environment was nothing to her; it did not, for example, constitute an additional reason to start the new programme, which it could have done. It is easy to imagine alternative cases in which the chairman does take helping the environment to constitute an additional reason:

1 Both increasing profits and helping the environment are, independently of each other, sufficient reasons to start the new programme;

2 Neither increasing profits nor helping the environment is alone sufficient, but they are jointly sufficient reasons to start the new programme;

3 Helping the environment is a sufficient reason, while increasing profits isn't;

4 Increasing profits is a sufficient reason while helping the environment is not, but it is still a positive consideration which speaks for the new programme.

Those are all cases where helping the environment does not count as Duff's irrelevant effect but is rather taken by the agent to be, in one form or another, a consideration in favour of starting the new programme. But the original case is different: that the new programme helps the environment does not make any difference to the chairman's decision, so that we may be entitled to suppose that, say, if the new programme which will increase profits may also be made to help the environment by increasing the new investment by 1 per cent, the chairman would not have been prepared to invest 1 per cent more in order to help the environment.

Similarly, the chairman's reaction warrants the inference that – should the programme unexpectedly turn out to actually not help or even harm the environment – the chairman would neither stop it because of that nor regret this unexpected consequence. The chairman is, in one word, just lucky that her programme turns out to also help the environment – and she can't even see her luck! So, one could suggest, we should not praise her for starting the new programme, even though she knew about this further effect and even though she could have avoided this further effect by not starting the new programme.[8]

As we now know from the Knobe Effect (Knobe 2003), this judgement is asymmetric insofar as even though folk will not praise the chairman for helping the environment, they will blame her for harming the environment. So despite the two cases' apparent symmetry, the chairman seems to be responsible in one case (harm) while she is not responsible in the other case (help). What is going on here? Probably the following: folk think that, in both cases, the chairman should have done something that she did not do, namely acknowledge harming/helping the environment as a relevant consideration.[9] Because she did not acknowledge helping the environment as a positive consideration, folk punish the chairman by not praising her. And because she did not acknowledge harming the environment as a negative consideration, folk punish the chairman by blaming her.[10] So the chairman is responsible in both cases because both cases – to use Duff's terminology – are such that observers do not share the agent's perspective on things but rather correct it by pointing out that the agent *should* have acknowledged the relevant effect *as* relevant but she did not.[11]

But does not the Knobe Effect itself speak against understanding folk to be holding the chairman responsible in the help case? After all, the whole point of the Knobe Effect is exactly that in the help condition – along with low praise – we also have low intentionality attribution. Intuitive responses say both that the chairman did not intentionally help the environment and that the chairman should not be praised for helping the environment; and combining the two we get the plausible explanation according to which the chairman should not be praised for helping the environment because she did not intentionally help the environment. Doesn't this speak against the chairman's responsibility?

I won't deny that this is an attractive alternative, and it has the virtue of simplicity. But, as the last decade of debate on the Knobe Effect has shown, there is the drawback of having to explain the asymmetry, which is proving to be a difficult task.[12] But I think what is going on is something different: in both conditions, something is wrong (morally speaking, I mean) about the chairman's behaviour. In the help case it is the chairman's disregard for a positive consideration; in the harm case it is the chairman's disregard for a negative consideration. And in both cases the chairman is being punished for her dubious behaviour (or at least for her dubious values and attitudes, anyway): the punishment takes, though, different forms. In the help case, the chairman is punished by not being praised for bringing about a positive effect. And in the harm case the chairman is being punished by being blamed for bringing about a negative effect.

So there is no asymmetry: the cases, just as their superficial structure suggests, are indeed symmetrical. And this symmetry is being mirrored by the respondents' reactions: in both cases respondents are condemning the chairman. And this, supposedly, depends on the chairman's responsibility for her disregarding the relevant effect: in both cases the chairman is aware of the effect and could also acknowledge it as relevant, but she still disregards it notwithstanding the moral relevance of the effect; and those can easily be considered actions; some of them are certainly speech acts: 'I don't care at all . . .', for example. This is, then, what the chairman is responsible for in both cases and what she is being blamed for in both cases: she is responsible for disregarding a morally relevant effect.[13]

Note that this is in line with standard accounts of responsibility (as, for example, what Hart refers to in the passage we quoted earlier): the agent is aware of the relevant effect and she is in control over whether she will take notice of the effect's moral relevance or not and that is what she is responsible for in both cases: and that is what respondents are blaming the chairman for in both cases.[14]

Whether or not I have here offered a plausible explanation for the Knobe Effect is not important here: explaining the Knobe Effect was not my main concern (if at all). I just needed to deal with a plausible challenge to the view that agents are responsible for merely foreseen side effects. This I have done by arguing that it is exactly by not praising someone for a positive effect which she was conscious of and she could have avoided that we blame the agent for having disregarded the moral relevance of that effect. So agents are responsible even for good effects that they have disregarded (viz. not acknowledged for what they were) and that we do not praise them for.

3 The moral correlate of sentencing

So far we have argued that double effect does not make a difference to responsibility attributions. This is in line with what we quoted from Hart earlier about the stage of conviction: in determining whether someone is responsible for a crime, the law does not normally require for the agent to have intended some effect; it is enough that the agent foresaw that effect.[15] But what about the stage of sentencing, namely when a court or jury is no longer asked to decide whether the accused is guilty but rather how much she should pay for her crime? Sentencing is where, in the absence of justification or excuse, mitigating circumstances (or, indeed, aggravating circumstances) may count in determining the amount of punishment that the convicted will be sentenced to.

Given that we are not doing philosophy of law, here I am interested in what one may call the *moral correlate of the stage of sentencing*. Let us try to explain what that may mean: if the moral correlate of the stage of convicting is for an observer to determine for herself whether the agent is to blame for what has happened, I guess the moral correlate of sentencing must be something like the observer's resulting opinion of the agent and how she is going to deal with the agent in the future as a result of what the agent has done. Has the observer changed for better or worse her pre-existing opinion of the agent because of what has happened? Does she now think less of the agent? Will she still want to have anything to do with the agent in the future? In case the observer did not know the agent before: does she now have a negative opinion of the agent as a result of what has transpired? Obviously, this is far too vague: but the point is only to provide a structure within which individuals can not only make moral judgements but also articulate them to the point of forming a motivated opinion about someone; an opinion which will, among other things, influence the way they will relate to the agent in the future.

After all, we are often positively surprised by other people; but also bitterly disappointed; sometimes we admire the courage of a stranger, but it also happens that we start avoiding someone because we have become suspicious of their motives; or we find ourselves slowly changing attitudes towards someone only to find out that we no longer think them self-interested. In short, our moral judgements – just like legal judgements – are not just a matter of right and wrong, guilty or innocent: sometimes we care enough to articulate our opinion of someone else in much more detail. This process is what I call the *moral correlate of legal sentencing*.[16]

Take the example of forgiveness, which I think is a particularly good case to illustrate the phenomenology of the moral correlate of sentencing. When we forgive someone or are forgiven by someone, that does not necessarily mean that we have switched our moral judgement about what the person did or that they have switched their moral judgement about what we did: one may still find that what the other did was wrong and nonetheless forgive them for it. Indeed, it could be argued that a continuous negative judgement is necessary for the phenomenon of forgiveness, because when we no longer blame someone because we have come to see what they did as right or justified, then what takes place is not forgiveness. Forgiving seems to require that we still find the action wrong and nonetheless we stop blaming the agent.[17]

This suggests that what has changed is not our moral judgement of what the person did, but maybe our view of the person's attitudes; most notably, in the case of forgiveness, our view of how the person dealt with what she did in its aftermath: has she come to see it as wrong? Does she regret it? Has she apologized? Those things will not and should not change our original moral judgement; but that does not mean that those things should not make any moral difference. The point seems to be that they make no moral difference to the justification and permissibility of the behaviour in question, but they may still make some moral difference to our view of what the person did. So if you think that forgiveness is a moral phenomenon (which does not need to mean that you think that forgiveness is always good or even ever good, just that it is morally relevant), the considerations that count for this moral phenomenon do not have to do with classic moral justification or moral permissibility. And my suggestion here is that those considerations have rather to do with what I am calling the moral correlate of sentencing.

Whatever you want to call this phenomenon, it deserves its own book because it certainly has its own moral phenomenology. And as we are already at the end of one book, this is not the place to start a treatise in moral phenomenology. I only want to explore this one possibility, namely that there may be a place for something like the distinction between intending and merely foreseeing (with emphasis on 'something like', because I am going to argue that it is something more fundamental than that which does the work here) in the moral correlate of sentencing.

Take Strategic Bomber and Terror Bomber: we have seen already in Chapter 2 how the so-called counterfactual test is hopeless in distinguishing their attitudes; because if we try and say that Strategic Bomber does not intend to kill the children because she would not do it if there only were a different way of destroying the munitions factory in order to win the war, then we see that we can also say that Terror Bomber would not do it if there only were another way of demoralizing the enemy in order to win the war (and, as we have seen in discussing the problem of closeness in Chapter 6, philosophers have unsurprisingly come up with plenty of alternative ways of achieving that). But who would you rather have suddenly showing up for Sunday roast at your daughter's side?[18] Well, that depends on their attitudes towards killing school children. And their attitude towards killing school children is not a matter of intention; it is rather a matter of values, principles, beliefs, desires, habits and emotions; whatever it is that constitutes our character: this can inform and determine intention but it does not need to.

A negative attitude towards killing the children is compatible with both Terror Bomber and Strategic Bomber, up to a point: and the point happens to be the same one, namely the one where the negative attitude becomes an obstacle on the way to winning a just war – and this is, by the way, just another way of formulating my critique of the Doctrine of Double Effect. One way of expressing that negative attitude would be regret; another way would be to hesitate; a further would be to at least consider the death of the children as a reason which speaks against the mission but which is outweighed by the overall benefits of winning the war; even though quite obviously a more significant way would be to disobey the order, to desert or even to turn back.

Similarly, a positive attitude towards killing the children is also compatible with both: ways of expressing that would be enjoying the mission, carrying it out with enthusiasm, perceiving the death of the children as an extra reason in favour of the mission, etc. These possibilities are, importantly, in no way restricted to Terror Bomber: one could imagine a particularly wicked Strategic Bomber who enjoys a mission involving the killing of children: her plan may still be focused on the munitions factory but that does not rule out a positive attitude towards the further consequence of the plan.

Note by my choice of examples and language that I am not only talking about reasons-giving attitudes such as 'perceiving the death of the children as a consideration in favour/against the mission'; one could imagine a further kind of adverbial attitudes which do not necessarily need to be reasons-giving in this case but that may still make a difference to the opinion we are going to form about what the agent did: this would be maybe the case of 'carrying out the mission with enthusiasm'.

I suggest that, when judging what the agent did, we not only judge what they do and why they do it but also the attitudes (values, principles, beliefs, desires, habits, feelings, emotions) *with which* a certain action was performed. Those can but must not be in line with the agent's plans and intentions: agents may accept to carry out a particular plan while wishing all the time that the plan would not involve a particular effect that they are uncomfortable with; similarly, agents may be more than happy to execute a plan which involves a pleasant further effect which though, alone, would not have sufficed to motivate them to execute the plan in question. Those attitudes *colour* our actions whether or not they provide reasons for or against them. And this last point is also dialectically important because it is one of the elements which distinguishes my proposal here from Scanlon's recent proposal to understand the appeal of double effect by distinguishing between, on the one hand, the *critical* use of principles and, on the other hand, the *deliberative* use of principles (2008: 20–36).

Here we finally come to the role of character: this colour is not so much part of our character but rather the very expression of our character. Sometimes we act *in line* with our character, but sometimes we need to act *out of* character; sometimes our plans are *barely compatible* with our character, other times they are its *truest* expression. Accordingly will the colour of our actions sometimes fade and sometimes shine; still, all the time it will affect what people think of us and of our actions.[19]

You may observe a pilot struggle with the order to carry out a mission involving the effect of killing school children: you may watch her hesitate, protest and look for alternatives. In the end, if she still decides to go ahead with it, you may find yourself allowing those considerations to make their way into your opinion of the pilot and of what she did; into the way you will behave towards the pilot in the future, for example. Still, you won't change your judgement: nothing justifies the killing of children.

3.1 The moral correlate as an anti-consequentialist constraint

I should note an interesting feature of the moral correlate of sentencing: it is an anti-consequentialist constraint. This is important because it shows that one need not be a consequentialist in order to reject double effect and also – which is not quite the same – that the plausibility of the moral correlate of sentencing as an alternative to double effect does not depend on embracing some form of consequentialism. This, in turn, is not supposed to mean that the moral correlate of sentencing cannot be consequentialized: but, and that's my only point, it need not be.[20]

I take this to be an advantage of the moral correlate of sentencing: but I can easily imagine consequentialists complain that it does not go far enough; that double effect may happen to be about distinctions such as the one between intended means and merely foreseen side effects, but that at the end of the day what is at stake in the debate on double effect is really the truth of consequentialism. There is a part of this position that I empathize with: it is true, I think, that double effect could be conceived as a move to defend Kantian approaches to morality. What I mean is that one can see the Doctrine as a way for Kantians to argue both that consequentialists cannot make sense of some important moral distinctions but also that (at least) utilitarian consequentialism is not as big a challenge to Kantian approaches as it would be if Kantians could not appeal to double effect.

To illustrate this point, take the collateral damage case: utilitarians could argue that Kantians are just too restrictive and that they must allow for some killing of innocents in war. Nobody is ever going to be able to fight a war if you don't allow for some killing of innocents, could the utilitarian challenge go. And some wars ought to be fought for the sake of humanity (insert here just the war of your choice). Now the Kantian here could just bite the bullet and point to the atrocities involved in any war; or she could challenge the empirical premise about the necessity of collateral damage or alternatively she could challenge the normative premise about just wars. But there is another move that the Kantian can make: namely appealing to the Doctrine of Double Effect in order to show that she, the Kantian, is indeed able to allow for some just wars because through the Doctrine she is able to allow for some collateral damage.

So I do accept the point about the Doctrine being a Kantian device against some consequentialist counterexamples (at least utilitarian ones, anyway). But that is far from saying that any critique of the Doctrine needs to be a consequentialist one or that any discussion of the Doctrine of Double Effect needs to come up with a verdict on the truth of consequentialism. It may rather be that the problem of the Doctrine is not that it relies on anti-consequentialist constraints, but rather that it relies on the wrong kinds of anti-consequentialist constraints: intention – this book has shown – is the wrong one to appeal to.

3.2 Actions rather than agents

I want to deal with one final objection to the moral correlate of sentencing: it could be argued that it won't do as an alternative because it deals with and judges *agents* rather than their *actions*. Talking about the evaluation of agents rather than actions in the context of double effect would not be very new, whatever its merits; an influential example here is Judith Thomson, who talks about 'a failure to take seriously enough the fact – I think it is plainly a fact – that the question whether it is morally permissible for a person to do a thing is just not the same as the question whether the person who does it is thereby shown to be a bad person' (1999: 517).

The first thing to note about this objection is that pointing out that the moral correlate of sentencing is about persons rather than actions would – even if true – be no objection at all: a judgement about persons may be all that can be rescued from the wrecks of double effect. This is a fair dialectical point, but here I actually want to argue that the moral correlate of sentencing is also about actions and not only about persons.

Let us start by taking the original sentencing. Legal sentencing is indeed about what is going to happen to agents rather than to their actions; but, first of all, that's the case with convicting too; in that respect, judgement is always about agents. Secondly, and more importantly, those are not general judgements about agents but only particular judgements about what agents have done in specific cases. Another way of seeing that those judgements are about actions and not just about agents is again through the sentencing metaphor: I am no legal expert, but I suppose that previous sentences have an influence on future ones for similar crimes; now, if sentencing was just about persons, then it could not carry over to other persons; that it does goes to show that it is not just about persons.

Take the example of forgiveness that we have used to illustrate the moral correlate of sentencing: it is not as if we forgive a person full stop; we rather forgive them for having done something; for having performed a particular action. And our forgiveness is often a change in attitude on our part which is directly related to a change in attitude of the agent not in general but with regards to what she has done. So that normally we do not forgive someone because they have started being much nicer to us or because they have become more generous in general; we forgive someone because we notice that they have come to truly regret what they have done and to make amends for it. Forgiveness then, just like sentencing, is about particular actions.

An example may help, here: people often come to really dislike someone that they used to be really close to: a former partner, a parent, an old friend. Sometimes this dislike blinds them, but not always: in many cases, they will still be able to forgive particular actions of the former partner, parent or old friend. They can come to see what they have done in a particular situation in a new light, but that does neither mean that they will now justify that action nor does it mean that they will now cease to dislike the other person. The general opinion about the person remains a negative one and the judgement about the action too, and still there is place for forgiving that action. This is just to show that one does not need to understand the moral correlate of sentencing as being just about agents: it is rather – and in this respect it is just like the whole of moral judgement – about *agents' actions.*

The point is not that our attitude towards Strategic Bomber may or should be also influenced by everything else we know about Strategic Bomber or by what she has done in the past or what kind of person we know Strategic Bomber to be (even though all these considerations may be good epistemic guides);[21] the point is that our attitude towards Strategic Bomber's killing of the children may or should be influenced by the way she goes about bringing about that very effect: did she hesitate? Did she look for alternatives? Did she protest when receiving the order? Did she enjoy it? Those things, again, may but need not be reflected in the agent's intention: when they are not reflected in the agent's intention, then we have moral differences that double effect cannot account for; and when they *are* reflected in the agent's intention, then we have a more fundamental explanation of what is – in these cases – actually doing the moral work.

4 Ends, *Mends* and Means

In this section, I propose a way of looking at double effect cases which does not depend on the concept of intention, and I show that by appealing only to the concept of intention we fail to draw some important distinctions.

There are different ways in which some foreseen consequence or effect can motivate an agent to act; or – which I take to be an equivalent formulation – an agent who is motivated to act by some foreseen consequence or effect can be in various different relations to the foreseen consequence or effect which motivates her to act. Let us look at some of these possibilities.

1 **Ends**: having fun. One doesn't have fun with any further aim; it is something that is done – normally – *only for its own sake* (you may imagine alternative cases, but that's not crucial here).

2 *Mends*: sometimes we do things not *only* for their own sake but *also for their own sake.* Those things serve a further purpose but they do not *only* serve a further purpose because we are not indifferent to serving the further purpose

through *those* means rather than other means and we may be interested in the thing itself and not only in its serving the further purpose. When I choose to play football in order to have fun instead of playing videogames in order to have fun, playing football serves the purpose of having fun but it is not all about that purpose as I am not indifferent to how I have fun: I prefer – at least as far as having fun is concerned – playing football to playing videogames, say.[22]

3 **Means**: sometimes we do things *only for the sake of some further purpose*. Often it is all about the further end and not at all about the means to that end: I may be indifferent to the alternative between playing football and playing videogames (and the disjunction may be much longer than this), as long as each similarly satisfies my end of having fun.

What happens when we map onto these three possibilities a reality made of actions having multiple foreseen consequences, just like in double effect cases? Playing football, say, has for me both the foreseen consequence of having fun and the foreseen consequence of being marginally beneficial to my health (and many other: wearing down my shoes is a famous one in this literature, from Bratman 1984).

Playing football may be an *End* which does not even have to serve any further purpose in order to be attractive to me. It may be a *Mend* which also serves the purpose of having fun, purpose which could be served by other means; to these others means, though, I prefer playing football. This is a case where there are *multiple means* that would satisfy the end I am after, and I have a clear preference towards one of these means over the other ones. Note that this may also need to be dealt with counterfactually: namely, as it happens it may be that the only means to have fun – for me – is playing football. But that if there were for me other means to have fun, then I *would* still prefer playing football over these alternatives.

Playing football may also be a *Means* for me in order to have fun. Namely I am interested in any means to have fun and I do not have preferences between all the different means that would similarly satisfy my goal of having fun: Buridan-like. This, again, may have to be dealt with counterfactually too; because it may be that as it happens the only available means in order to have fun is playing football; but that if there were alternatives, then I would have no preference for football over these alternatives. My preference, in short, is *only* for whatever serves the purpose of having fun.

The difference between Mends and Means could be put simply in the following terms: the agent would have still a reason in favour of the former (Mends) but she would not have a reason in favour of the latter (Means) even if the means did not serve the relevant end. Notice that this is different from a counterfactual saying that the agent would still play football in the former case while she would not do it in the latter case; this latter counterfactual is too strong because it presupposes that the independent reason in favour of playing football is a sufficient one to motivate the agent to play football even once the fun is removed – and this need not be the case in order to distinguish the two cases.

Now enter the further foreseen consequence of the marginal health benefit (and wearing down my shoes and whatever else is normally involved in playing football). We seem to have different possibilities:

A Both having fun and the marginal health benefit are independently sufficient to motivate me to play football, so that my playing football is motivationally overdetermined. So both having fun and the marginal health benefit are, when it comes to reasoning as to whether to play football, positive considerations; and they are both strong enough considerations to motivate me independently of the other consideration. Counterfactually here one would say that, in the case in which my playing football is overdetermined, I would have played football even if I hadn't believed that I would have had fun and I would have played football even if I hadn't believed that it had a marginal health benefit but I would not have played football if I hadn't believed that I would have had fun AND I also hadn't believed that it had a marginal health benefit. This just means: neither necessary, each sufficient.[23]

B Having fun and the marginal health benefit are only together sufficient to motivate me to play football; as neither is alone sufficient, they are both necessary. Again, both are positive considerations but neither is strong enough to, alone, motivate me to play football; but given that I foresee both consequences, I am motivated to play. Counterfactually here one would say that, I would not have played football if I hadn't believed that I would have had fun – whatever my beliefs about the marginal health benefit; and I also would not have played football if I hadn't believed that it had a marginal health benefit – whatever my beliefs about having fun.

C   Only having fun is sufficient while the marginal health benefit is not (where this is compatible with both playing football being a Mend and with playing football being a Means). If I hadn't believed that I would have had fun I would not have played football independently of my beliefs about the marginal health benefit of it. Here the insufficient consideration of the marginal health benefit can play different roles:

C1   the marginal health benefit may be an additional consideration **in favour** of playing football, one that I do not need in order to be motivated because having fun is alone already enough; and also one that alone would not motivate me; but still something that I see as a positive feature of playing football. In this case, the additional positive consideration of the marginal health benefit could be for example relevant in picking out playing football over something else as a means to have fun. Say, playing football has the marginal health benefit; playing videogames does not; so even if they would similarly serve my purpose of having fun, I am more inclined towards the former than towards the latter because of this additional consideration. This case should be distinguished, by the way, from a case in which both playing football and playing videogames similarly serve the purpose of having fun but I prefer playing football because *it is* playing football rather than because of its additional feature of having a marginal health benefit. Both these cases, though, can be classified as *Mends*.

C2   the marginal health benefit may be a consideration **against** playing football, but one that is overridden by the foreseen consequence of having fun (I don't know how plausible this is, but try to imagine someone who is afraid of getting (too) fit in case she gets additional tasks either at home or at the office; or someone whose social reputation and standing are incompatible with health benefits or fitness in general). This may be then the case of someone who – should both playing football and playing videogames be available as similarly fulfilling of the goal of having fun, may have reason to prefer playing videogames to playing football because of the negative consideration which is attached to playing football but not attached to playing videogames.

C3 the marginal health benefit is, as far as I am concerned, **irrelevant** to my reasoning as to whether to play football. It neither speaks in favour of playing football nor does it speak against playing football: it is, in a slogan, *silent* on the matter of playing football (it is important to note that the point here is only meant to be relative to playing football and not general and also, obviously, should be understood in terms of the agent's perspective and not in agent-independent terms). This case would then represent someone who – should both playing football and playing videogames similarly fulfil her goal of having fun – would have no reason to prefer either playing football or playing videogames on the grounds of the marginal health benefit being either a positive or a negative consideration. All other things being equal, then, only in terms of having fun and the marginal health benefit, the agent in this case would not have a way to choose between playing football and playing videogames.

D Only the marginal health benefit is sufficient while having fun is not. By replacing 'having fun' with 'the marginal health benefit', what I say under (C), (C1), (C2) and (C3) applies here to (D) too.[24]

Let me now say why I think that the traditional distinction between intended means and merely foreseen side effects at the centre of the Doctrine of Double Effect cannot account for the distinctions that I have just made. Could we distinguish, for example, Mends and Means in terms of intention? One could propose that we do not intend Means because there it is all about the further end and the agent does not have any further reason which speaks for Means apart from the further end so that the agent does not have any particular reason to choose one set of Means over all the other sets of Means that similarly serve the further end.

According to this proposal, then, one would only intend Ends and Mends; but then the concept of intention could no longer be usefully applied to the Doctrine of Double Effect as it would allow most, if not all, of the things that the Doctrine does not want to allow for. To take classic examples, neither Terror Bomber nor *Fat Man* need be understood in terms of Ends or Mends: Terror Bomber may not have any reason to kill the children other than to demoralize the enemy and win the war and the bystander may not have any reason to push off the fat guy other than saving the five; so that one could imagine that if there were alternative ways for Terror Bomber to pursue winning the war and for the bystander to pursue saving the five, they would have no preference for killing children or pushing the fat guy over those alternatives.

What about biting the bullet and accepting that Ends, Mends and Means are all intended? Then at least the Doctrine of Double Effect would have the following problem: because it rules against intended effects, it would forbid all these cases in which the agent had a positive preference for alternative consequences which were unfortunately not available, so that it would rule not only against the case in which the bystander in *Fat Man* positively wishes that next to the fat guy were a stone which could also do the job but also against the case in which the bystander at *Bystander at the Switch* positively wishes that nobody were on the side track.

Also, the classic distinction between intended means and merely foreseen side effects does not seem to be able to deal with the difference between some foreseen effects being merely sufficient, merely necessary or both necessary and sufficient. Could one, for example, suggest that we intend only the foreseen consequences which motivate us? Then we would not intend foreseen consequences in cases like (A) where there is some other foreseen consequence that would have also been sufficient to motivate us to act. But this cannot be right; otherwise, the Doctrine would again allow for monstrosities: such as the case where I divert the trolley onto the side track because I want to kill my worst enemy who is trapped on the side track while knowing all the time that this will also save the five on the main track and that this latter consideration would have also, alone, been sufficient.

Finally, the concept of intention does also not tell us – in cases where some foreseen consequence is neither alone nor in combination sufficient to motivate us – what kind of attitude we have towards the foreseen consequence in question. We can't expect the concept of intention to map positive attitudes so that we intend all and only the foreseen effects towards which we have a positive attitude. Imagine a Strategic Bomber for which the foreseen consequence of destroying munitions is enough to motivate her to drop bombs; the further foreseen consequence of killing children would not have motivated her to drop bombs because she did not believe that killing children would have had any positive effect towards winning the war; but this particular Strategic Bomber is a monster who is actually delighted that her mission will also have the consequence of killing children – which she considers a bonus. We want to distinguish between this Strategic Bomber and a Strategic Bomber who considers the killing of children to be a reason against the mission, but the concept of intention does not allow us to do that either.

5 Conclusion

In this chapter, I have argued against the idea that double effect can make a difference to responsibility attributions; also, I have proposed both a way of looking at the normative issues behind the Doctrine of Double Effect – what I have called the *moral correlate of sentencing* – and also a way of looking at the action-theoretical issues behind the Doctrine of Double Effect and the reasoning involved in double effect cases by distinguishing between Ends, *Mends* and Means.

NOTES

Chapter 1

1   Some, like me, could maybe even claim that – if we didn't have to worry about earning money – we would do exactly what we are already doing anyway.

2   Just today I was reading in the *Frankfurter Allgemeine Sonntagszeitung* about Heinrich George – one of the most famous actors in Nazi-Germany – and his version of the 'I was only following orders' defence: 'Ich wollte nur spielen' (I just wanted to act).

3   The radio case is one that I have used in the past (Di Nucci 2009a); I must admit that I am now aware – but that I wasn't as I used the case the first time – that it has an illustrious precedent in Hart (1968).

4   This is, for example, how Anscombe famously suggested we distinguish between intentional and unintentional actions (1957).

5   One may disagree about the case where I see the lights and fail to draw the inference qualifying as a case of intentional action; I do think that this is a difficult case where we are tempted to deny the possibility of not drawing such simple inference; but I won't get into these difficulties here; I just wanted to illustrate cases where intentionality and responsibility may come apart.

6   Here one could be tempted to suggest that the third case of the agent turning on the radio in order to listen to the news and in order to wake up her neighbour is somewhere in between the other two; I don't know about that, it seems rather to belong together with the former case.

7   This is not the place to get into the details of the Doctrine of Double Effect (see the next chapter about that), but at least one general point is in order: the most natural way of describing our example is in terms of one case being such that the agent has the end of waking up her neighbour and turns on the radio in order to achieve that end and the other case being such that waking up the neighbour is a foreseen side effect of turning on the radio in order to listen to the news. In between these two cases there is a possible case in

which waking up the neighbour is an intended means rather than an intended end or a merely foreseen side effect: say the agent doesn't simply enjoy annoying her neighbour but rather wants her neighbour to move out so that she can buy the flat next door too, so that waking the neighbour up in the morning is part of her strategy.

8   Let me just clarify at the outset that I will be using throughout the book 'moral permissibility' and 'moral justification' as interchangeable: an action is morally permissible iff it is morally justified (the small dialectical assumption here being that morally obligatory actions are also morally permissible and not an altogether different category, because obviously morally obligatory actions are morally justified too).

9   http://www.vatican.va/archive/ENG0015/__P7Z.HTM#$2C1

10 http://www.vatican.va/archive/ENG0015/__P7Z.HTM#$2C1

11 http://www.vatican.va/archive/ENG0015/__P7Z.HTM#$2C1

12 http://www.vatican.va/archive/ENG0015/__P7Z.HTM#$2C1

13 http://www.vatican.va/archive/ENG0015/__P7Z.HTM#$2C1

14 http://www.vatican.va/archive/ENG0015/__P7Z.HTM#$2C1

15 On the face of it this last statement of the Catechism seems particularly strange, as it first allows for unintentional killing to then forbid killing without the intention to do so (if there is no proportionate reason to do so): we will explain in the next chapter that there is a conceptual difference between 'intentional' and 'intended' and that the Doctrine of Double Effect distinguishes morally between intended and unintended negative effects and not between intentional and unintentional negative effects; the Catechism is here implicitly appealing to that distinction by allowing for unintentional killing and then saying that unintended killing can only be justified through proportionate reasons. What this means is that the prohibition that the Catechism formulates in terms of 'intentional killing' is really a prohibition against 'intended killing' – see Chapter 2 for details on these issues.

16 http://www.vatican.va/archive/ENG0015/__P7Z.HTM#$2C1

17 http://plato.stanford.edu/entries/double-effect/

Chapter 2

1   Here is an alternative translation of Gury's Latin from Boyle: 'It is licit to posit a cause which is either good or indifferent from which there follows a twofold effect, one good, there other evil, if a

proportionately grave reason is present, and if the end of the agent is honourable – that is, if he does not intend the evil effect' (1980, but page numbers here and throughout refer to the 2001 edition: 8).

2 This is the standard translation of the *Fathers of the English Dominican Province*. The Latin original goes as follows: 'nihil prohibet unius actus esse duos effectus, quorum alter solum sit in intentione, alius vero sit praeter intentionem' (IIª-IIae q. 64 a. 7 co.)

3 Full disclosure: I am the editor of the PhilPapers Section on the Doctrine of Double Effect and the author of the above definition. For that reason, I will not use the PhilPapers definition here, but I stand by it.

4 Roughley (2007: 94) makes a similar point.

5 This simple point has important consequences, as once we recognize that we do not need metaphysically independent effects but rather only different action descriptions in order to be able to talk of double effect, then we quickly realize that the scope of application of the Doctrine is, as we mentioned at the beginning of the previous chapter, very wide if at all limited.

6 Interestingly enough, only Boyle's Gury talks of 'intended' while Mangan's Gury does not. But as Mangan's own formulation of the Doctrine is supposed to be a truthful modern rendition of Gury's Latin, then we should not worry about that.

7 Here are some representative contributions to this debate: Bratman 1984, Adams 1986, Bratman 1987, McCann 1991, Di Nucci 2009a, McCann 2010, Di Nucci 2010a, McCann 2011 and Di Nucci 2013. Something like this question features already in Anscombe's *Intention* (1957).

8 So if we take the uses of 'intended' and 'intentional' seriously here, the versions of double effect of, on the one hand, McIntyre and Woodward and, on the other hand, Gury and Mangan are not – at least on the face of it – interchangeable: they would indeed come up with opposite judgements of Bratman's case. On the version of double effect endorsed by Gury and Mangan, Strategic Bomber would be morally justified in killing the children (provided that the case meets the other conditions, obviously) because Strategic Bomber does not intend to kill the children. But on the version of double effect endorsed by McIntyre and Woodward, Strategic Bomber would NOT be morally justified in killing the children because Strategic Bomber kills the children intentionally. The two versions of double effect result here in two different (and incompatible: morally justified vs. not morally justified) conclusions.

9 Page numbers from Woodward 2001.

10 Page numbers from Woodward 2001. I should note that the conditions are numbered differently by Boyle. His four conditions are as follows: '(1) the agent's end must be morally acceptable (*honestus*), (2) the cause must be good or at least indifferent, (3) the good effect must be immediate, and (4) there must be a grave reason for positing the cause' (1980: 8). Boyle swaps 1 and 2 with respect to Mangan: this is a bit confusing but does not change matters in any way.

11 On this issue, see also Roughley 2007: 96–7.

12 For the sake of comparison, here is how Frances Kamm formulates the counterfactual test: 'This test asks us to consider an effect, such as the hitting of the bystander, and imagine that (contrary to the laws of nature) it would not occur if we performed the act that we wish to perform, but everything else would remain the same. Would we still continue to perform the act? If we decline to perform the act because the act would not bring about the effect, it is said that this shows that we intended to produce the effect' (2007: 96).

13 Here I will not deal with Kamm's argument against the counterfactual test (2007: 95–6), because it depends on claims of hers that I take issue with elsewhere – namely in Chapter 7.

Chapter 3

1 See also tinyurl.com/7p722gy. This blog post and Pakaluk's piece are the only two cases known to me in which this suggestion is made.

2 A peculiarity of the second example is that, supposedly, if I did not throw goods overboard to rescue myself and my crew, the goods would still get lost in the shipwreck. This is like imagining that, in the first example, the tyrant would tell me that if I did not do something base, then he would kill my family and also bring about that very same base thing. This does indeed make a possibly significant difference, both action-theoretically and morally, so that it is just best to imagine a case in which, if I did not throw the goods overboard, myself and the crew would die but the goods would be somehow saved (maybe to avoid shipwreck I must throw the goods overboard here and now, and if I don't the ship will sink there and then, and *here* the goods cannot be recovered by divers but *there* the goods can be recovered. The peculiarity discussed here is pointed out by Pakaluk (2011: 215) as well, who does not though suggest reading the second example as I do here.

3 I did not want to unnecessarily complicate this discussion, but there may be still another sixth kind of action in Aristotle's text, distinct

from the five discussed here: 'Acting by reason of ignorance seems
also to be different from acting *in* ignorance; for the man who is
drunk or in a rage is thought to act as a result not of ignorance but
of one of the causes mentioned, yet not knowingly but in ignorance'
(emphasis in the original, 1110b–25). Here the distinction seems to
be between ignorance in the sense of not knowing, like Oedipus, and
ignorance in the sense of a sort of unawareness or unconsciousness,
like the drunk. These two are genuinely different, and it is an
interesting open question what the contemporary causal account that
we have been comparing Aristotle to has to say about the case of the
drunk, who does not seem to act intentionally under any description,
but who will have to be held responsible for the damage that she
might cause.

4 Charles revises the third condition twice: '(3) "z is caused by S's
desire to do a z-type action either for its own sake or as the means
to achieving a further goal which he desires for its own sake . . . (3)"
"z is an action which is caused either by S's desire to do a z-type
action (for itself or derivatively) or by his desire to do a y-type action
(for itself or derivatively), when S knows that in doing y he is also
doing z" (1984: 61). Here I shall ignore the possible circularity in 3'.

5 For a recent introduction to deviant counterexamples, see Stout
(2010).

6 This has the interesting consequence that if we follow Charles in
taking Aristotle's voluntary actions to be what current philosophy
of action refers to as intentional actions, then animals and children
would, according to Aristotle, be capable of acting intentionally –
which is a pretty strong thesis (on this point see Steward 2009, Glock
2009 and Stoecker 2009).

7 See also Pakaluk's discussion of mixed actions and necessitation
(2011: 218).

8 These five cases are, for example, cited by McIntyre in her
introduction to Double Effect for the Stanford Encyclopedia of
Philosophy (she adds self-sacrifice to the list). Nothing really hangs
on whether all of these cases are proper illustrations of double effect
(self-defence may not be, for example): I mention them as illustrative
of the Doctrine and of the debate and as cases that are similar to
Aristotle's two examples.

9 '. . . he is the driver of a runaway tram which he can only steer from
one narrow track to another; five men are working on one track and
one man on the other; anyone on the track he enters is bound to be
killed. . . . The question is why we should say, without hesitation, that
the driver should steer for the less occupied track' (1967: 147).

10 Here it is again worth emphasizing the disanalogy between Aristotle's two examples: while Aristotle endorses the throwing of goods overboard, it is not clear that Aristotle would also endorse doing something base to save your family. Indeed, Aristotle states that '. . . some acts, perhaps, we cannot be forced to do, but ought rather to face death after the most fearful sufferings' (NE III.1 49). But that is not a problem, as the example involving doing something base to placate a tyrant is left open without specifying what the base deed should be (so that only the good effect is morally clear and assessable – saving one's family – while the bad effect is left as a variable). Pakaluk, for example, suggests that Aristotle may rather tend not to endorse doing something base for the sake of saving one's family, providing some Socratic applications: 'Often it is supposed that Aristotle is presuming that the agent will act to save his family, and yet the passage gives no grounds for holding this. Actually, there is no need to suppose that Aristotle even meant to suggest a "right" answer to the dilemma, which serves its purpose if both alternatives appear unpalatable. But suppose the dilemma was formulated in the Academy as an intensification of dilemmas that Socrates faced–it's being wondered how Socrates would have acted in these more trying circumstances–then it is natural to think that Aristotle, if, as seems right, he took Socrates as a model of virtuous action, would at least have taken seriously that the agent should refuse to do the shameful thing. The two cases actually faced by Socrates were: the Thirty Tyrants commanded him to arrest an innocent man, and he refused; his friends tried to persuade him to escape from prison for the sake of caring for his family, and he refused. These dilemmas are intensified if one imagines that it is not Socrates but those he cares for who will suffer through his refusal to heed the Tyrants' command, or that the cost of his refusing to do something shameful, such as deliberately break the law in escaping from prison, was not merely that his family suffer from his absence, but also that they be tortured and killed' (Pakaluk 2011: 215–16).

11 This is, admittedly, not always so clear, as in the hysterectomy case where, at least on the supposition that the foetus would otherwise survive, some may not necessarily prioritize the sick mother over the healthy foetus.

12 Here my reference to utilitarianism is admittedly quick and one should really distinguish between different possible versions of consequential-ist approaches. But my point is just a dialectical one and in this respect I don't think it needs much specifying: dropping Condition 3 makes double effect as unpalatable as its consequentialist alternatives.

13 Let me clarify my talk of the 'same action' here: I am not referring to the action individuation debate nor do I mean the thick–thin

action-type distinction by Wedgewood (2011b): I simply mean that the kinds of movements involved are different, as in flipping a switch as opposed to pushing a person.

14 The same is true of the abortion case and of self-defence, even though the case of death-inducing pain alleviation is slightly different: there it is life against pain. Still, that is also a case in which the most fundamental interests of persons are at stake, rather than, say, commercial interests.

Chapter 4

1 http://plato.stanford.edu/entries/double-effect/

2 See Cavanaugh (2006) for an example of someone who thinks that the Doctrine of Double Effect is not an exception to moral absolutism, but rather a way to defend it. Also, as I mentioned in Chapter 1, the Catholic Church explicitly uses the Doctrine in its Catechism in order to defend absolute principles such as the Ten Commandments.

3 Page numbers are from Woodward 2001.

4 Trams became Trolleys when Judith Jarvis Thomson exported the thought-experiment to the States (1976 and 1985).

5 http://news.bbc.co.uk/2/hi/uk_news/magazine/4954856.stm

6 http://moral.wjh.harvard.edu/index.html

7 Consider the story, well known to philosophers, of the fat man stuck in the mouth of the cave. A party of pot-holers have imprudently allowed the fat man to lead them as they make their way out of the cave, and he gets stuck, trapping the others behind him. Obviously the right thing to do is to sit down and wait until the fat man grows thin; but philosophers have arranged that flood waters should be rising within the cave. Luckily (luckily?) the trapped party have with them a stick of dynamite with which they can blast the fat man out of the mouth of the cave. Either they use the dynamite or they drown. In one version, the fat man, whose head is in the cave, will drown with them; in the other, he will be rescued in due course. Problem: may they use the dynamite or not? [The example is introduced in part] because it will serve to show how ridiculous one version of the doctrine of the double effect would be. For suppose that the trapped explorers were to argue that the death of the fat man might be taken as a merely foreseen consequence of the act of blowing him up. ('We didn't want to kill him . . . only to blow him into small pieces' or even '. . . only to blast him out of the cave.') I believe that

those who use the doctrine of the double effect would rightly reject such a suggestion, although they will, of course, have considerable difficulty in explaining where the line is to be drawn. What is to be the criterion of 'closeness' if we say that anything very close to what we are literally aiming at counts as if part of our aim? (1967: 145–6).

8   Another consideration that is particularly relevant to this new case given that it involves self-sacrifice is the gap between the reports and what respondents would actually do were they really in such a situation.

9   I don't suppose that FitzPatrick ever meant it as a full-blown general principle, because, understood as not only necessary but also sufficient, it justifies, among others, psychopaths, mass-murderers and in general most, if not all, of the major wrong-doers of this world.

10 This should not be overstated as Thomson's general conclusion that intervening in *Bystander at the Switch* is not permissible clearly clashes with general intuition, as 90 per cent of respondents disagree with Thomson. But fortunately we haven't yet reached a point where these kinds of surveys alone are sufficient to refute normative claims.

11 Option (ii) is diverting the trolley towards the one workman.

12 Here I leave unanswered the question of which interpretation is actually closer to Thomson's original: it may be that my interpretation is preferable, and then what I offer here is a defence of Thomson. Or it may be that FitzPatrick's interpretation is closer to the original, and then what I offer here is my own argument, based on one by Thomson (and there is certainly something to say in favour of FitzPatrick's interpretation, as Thomson, after having considered the value of dying for strangers, writes 'Perhaps you disagree. I therefore do not rely on that idea' (2008: 367), and goes on to talk about consent). I think this is just a question of copyright: nothing in the content of my argument hangs on whether it is more appropriately attributed to Thomson or myself.

13 No one else will save those on waiting lists: 'In the U.S. alone, 83,000 people wait on the official kidney-transplant list. But just 16,500 people received a kidney transplant in 2008, while almost 5,000 died waiting for one' (WSJ 8.1.10).

Chapter 5

1   A BBC online survey had broadly similar, if not so dramatic, results: 76.85 per cent said it was permissible to intervene in *Bystander at the Switch*, while 73.12 per cent said it was not permissible to intervene in *Fat Man* (http://news.bbc.co.uk/2/hi/uk_news/magazine/4954856.stm).

2   Page numbers refer to the pre-print available here: http://www9. georgetown.edu/faculty/lbh24/MJAASS.PDF

3   The results are statistically significant: χ^2 (2, N: 152) = 9.31, p < 0.01.

4   Answers to the trilemma for condition (a): do nothing, 37; flip to the right, 26; and flip to the left, 11.

5   Answers to the trilemma for condition (b): do nothing, 14; flip to the right, 15; and flip to the left, 13.

6   Answers to the trilemma for condition (c): do nothing, 11; flip to the right, 9; and flip to the left, 11.

7   The results are statistically significant: χ^2 (1, N: 120) = 8.82, p < 0.01.

8   This claim needs to be qualified: while there is no statistically significant difference between (b) and (c) (χ^2 (1, N: 77) = 0.87, p < 0.01), which suggests that a trilemma which does not involve self-sacrifice has no significant effect on the answers to the traditional dilemma, the chi-square between (a) and (c) also fails to reach statistical significance (χ^2 (1, N: 107) = 2.82, p < 0.01), weakening the claim that it is exactly the self-sacrifice element that induces subjects to then not kill the one in the dilemma.

9   Here there are other theoretical options that Thomson does not discuss: it could be argued, for example, that it is not enough for the bystander to ask herself whether she would be willing to sacrifice her own life and then, in case she gives herself an affirmative answer, then she may kill the one. Maybe the bystander must know that she would sacrifice herself, or at least she must be justified in believing that she would kill herself – and introspection may not be the right sort of justification here. In general, it can be argued that the epistemic burden on the bystander, in order to be allowed to kill the one in the traditional dilemma, is much heavier than just a Yes or No answer to the relevant hypothetical question.

Chapter 6

1   Some of the items on the list are more appropriately characterized as illustrations of the intending/foreseeing constraint, for example the Trolley Problem. Others, such as collateral damage, have had a dual role in the debate: collateral damages in war is one of the most discussed applications of the intending/foreseeing distinction and double effect in general, and the thought-experiment involving Terror Bomber and Strategic Bomber is one of the most influential illustrations of the distinction and the Doctrine. But the point about the moral relevance of the distinction between intending and merely

foreseeing is so general that most if not all ethical issues (and many non-ethical issues too) could be potentially added to this list. Indeed, as morally and politically loaded cases such as terror bombing or the bioethical cases have played such a major role in the debate, I think that setting up the discussion by using one of these cases to illustrate the distinction will also already bias the argument somewhat, and that is why I have chosen to illustrate the distinction with a non-moral scenario which is, though, modelled on the classic cases.

2   The simple equation, here, is: losing to sport as harm to ethics.

3   In *Modern Moral Philosophy* Anscombe famously attributes such a view of intention to Sidgwick: 'From the point of view of the present enquiry, the most important thing about Sidgwick was his definition of intention. He defines intention in such a way that one must be said to intend any foreseen consequences of one's voluntary action. This definition is obviously incorrect, and I dare say that no one would be found to defend it now' (1958: 11).

4   This is somewhat similar to two cases usually attributed to David Lewis (see Quinn's (1989: 343) discussion among others for a description of this case) and Mark Johnston (Delaney 2008), where the Terror Bomber knows that the enemy will be convinced of the death of the civilians by just observing the explosion from either far away (David Lewis's version) or through monitors at a segregated location (Mark Johnston's version). On this, see also Predelli (2004).

5   FitzPatrick often speaks of a 'merely causal' relation as opposed to a constitutive relation. This could lead one to think that FitzPatrick takes constitution to be a kind of causal relation. This would be problematic: if x is constitutive of y, then x is not independent of y, and if x is not independent of y, then x cannot be a cause of y because the cause must be independent from the effect at least according to traditional Humean accounts of causation.

6   This is supposed to avoid worries mentioned by Hart (1967) and Quinn (1989) with the relation between types.

7   Pruss (forthcoming 17–18) has already raised some problems for FitzPatrick's proposal.

8   This very last point is obviously not a general argument against Hills's proposal as a solution to the problem of closeness but only a particular argument against Hills's solution being deployed in defence of the Doctrine of Double Effect. Also, for my own bioethical writings please see Di Nucci (2009b, 2009c, 2011c, 2012b and forthcoming a–g).

9   By the way, Hills would have only needed this second point without having to make any moral judgements. That she still did commit to

the cruelty of causing injury without killing may then suggest that the second point needed, even from her perspective, to be substantiated, and she chose to do so by making moral judgements about the value of killing.

10 FitzPatrick (2003) has tried to reply to this kind of criticism by Thomson, Rachels and Scanlon exactly by stipulating what Hills concedes: namely that in the double effect debate what is at issue is not what the agents actually intend but only what they *can* intend. So whatever the success of FitzPatrick's reply, it won't help Hills here. More on these issues in Chapter 11.

11 This is an appropriate place to note one peculiarity about Foot's cave as opposed to many other double effect scenarios: as the issue is the agents' own survival, it is not clear that there would be overwhelming intuitions that what the explorers do is morally wrong the way there are, supposedly, for terror bombing or the *Fat Man* scenario of the Trolley Problem (see, on the latter, Hauser 2006). Whether that is in itself an argument for some form of utilitarian consequentialism is not a question that I can answer here.

12 I think it is not implausible here to interpret Kant as a sort of package-deal theorist according to which the rational agent must will all the indispensably necessary conditions to the achievement of her end (at least all of those she is aware of): which would mean that Kant did not distinguish between means and side effects. But, obviously, one can also interpret Kant differently here and claim that Kant is only talking about means and that therefore nothing Kant says here has anything to do with the distinction between intended means and merely foreseen side effects that is central to the Doctrine of Double Effect. This interpretative question is an issue in its own right which I cannot resolve here, but whichever of those two plausible interpretations of Kant one adopts here, no help for Delaney will come of it. More on Kant in the next chapter.

13 This is another way of saying that, even if Wedgwood's solution could resist every one of my objections raised in this section, it would at best be just another version of Quinn's attempt, which I discuss in Section 9.

14 Other counterexamples against the necessity of the strict definition are all Lewis-like terror bombing cases, many of which we have already discussed here (see also Quinn 1989; Fischer et al. 1993; FitzPatrick 2006); in the next section, we shall present other scenarios which make trouble for Quinn's proposal: those cases happen to also work as counterexamples to the strict definition here.

15 The Loop Variant is, in fairness, a general challenge to double effect and not just a particular challenge to Masek's defence of it. I discuss this case in some detail elsewhere: see the next chapter.

16   Another recent contribution to the debate on double effect which
     addresses some closeness cases is Alexander Pruss's (forthcoming).
     Pruss has put forward a defence of the Doctrine based on replacing
     the intensional concept of intention with the extensional concept
     of accomplishment as a condition of the Doctrine of Double Effect.
     Pruss accordingly reformulates the Doctrine as follows: 'An action
     that results in an evil is permissible if and only if it satisfies NWO,
     GI and PROP, and the evil was not accomplished in the action' (9,
     where NWO, GI and PROP are respectively the first, second and
     fourth condition of the traditional doctrine). This isn't supposed
     to be a solution to the problem of closeness in terms of giving
     criteria for what counts as too close but Pruss does claim that his
     'accomplishment' account can deal with a couple of cases of his
     own making. Pruss's account is only extensional to a point though,
     as he says that 'Whether something in the world counts as my
     accomplishment in a particular action depends on what my plan was,
     i.e., on whether the thing was a part of the actualization of the plan'
     (8); because of this, Pruss admits that, in the *Fat Man* scenario of
     the trolley problem, killing the fat guy will not count as the agent's
     accomplishment: 'what has been accomplished is that the body of
     the bystander has absorbed the kinetic energy of the trolley, and
     this was intended. This absorption of kinetic energy is the cause of
     death, and hence is not identical with the death itself. The absorption
     of kinetic energy is not an evil. The evil of death has neither been
     intended nor accomplished' (13). Pruss does not discuss cases that
     we have taken as examples of the problem of closeness throughout
     such as craniotomy and Foot's cave, but it is easy to see how the same
     concession would have to be made for such cases, as killing the fat
     guy in Foot's cave and the foetus in craniotomy would not count as
     the agent's accomplishment as they are not part of the agent's plan.
     In short, then, Pruss's reformulation of the Doctrine of Double Effect,
     whatever its other merits, does not even make a start at solving the
     problem of closeness – and that's no surprise if what counts as an
     accomplishment will be determined by what is intended.

17   Other counterexamples to Quinn have been generated by modifying
     versions of the terror bombing thought-experiment: see, for example,
     Kamm 1992; Fischer et al. 1993; FitzPatrick 2006.

Chapter 7

1   Anscombe: 'What distinguishes actions which are intentional from
    those which are not? The answer that I shall suggest is that they

are the actions to which a certain sense of the question "Why?" is given application; the sense is of course that in which the answer, if positive, gives a reason for acting' (1957: 9). Davidson: 'To know a primary reason why someone acted as he did is to know an intention with which the action was done' (1963: 7).

2 Let me warn against the ambiguity of the use of 'only' here: 'only' here is meant, as it is traditional in philosophy, to mention a necessary condition; namely that it was a necessary condition of the agent's doing what she did that she at least believed that doing what she did would have the effect that her friends would feel indebted. So indebtedness was a necessary condition of her acting and she only acted because she believed that they would feel indebted in the sense that had she not believed that she would not have acted. There is a different use of 'only', though: think of 'I did it only for you'. This use is one where only signals that there was no other reason why one did it – so necessary and sufficient; but it may also signal that the other person was a sufficient (but not necessary) reason to do something: as in 'I lied only to save you' where there may be a handful of other people in the world for the sake of this one would lie. Here, though, whenever we are talking about indebtedness and similar effects, both Kamm and I mean 'only' as simply a necessary condition.

3 I am not proposing that we actually endorse this position; I am only saying that the fact that this standard position remains available shows that Kamm's suggestion fails to make progress on this difficult issue for the Doctrine of Double Effect. As a matter of fact, I think that the position in question – if understood in terms of 'hitting the one' is intended but 'killing the one' is merely foreseen – is subject to the usual issues related to the problem of closeness, and that it is therefore not a plausible way in which the Doctrine of Double Effect can deal with the Loop Variant.

4 Those parts of the text which are in *italics* are those that I have modified to generate Party (organizing) Case out of the original Party Case; the rest of the text is identical with Kamm's original.

5 I mention this because there is some textual evidence, in Kamm's *Intricate Ethics*, that she – differently from Bratman and other critics of the Simple View of intentional action – does not distinguish between 'intended' and 'intentional' but rather uses 'intentionally' and 'not intentionally' to refer to whether the action was intended or not intended. I will here neither engage with this issue nor mention the cases where Kamm does that in any detail, but one representative example is: 'What I may not bring about intentionally (for reasons of cost), I may permissibly bring about as a mere side effect'

(2007: 109). The fact that Kamm contrasts 'intentionally' with 'mere side effects' suggests that she means intended and that she therefore does not distinguish between 'intentional' and 'intended'. Bratman, on the other hand, distinguishes between 'intended' and 'intentional': 'Though Strategic Bomber has taken the deaths of the children quite seriously into account in his deliberation, these deaths are for him only an expected side effect; they are not – in contrast with Terror Bomber's position – intended as a means. . . . In saying this I do not deny that Strategic Bomber kills the children intentionally' (1987: 139–40).

6   The italics in the original stands for Kamm's reformulations of Bratman's three roles; Bratman himself (1987) talks of (i) posing problems for further reasoning; (ii) constraining other intentions; and (iii) issuing in corresponding endeavouring. Here I will not take issue with Kamm's rendering of Bratman's discussion, but I append here for the reader his original, applied by Bratman to the well-known case of Terror Bomber and Strategic Bomber: (i) 'Terror Bomber must figure out, for example, what time of day to attack and what sorts of bombs to use' (1987: 141). (ii) 'So Terror Bomber's prior intention to kill the children stands in the way of his forming a new intention to order the troop movement' (1987: 141). (iii) 'If in midair he learns they have moved to a different school, he will try to keep track of them and take his bombs there' (1987: 141–2).

7   Later on in the chapter where she discusses Bratman's three roles of intention, Kamm introduces a version of the case I have just presented – she calls it Double Track Case – and she admits that it would be much more difficult to argue for unintended means in such as case – in her passage on the Double Track Case (2007: 112–13), Kamm seems to be genuinely undecided (but I won't engage in exegesis here). Interestingly enough, Kamm does not explicitly link her remarks there with the previous discussion of the three roles of intention – even though, as we just saw, a case such as her Double Track Case does seem to be relevant for at least Bratman's first role of intention, 'posing problems for further reasoning'.

8   I accept that one could object to this case on the grounds that if there actually was a side-side track, then we could just save the five by having the trolley remain, forever, in this mini-loop. But this strategy does have some drawbacks: first of all, we would have to sacrifice one our life in order to keep pushing the button which diverts the trolley every time; how many people would be willing to engage in this endless sacrifice in order to save five lives? Judging by our current societies, not very many – whatever the value of such sacrifice is supposed to be. But there are other ways to deal with this objection

without appealing to self-sacrifice: first, even if we were willing to keep the trolley on this mini-loop forever, we would probably fall asleep sooner or later (and anyway die on day, even though by then the others may be dead or gone too) and then the trolley would kill the five or the one. Also, we have no guarantee that, by keeping the trolley on the mini-loop, it won't kill the one: after all, the mini-loop includes the point where the one is, by stipulation. Finally, and more simply, we could just imagine that we cannot divert the trolley onto the mini-loop ad infinitum but just the once or maybe twice: we would still be committed to try given the rest of our commitments.

9   In fairness, talking of *despite* the fact that some effect will be caused appears to suggest a negative attitude; but this need not be the case, as an agent may be indifferent to some effect being brought about by her actions; the case of indifference would still not be a case of 'because of', as the agent's indifference to the effect means that the agent does not bring about the action because it has that effect. Whether or not the case of indifference can be terminologically rendered by 'despite' is a minor issue here, as it is whether we should rather talk of four different attitudes instead of three only so that we give indifference its due.

10 Again, here we assume that the mess is negative, but as the negativity of the mess is merely an intensional one, the agent may be indifferent to the mess rather than against it; so that it may be more correct to say that two count in favour of the action and that the third one does not count in favour, but I will leave as is in the main text in order to maintain the dialectic tension between the different attitudes.

11 Let me make something obvious and explicit here: even though I sometimes purely talk of property, I always mean intensional properties, namely properties that the agent believes her actions to have rather than actual properties of the action.

12 Those are interesting questions in their own right, which I cannot properly deal with in any detail here: both the question of whether, in this and similar cases, the agent is under rational pressure to maximize indebtedness; and the question of whether if the agent is not under rational pressure to maximize indebtedness, then that may be the distinctive feature which sets overall aims apart from secondary aims and means. Just on the fly I would say that probably the agent is not under rational pressure to maximize, only to get enough indebtedness for her aims – namely enough indebtedness so that she does not have to clean up alone. But this is complicated by the fact that if the agent's priority is not to have to clean alone afterwards, that may suggest that she will have reason to maximize indebtedness in order to minimize her cleaning effort – so up to the

point where she needs to do no cleaning. On the other hand, nothing in the set-up of the example speaks against taking the agent to prefer cleaning together with her friends to both cleaning alone and having her friends do all the cleaning. Anyway, as anticipated, these issues cannot be dealt with here properly, so I will leave it at these remarks.

13 There is no reason to discuss Kamm's criticism of the other two principles (Anscombe's reason-intention and the Doctrine of Double Effect), as this depended solely on the putative distinction between 'in order to' and 'because of' that we have criticized throughout. Just one thing though: having criticized an alternative to the Doctrine of Double Effect – as we have done here arguing against Kamm's Doctrine of Triple Effect – is in itself no argument in favour of the Doctrine of Double Effect. Indeed, the discussion here should have made clear that some problems are shared by both doctrines.

Chapter 8

1 For the earliest examples known to me, see Ryan 1933 and Ford 1944. Gury also talks about the killing of non-combatants in the context of his seminal discussion of double effect (see Boyle 1980: 528–9).

2 Here the terminology is a bit confusing: in modern philosophical discussions, the talk is always of 'terror' bombing and 'strategic' or 'tactical' bombing. Some (e.g., Cavanaugh 2006: xii) distinguish between 'strategic' and 'tactical' on historical grounds, finding the latter more appropriate. Others (e.g., Ford 1944: 263) object to both 'strategic' and 'tactical' and opt for 'precision' bombing. Other terms for 'terror' bombing are 'obliteration' bombing, 'area' bombing and 'indiscriminate' bombing (Walzer 1971: 11). To make matters more confusing, the adjective 'strategic' is sometimes used for 'terror' bombing as well. I stick to 'terror' bombing and 'strategic' bombing throughout because it is the most common usage in the literature (as a brief Google search revealed).

3 Reference found in Walzer (1971: 11).

4 This and the following quotes are taken from Ford 1944: 262 ff.

5 The epistemic characterization is important here, but it can vary: we can talk of certainty, high probability or even just possibility, as long as there is no epistemic gap between the two cases.

6 From the point of view of military ethics in general and just war theory in particular, there is an important difference between talking

about 'civilian casualties' in general, as Bennett does, and talking about school children, as Bratman does. The civilian casualties referred to by Bennett may very well be the munitions factory workers, and their moral status is controversial. On this, see debates on non-combatants, civilians-m, and civilians-w (where 'm' and 'w' distinguish between those civilians which provide military equipment such as munitions and those which provide welfare equipment such as food); in particular, see Fabre 2009 and McMahan 2009. While Bennett's reference to 'civilian casualties' may be a reference to civilians-m who may actually turn out to be liable to attack, Bratman's reference to school children simplifies the thought-experiment by providing a group (school children) which none of the contrasting views would consider liable to attack. That is why I shall stick to Bratman's school children throughout, which help identify the double effect debate on terror bombing and strategic bombing as independent from the non-combatant debate.

7   This point does not depend on claiming that there is no munitions factory in the world of Terror Bomber. The same point can be made by supposing that there is a munitions factory but that Terror Bomber does not know that or that the orders Terror Bomber receives do not mention one (this fits Bratman's talk of 'options').

8   Here my talk of causal beliefs does not presuppose causalism about action-explanation: I say that the beliefs are 'causal' to refer to their being beliefs about the causal structures of the world, such as the causal effectiveness of different strategies. Elsewhere I have criticized causalism in action theory (Di Nucci 2008, 2011b, 2011d and 2013), but my argument is here supposed to be independent from the truth or falsity of causalism.

9   Still, some of these irrational combinations may still play a role in the intuition that our moral judgement on Terror Bomber should be different from our moral judgement on Strategic Bomber. Take the following:

- Terror Bomber does not believe that killing children will weaken enemy *and* she does believe that destroying munitions will weaken enemy.
- Strategic Bomber believes that destroying munitions will weaken enemy *and* she does not believe that killing children will weaken enemy.

This is a permutation in which Terror Bomber and Strategic Bomber have the same causal beliefs, but I have excluded it because it involves Terror Bomber in criticizable irrationality: why does she embark on the plan to kill the children in order to weaken enemy if she does not believe that killing children will weaken enemy? Still, maybe this possible combination of the two agents' beliefs may be at least a part of the intuition that Terror Bomber is morally criticizable while Strategic Bomber is not morally criticizable. But this would be seemingly unfair: the two, in such a case, have the same beliefs and cause the same amount of suffering. Can we possibly blame Terror Bomber more just because of her error of judgement? It seems not, because it was not an error of *moral* judgement (if it were, then Strategic Bomber would have committed the same error).

10 This is, indeed, the core of Bratman's non-reductive planning theory of intention; and here I am not offering a general critique of Bratman's theory, which I have discussed at length elsewhere (Di Nucci 2008, 2009a and 2010a).

11 Delaney (2008) proposes a similar scenario. For my critique of his own position please see Chapter 6.

12 Let me here note that even though I have imported the structure of the trolley problem, the two thought-experiments remain different in that in the trolley problem there are obvious non-psychological differences (the bridge, for example) which need not be the case in the terror–strategic thought-experiment. Also, it may be argued that there is a further difference in that the agent in *Fat Man* physically uses the fat guy for her purposes, while the agent in Strategic Bomber does not physically use the children for her purposes – the difference being, supposedly, that the agent in *Fat Man* physically pushes the fat guy while the agent in Strategic Bomber does not have any such contact with the children. Here I would be worried that we would then be just talking, as in Harris's irony, about the difference between throwing people at trolleys and throwing trolleys at people (or throwing bombs at people and throwing people at bombs).

13 Bentham (*An Introduction to the Principles of Morals and Legislation*) famously distinguishes between *oblique* intention and *direct* intention. The talk of immediacy takes us back to Gury and Mangan's definitions of double effect. To see that immediacy, when talking about double effect, is a way of denying that the relevant effect is a means, think of its German translation 'unmittelbar', which already includes in itself the denial of 'means' (mittel).

14 This is indeed very plausible, but it is an historical hypothesis and this is not the place to defend it.

15 Another possibly interesting question about the Doctrine of Double Effect with relation to the history of WWII is whether we find it plausible that the Doctrine offers different judgements for what the

RAF did in the first part of 1940 and for what they did in the second part of 1940 – even though we must be careful in not overstating the application of the Doctrine to WWII: the technology was such that only 22 per cent of bombers dropped their load within 5 miles of the target (Walzer (1971: 15) and Frankland (1970: 38–9)); with this kind of success rate it is likely that we are not even allowed to talk of intentions in the first place, as we would violate belief constraints: the bombers' attitude towards their targets was at the time more one of hope than one of intention, at least if we accept rational constraints on intention (Bratman 1984, 1987; McCann 1991, 2010, 2011; Di Nucci 2009a, 2010a).

Chapter 9

1 A note on the methodology: every participant only had access to one of the two stories and to one of the six questions; and every participant only answered one of the six questions.

2 These results are statistically significant: χ^2 (1, N: 96) = 31.85, $p < 0.01$.

3 These results are not statistically significant: χ^2 (1, N: 117) = 0.08, $p < 0.01$.

4 These results are only marginally significant: χ^2 (1, N: 85) = 5.94, $p < 0.05$.

5 These results are not statistically significant: χ^2 (1, N: 86) = 0.49, $p < 0.01$.

Chapter 10

1 Here I don't mean to argue that the sacrifice involved would be obviously immoral but only that it is not obvious that the proportionality condition would be met because the sacrifice is very significant. An anonymous referee pointed out to me, for example, that even if more persons died prematurely after birth than did not die prematurely after birth, we would still think it was worth creating persons, at least if there was no alternative. I am not sure about this: could we really justify such great sacrifice of persons? Could we legitimately conceive and bring to bear a baby knowing that her chances of after-birth long-term survival would be less than 50 per cent? How many potential parents would still do that? Also, maybe it would still

be *worth* creating persons to avoid the extinction of humanity but the practice would nonetheless be immoral: the survival of the human kind must not be necessarily reduced to an ethical issue. These remarks are not meant to be conclusive but only to clarify that the proportionality condition is not at all obvious in in vivo conception. And normally in double effect cases, the proportionality condition is very obvious, as in the five against one of the trolley problem.

2   On the issue of proportionality, see also Devolder's already mentioned forthcoming critique of Murphy. Here I don't have the space to take issue with Devolder's critique as well as with Murphy's argument, so I limit my discussion to the latter. Let me just say that my critique is more radical than Devolder's in two crucial respects: first, it goes at the heart of the application of double effect to embryo debates and the supposed distinction between in vivo and in vitro in challenging the idea of unintended in vivo versus intended in vitro, and not just the issue of proportionality; secondly, my argument challenges the use of double effect in this debate in general and not just Murphy's particular application.

3   http://plato.stanford.edu/entries/stem-cells/

4   It has been suggested to me that one moral difference between in vivo conception and the transplant case may be that each of the embryos receives the best chance at survival while the patient from whom we take the organs stands no chance to survive. Coming out of the transplant analogy, the idea would be that an embryo in stem cell research stands no chance to survive while each of the embryos receives the best chance to survive in in vivo conception. The problem here is that this suggestion alters the necessary epistemic balance between the two cases by suggesting that death is only sure in one case but not in the other. But across cases the number of deaths must be supposed to be equal and therefore the probability of death in the one case must also be equal between the two scenarios.

Chapter 11

1   Jonathan Bennett (1980: 97) calls those two sorts of questions first-order morality and second-order morality. I find this way of speaking a bit unfortunate because the distinction may then be easily confused with the one between normative ethics and meta-ethics.

2   This should include my own past actions.

3   Some prominent examples: Bennett (1980: 96–8), Thomson (1991: 293) and Scanlon (2008: 19–20).

4 Note that the school has become a hospital in this variant, but obviously nothing is supposed to depend on that.

5 Scanlon acknowledges Thomson for the thought-experiment, even though he oddly enough fails to cite Thomson's original version.

6 This particular world may only dream of military pilots who go questioning their orders to some moral authority, but this hopefully does not compromise the plausibility of the thought-experiment.

7 Given that Wedgwood does not want to talk about moral permissibility ('The central claim of my version of the DDE, then, is that there is normally a stronger reason against an act if the act has a bad state of affairs as one of its intended effects than if it has that bad state of affairs as one of its unintended effects' (2011b: 2)), then this should be reformulated accordingly; but whatever the specific content of the answer, the point here is simply that there is some moral answer to the pilot.

8 In fairness, an extensional principle would not have problems with the question of this chapter on whether double effect can tell us how we may permissibly act; exactly because an extensional principle would not have to appeal to either actual or possible intentional states of agents but only to the mind-independent world.

9 Also, the following remarks by Wedgwood on Thomson go in the same direction: 'But does the DDE really have to deny this thesis? Suppose that it is true of you that if you did A, you would do it with a bad intention. Must the DDE then say that you may not do A? Surely the answer is No. What the DDE must say is merely that you may not do-A-with-this-bad-intention; it need not say that there would be anything wrong at all with your doing A with a *different* intention.' (http://peasoup.typepad.com/peasoup/2009/03/defending-double-effect.html).

10 A point of caution: here it could be objected that I have granted too readily to Wedgwood and FitzPatrick the point about possible rather than actual motivational states. Indeed, my discussion has been rather brief; but there is a good dialectical reason for that, namely charity – as we have shown that if we wouldn't even grant them the point about possible motivational states, their argument would be a non-starter. So my discussion here should not be understood as an endorsement of the point about possible rather than actual motivational states.

11 Here one could try to apply Wedgwood's proposed solution to the problem of closeness – which I have discussed at length in Chapter 6 – to this issue too: since I have rejected Wedgwood's argument already in Chapter 6, I will not engage in that discussion again here.

Chapter 12

1   You will find a good discussion of why double effect won't do as a
    responsibility-diminishing principle in Roughley 2007.

2   Interestingly enough, it happened to fall on Hart himself to revive
    the debate on double effect in the post-war period: you can trace
    pretty much all of the literature on double effect of the last half a
    century back to Hart's *Intention and Punishment* (from which I take
    the above quote) through Philippa Foot's The *Problem of Abortion
    and the Doctrine of Double Effect*, which was a direct response to
    Intention and Punishment; both articles appearing within a year,
    In 1967, in the same journal, the *Oxford Review*.

3   And this assumption is not question-begging because just now we are
    only discussing possible accounts of responsibility and not the truth
    of the Doctrine.

4   Just to point out that one may take Kant to hold the opposite view: we
    are only free when we do the right thing, so that – one may argue – we
    are only responsible for our morally right actions.

5   My own position on the issue of responsibility for unintentional
    actions is that cases of negligence and culpable ignorance show that
    we must be also responsible for at least some of our unintentional
    actions: this is somewhat relevant to the present issue because if
    we are responsible even for some of our unintentional actions –
    and intended actions are a sub-class of intentional actions – then,
    a fortiori, we are also responsible for some unintended actions
    too – which is exactly the point at issue here. For my own
    writings on agency and responsibility, please see, on top of what
    has already been cited throughout the book, Di Nucci 2010b, 2011a
    and 2012a.

6   Let me say that I am here interested in Duff's discussion of double
    effect only insofar as it discusses responsibility and it is therefore not
    a primary importance for me, here, to take a stand on Duff's claim
    that one can identify three different kinds of attitudes towards an
    effect rather than, say, just two: namely that an effect speaks for or
    against some action or (alternatively) that an effect either speaks
    or does not speak for an action – indeed, if one were to opt for the
    latter alternative just mentioned, that would include in the second
    disjunct 'does not speak for an action' both Duff's second and third
    attitude. I do not want to take a stand on this issue in itself because
    there are quite a few things to say about it that I cannot go into any
    detail here: for example, that one should distinguish between some
    effect being at least in part motivating (as in Duff's first option) and

some effect speaking in favour of an action; because one can easily generate cases where some effect does speak in favour of an action but does not at all motivate the agent simply because the agent has independent sufficient reasons to perform the action in question (more on this later on in this section). Also, Duff's conditions do not seem to be mutually exclusive, so that Terror Bomber may represent a case of an agent which is both motivated to act by the effect killing the children (because it is a means to demoralize the enemy) and also sees killing the children as a consideration against the mission which is outweighed by other considerations (winning the war).

7   There is an interesting discussion to be had about the normative status of 'I don't care': if we take it to be a statement of indifference, should that then be interpreted as negative or neutral (or even positive as in the case of indifference to temptation)? Again, I do not have the time to go into this interesting issue here, even though some of the stuff I say in the rest of the paper may then be re-used to answer this particular question.

8   I wonder if one may not be able to distinguish between a case in which the chairman takes 'helping the environment' as an additional consideration in favour of the new programme and a case in which the chairman does not take 'helping the environment' as an additional consideration in favour of the new programme but she is still happy to find out that the new programme will help the environment. What speaks against this distinction is that it could be argued that the chairman's happiness at the news that the new programme will also help the environment must be interpreted in terms of 'helping the environment' being at least in some sense a positive reasons-giving feature: if not in this case, at least in related cases: say cases in which the chairman has to choose between two programmes which are identical in financial terms but one also helps the environment and the other one does not. I am not sure whether we are committed to say that, in this related case, the chairman would have to choose the programme which helps the environment if in the original case she is happy to find out that the programme helps the environment: maybe the chairman has a policy of not letting any consideration other than financial considerations play a role in her decision making – so that in the new case she would be in a Buridan case and would toss a coin – but she can still privately rejoice that in the original case the programme she is choosing on purely financial grounds happens to help the environment (just as she will rejoice in case the environment-helping programme wins the coin-toss in the new case). I am not sure about this but I do not think that we need to settle this particular issue just now.

9 Here there is an interesting issue about the status of 'acknowledging something as a relevant consideration'; is that a judgement, a mental act, a decision, an action? Given that in the scenarios the chairman performs explicit speech acts, this isn't pressing for my argument; but whatever one says about the status of 'acknowledging', since I am proposing that the chairman is being blamed for that, it better be something compatible with the 'ought implies can' principle.

10 Here we shouldn't read too much into talk of 'punishment', which I am using metaphorically to bring out the negative attitude of respondents in both cases.

11 As I said, my guess is that Duff meant just this in endnote 9 (1982: 6).

12 Just check the 379 (and counting) Google Scholar citations for Knobe's original article (2003) to get an idea of the size and diversity of the debate.

13 Two things here: first, notice that one could consider the lacking attribution of intentionality in the help case also as part of the punishment for the chairman's disregard: after all, to attribute intentionality in the help case does amount to – at least to some extent – giving the chairman credit for helping the environment and to suggest that she meant to do that, while – in an important respect – she definitely did not, because she explicitly acknowledges 'helping the environment' as non-motivating. So one could consider the attributions of intentionality in both cases as part of the punishment. Secondly, I suppose that in both cases people would attribute intentionality to the chairman's attitude towards the environment: 'did the chairman intentionally disregard the environment?' is a question that, I suppose, would be answered positively by the majority of respondents in both cases. But I do not have the time to test this empirically here.

14 One could, for example, claim that the speech act 'I don't care at all' is the action to which responsibility is being attributed in both cases, so as to maintain the symmetry of the two conditions: in both conditions the chairman has control over the speech act in the sense of being aware of it and being in a position to avoid it (and the same goes to whatever motivates the speech act too, supposedly – in case one wanted to go one step back); so in both conditions, the chairman is responsible for her speech act; and in both conditions, respondents punish the chairman for her speech act: in the help condition because they do not praise even though the chairman has brought about something good; and in the harm condition because they blame the chairman for having brought about something bad. And – see previous endnote – the chairman can be said to intentionally perform the speech act 'I don't care at all' in both cases.

15 Here I will ignore issues about the role of intention in the definition of certain crimes. Those interested in the topic can do worse than start from Hart himself (1968). Also, the already cited Roughley (2007) deals with this issue too.

16 This is obviously not to say that the moral correlate of legal sentencing and legal sentencing itself are necessarily independent: indeed, I suspect that at least jury trials rely on the moral correlate of sentencing in order to arrive at actual legal sentencing; having said that, juries are not normally charged with sentencing but only with convicting.

17 Here I certainly do not want to commit myself to the view that forgiveness requires that one stop blaming the other; I take that to be just an example of one way of forgiving and nothing is supposed to hang on this point anyway. Also, the point about the necessity of not having changed judgement on the action that one is forgiving someone for should also be taken with a pinch of salt: there is at least one case which speaks against it, namely a case in which I have changed my judgement on a certain action for different reasons which are not the reasons which explain why I forgive the agent for that action. A conversation with Tobias Gutmann has helped me see this point and I thank him for that.

18 I know that the right answer here ought to be 'neither'; but unfortunately you can't choose who your daughter is going to fall for.

19 Here I won't get into the issue of whether this colour ought to affect the way we judge other people or merely may (in the sense of moral permissibility) affect the way we judge other people; since we are talking about an alternative to double effect, the latter weaker claim will be enough anyhow.

20 Since here I am not interested in the truth of consequentialism, I will ignore the obvious objection that could be raised here according to which for consequentialism it is enough if something *can* be consequentialized.

21 I admit that here there may be a disanalogy with the legal case: courts do take past behaviour into account when sentencing; but, interestingly for the analogy with the moral case, juries are normally kept as uninformed as possible about non-relevant facts about the accused; but I will admit that juries are not normally sentencing bodies.

22 Here one should distinguish the case in which the preference is merely relative to some goal from the case in which the preference is independent from the goal in question.

23 Here one should distinguish the case in which the agent does not believe that P from the case in which the agent believes that not P;

but I don't think that, here, this distinction makes an important difference.

24   Here I am only considering cases in which the agent acts and is therefore motivated; otherwise, there are obviously other combinations, such as, to mention only one, both considerations being in favour of playing football but neither alone nor together sufficient. Reality, it should be pointed out, is probably such a case: where only those two considerations alone would surely not be enough and there will have to be all sorts of background conditions to contribute to motivating the agent.

BIBLIOGRAPHY

Adams, F. (1986), 'Intention and Intentional Action: The Simple View', *Mind & Language* 1: 281–301.

Anscombe, G. E. M. (1957), *Intention*. Oxford: Basil Blackwell.

—(1958), 'Modern Moral Philosophy', *Philosophy* 33(124): 1–19.

—(1982), 'Medalist's Address: Action, Intention, and "Double Effect"', *Proceedings of the American Catholic Philosophical Association* 56: 12–25. Reprinted in Woodward 2001.

Aquinas, T. (1988), 'Summa Theologica II-II, Q. 64, art. 7, "Of Killing"'. In William P. Baumgarth and Richard J. Regan, S. J. (eds), *On Law, Morality, and Politics*. Indianapolis/Cambridge: Hackett Publishing Co.

Aristotle (Ross translation, 1925). *Nicomachean Ethics*. Oxford: Oxford University Press.

Bennett, J. (1980), *Morality and Consequences. The Tanner Lectures on Human Values*.

—(1995), *The Act Itself*. Cambridge: Cambridge University Press.

Boyle, J. M. (1980), 'Toward Understanding the Principle of Double Effect', *Ethics* 90: 527–38. Reprinted in Woodward 2001.

Bratman, M. (1984), 'Two Faces of Intention', *Philosophical Review* 93: 375–405.

Bratman, M. (1987), *Intention, Plans, and Practical Reason*. Cambridge, MA: Harvard University Press.

Brock, D. W. (2006), 'Is a Consensus Possible on Stem Cell Research? Moral and Political Obstacles', *J Med Ethics* 32: 36–42.

Cavanaugh, T. A. (2006), *Double-Effect Reasoning*. Oxford: Oxford University Press.

Charles, D. (1984), *Aristotle's Philosophy of Action*. Ithaca, NY: Cornell University Press.

Davidson, D. (1963), 'Actions, Reasons, and Causes', *Journal of Philosophy* 60: 685–700.

—(1973), 'Freedom to Act', in T. Honderich (ed.), *Essays on Freedom and Action*. London: Routledge and Kegan Paul, pp. 137–56.

—(1978), 'Intending', in Y. Yovel (ed.), *Philosophy of History and Action*. Jerusalem, Israel: The Magnes Press, The Hebrew University.

Davis, N. (1984), 'The Doctrine of Double Effect: Problems of
  Interpretation', *Pacific Philosophical Quarterly* 65: 107–23.
  Reprinted in Woodward 2001.
Delaney, N. (2007), 'Double-Effect Reasoning: Doung Good and Avoiding
  Evil by T. A. Cavanaugh', *Notre Dame Philosophical Reviews*.
—(2008), 'Two Cheers for Closeness: Terror, Targeting, and Double
  Effect', *Philosophical Studies* 137: 335–67.
Devolder, K. (forthcoming), 'Embryo Deaths in Reproduction and Embryo
  Research: A Reply to Murphy's Double Effect Argument. *J Med Ethics*.
Di Nucci, E. (2008), *Mind Out of Action*. Saarbrücken, Germany: VDM
  Verlag.
—(2009a), 'Simply, false', *Analysis* 69(1): 69–78.
—(2009b), 'Abortion: Strong's Counterexamples Fail', *J Med Ethics* 35:
  304–5.
—(2009c), 'On How to Interpret the Role of the Future within the
  Abortion Debate', *J Med Ethics* 35: 651–2.
—(2010a), 'Rational Constraints and the Simple View', *Analysis* 70: 481–6.
—(2010b), 'Refuting a Frankfurtian Objection to Frankfurt-Type
  Counterexamples', *Ethical Theory and Moral Practice* 13(2): 207–13.
—(2011a), 'Frankfurt Counterexample Defended', *Analysis* 71(1): 102–4.
—(2011b), 'Frankfurt versus Frankfurt: A New Anti-causalist Dawn',
  Philosophical Explorations 14(1): 1–14.
—(2011c), 'Sexual Rights and Disability', *Journal of Medical Ethics* 37(3):
  158–61.
—(2011d), 'Automatic Actions: Challenging Causalism', *Rationality
  Markets and Morals* 2(1): 179–200.
—(2012a), 'Priming Effects and Free Will', *International Journal of
  Philosophical Studies* 20(5): 725–34.
—(2012b), 'Double Effect and Assisted Dying', *British Medical Journal*
  (letter, 7 February 2012).
—(2013), *Mindlessness*. Newcastle: Cambridge Scholars Publishing.
—(forthcoming a), 'Fathers and Abortion', *The Journal of Medicine &
  Philosophy*.
—(forthcoming b), 'Killing Foetuses and Killing Newborns', *Journal of
  Medical Ethics*.
—(forthcoming c), 'Self-Sacrifice and the Trolley Problem', *Philosophical
  Psychology*.
—(forthcoming d), 'Withdrawing artificial nutrition and patients'
  interests', *Journal of Medical Ethics*.
—(forthcoming e), 'Double Effect and Terror Bombing', *GAP.8 Proceedings*.
—(forthcoming f), 'Embryo Loss and Double Effect', *Journal of Medical
  Ethics*.
—(forthcoming g), Habits, 'Nudges, and Consent', *American Journal of
  Bioethics*.

Duff, A. (1982), 'Intention, Responsibility and Double Effect', *The Philosophical Quarterly* 32: 1–16.

Fabre, C. (2009), 'Guns, Food, and Liability to Attack in War', *Ethics* 120(1): 36–63.

Finnis, J. (1995), 'A Philosophical Case against Euthanasia', in J. Keown (ed.), *Euthanasia Examined: Ethical, Clinical, and Legal Perspectives*. Cambridge: Cambridge University Press, pp. 23–35.

Fischer, J. M., Ravizza, M. and Copp, D. (1993), 'Quinn on Double Effect: The Problem of Closeness', *Ethics* 103: 707–25.

FitzPatrick, W. J. (2003), 'Acts, Intentions, and Moral Permissibility: In Defense of the Doctrine of Double Effect', *Analysis* 63(4): 317–21.

—(2006), 'The Intend/Foresee Distinction and the Problem of "Closeness"', *Philosophical Studies* 128(3): 585–617.

—(2009), 'Thomson's Turnabout on the Trolley', *Analysis* 69(4): 636–43.

—(2012), 'The Doctrine of Double Effect: Intention and Permissibility', *Philosophy Compass* 7: S.183–96.

Foot, P. (1967), 'The Problem of Abortion and the Doctrine of the Double Effect', *Oxford Review* 5: 5–15. Reprinted in Woodward 2001.

Ford, J. C. (1944), 'The Morality of Obliteration Bombing', *Theological Studies* 5: 261–309.

Frankland, N. (1970), *Bomber Offensive*. Ballantine Books.

Glock, H-J. (2009), 'Can Animals Act for Reasons?', *Inquiry* 52(3): 232–54.

Goldman, A. (1970), *A Theory of Human Action*. Englewood Cliffs, NJ: Prentice-Hall.

Grice, H. P. (1971), 'Intention and Uncertainty', *Proceedings of the British Academy* 57: 263–79.

Harris, A. T. (1995), *Despatch on War Operations*. Frank Cass & Co.

Harris, J. (2007), *Enhancing Evolution: The Ethical Case for Making Better People*. Princeton: Princeton University Press.

Hart, H. L. A. (1968a), 'Intention and Punishment', in H. L. A. Hart (ed.), *Punishment and Responsibility: Essays in the Philosophy of Law*. Oxford: Clarendon Press, pp. 113–35. Originally published in the Oxford Review 1967.

—(1968b), *Punishment and Responsibility*. Oxford: Oxford University Press.

Hauser, M. (2006), *Moral Minds*. New York: HarperCollins.

Hills, A. (2003), 'Defending Double Effect', *Philosophical Studies* 116: 133–52.

—(2007), 'Intentions, Foreseen Consequences and the Doctrine of Double Effect', *Philosophical Studies* 133: 257–83.

Holm, S. (2003), 'The Ethical Case against Stem Cell Research', *Cambridge Quarterly for Health Care Ethics* 12: 372–83.

Hornsby, J. (1980), *Actions*. London: Routledge & Kegan Paul.

Huebner, B. and Hauser, M. (2011), 'Moral Judgments about Altruistic Self-sacrifice: When Philosophical and Folk Intuitions Clash', *Philosophical Psychology* 24(1): 73–94.

Kamm, F. M. (1992), 'Non-consequentialism, the Person as an End-in-Itself, and the Significance of Status', *Philosophy & Public Affairs* 21(4): 354–89.

—(2007), *Intricate Ethics*. Oxford: Oxford University Press.

Kant, I. (1785/1993), *Grounding for the Metaphysics of Morals*. Translated by James W. Ellington. Indianapolis: Hackett Publishing Company.

Knobe, J. (2003), 'Intentional Action and Side Effects in Ordinary Language', *Analysis* 63(279): 190–4.

Korsgaard, C. (1997), 'The Normativity of Instrumental Reason', in G. Cullity and B. Gaut (eds), *Ethics and Practical Reason*. Oxford: Oxford University Press.

Liao, S. M., Wiegmann, A., Alexander, J. and Vong, G. (forthcoming), 'Putting the Trolley in Order: Experimental Philosophy and the Loop Case', *Philosophical Psychology*.

Mangan, J. T. (1949), 'An Historical Analysis of the Principle of Double Effect', *Theological Studies* 10: 41–61.

Marquis, D. (1991), 'Four Versions of Double Effect', *The Journal of Medicine and Philosophy* 16: 515–44.

Masek, L. (2010), 'Intentions, Motives and the Doctrine of Double Effect', *The Philosophical Quarterly* 60(240): 567–85.

McCann, H. (1991), 'Settled Objectives and Rational Constraints', *American Philosophical Quarterly* 28: 25–36.

—(2010), 'Di Nucci on the Simple View', *Analysis* 70: 53–9.

—(2011), 'The Simple View Again: A Brief Rejoinder', *Analysis* 71(2): 293–5.

McIntyre, A. (2008), 'The Doctrine of Double Effect', *Stanford Encyclopedia of Philosophy*.

McMahan, J. (2009), *Killing in War*. Oxford: Oxford University Press.

Mele, A. R. and Moser, P. (1994), 'Intentional Action', *Nous* 28: 39–68.

Murphy, T. F. (forthcoming), 'Double-effect Reasoning and the Conception of Human Embryos', *J Med Ethics*.

Nagel, T. (1986), *The View from Nowhere*. Oxford: Oxford University Press.

Otsuka, M. (1997), 'Kamm on the Morality of Killing', *Ethics* 108(1): 197–207.

—(2008), 'Double-Effect, Triple-Effect and the Trolley Problem', *Utilitas* 20: 92–110.

Pakaluk, M. (2011), 'Mixed Actions and Double Effect', in M. Pakaluk and G. Pearson (eds), *Moral Psychology and Human Action in Aristotle*. Oxford: Oxford University Press.

Petrinovich, L. and O'Neill, P. (1996), 'Influence of Wording and Framing Effects on Moral Intuitions', *Ethology and Sociobiology* 17: 145–71.

Predelli, S. (2004), 'Bombers: Some Comments on Double Effect and Harmful Involvement', *Journal of Military Ethics* 3: 16–26.

Pruss, A. R. (forthcoming), 'The Accomplishment of Plans: A New Version of the Principle of Double Effect', *Philosophical Studies*.

Quinn, W. S. (1989), 'Actions, Intentions, and Consequences: The Doctrine of Double Effect', *Philosophy and Public Affairs* 18(4): 334–51.

Rachels, J. (1994), 'More Impertinent Distinctions and a Defense of Active Euthanasia', reprinted in B. Steinbock and A. Norcross (eds), *Killing and Letting Die*, 2nd edn. New York: Fordham University Press, pp. 139–54.

Rawls, J. (1955), 'Two Concepts of Rules', *The Philosophical Review* 64(1): 3–32.

Roughley, N. (2007), 'The Double Failure of Double Effect', in S. Nannini and C. Lumer (eds), *Intentionality, Deliberation, and Autonomy*. Farnham, England: Ashgate.

Ryan, J. K. (1933), *Modern War and Basic Ethics*. Bruce.

Scanlon, T. (2008), *Moral Dimensions*. Cambridge, MA: Harvard University Press.

Sinnott-Armstrong, W. (2008), 'Framing Moral Intuitions', in W. Sinnott–Armstrong (ed.), *Moral Psychology, Volume 2: The Cognitive Science of Morality*. Cambridge, MA: MIT Press, pp. 47–76.

Sparrow, R. (2009), 'Saviour Embryos? Preimplantation Genetic Diagnosis as a Therapeutic Technology', *Reprod Biomed Online* 20: 667–74.

Steward, H. (2009), 'Animal Agency', *Inquiry* 52(3): 217–31.

Stoecker, R. (2009), 'Why Animals Can't Act', *Inquiry* 52(3): 255–71.

Stout, R. (2010), 'Deviant Causal Chains', in T. O'Connor and C. Sandis (eds), *Blackwell Companion to the Philosophy of Action*. Oxford: Blackwell.

Swain, S., Alexander, J. and Weinberg, J. (2008), 'The Instability of Philosophical Intuitions: Running Hot and Cold on Truetemp', *Philosophy and Phenomenological Research* 76: 138–55.

Sykes, N. and Thorns, A. (2003), 'The use of opioids and sedatives at the end of life', *The Lancet Oncology* 1: 312–18.

Thomson, J. J. (1976), 'Killing, Letting Die, and the Trolley Problem', *The Monist* 59: 204–17.

—(1985), 'The Trolley Problem', *The Yale Law Journal* 94: 1395–415.

—(1991), 'Self-Defense', *Philosophy & Public Affairs* 20: 283–310.

—(1999), 'Physician-Assisted Suicide: Two Moral Arguments', *Ethics* 109: 497–518.

—(2008), 'Turning the Trolley', *Philosophy and Public Affairs* 36: 359–74.

Walzer, M. (1971), 'World War II: Why Was This War Different?', *Philosophy & Public Affairs* 1(1): 3–21.

Wedgewood, R. (2011a), 'Scanlon on Double Effect', *Philosophy and Phenomenological Research* 83: 464–72.

—(2011b), 'Defending Double Effect', *Ratio* 24: 384–401.

Wiegmann, A., Okan, Y., Nagel, J. and Mangold, S. (2010), 'Order
    Effects in Moral judgment', in S. Ohlsson and R. Catrambone (eds),
    *Proceedings of the Thirty-Second Annual Conference of the Cognitive
    Science Society*. Austin, TX: Cognitive Science Society, pp. 2111–16.
Woodward, P. A. (1997), 'The Importance of the Proportionality
    Condition to the Doctrine of Double Effect: A Response to Fischer,
    Ravizza, and Copp', *Journal of Social Philosophy* 28: 140–52.
—(ed.) (2001), *The Doctrine of Double Effect*. South Bend, IN: University
    of Notre Dame Press.

INDEX